Library of
Davidson College

Two Nations Over Time

Recent Titles in Contributions in American History
SERIES EDITOR: Jon L. Wakelyn

Essays in Nineteenth-Century American Legal History
Wythe Holt, editor

A Right to the Land: Essays on the Freedmen's Community
Edward Magdol

Essays on American Music
Garry E. Clarke

Culture and Diplomacy: The American Experience
Morrell Heald and Lawrence S. Kaplan

Voting in Provincial America: A Study of Elections in the Thirteen Colonies, 1689–1776
Robert J. Dinkin

The French Forces in America, 1780–1783
Lee Kennett

Cold War Political Justice: The Smith Act, the Communist Party, and American Civil Liberties
Michal R. Belknap

The Many-Faceted Jacksonian Era: New Interpretations
Edward Pessen, editor

Manning the New Navy: The Development of a Modern Naval Enlisted Force, 1899–1940
Frederick S. Harrod

Riot, Rout, and Tumult: Readings in American Social and Political Violence
Roger Lane and John J. Turner, Jr., editors

The Long Shadow: Reflections on the Second World War Era
Lisle A. Rose

The Politics of Wartime Aid: American Economic Assistance to France and French Northwest Africa, 1940–1946
James J. Dougherty

The Oil Cartel Case: A Documentary Study of Antitrust Activity in the Cold War Era
Burton I. Kaufman

Two Nations Over Time
SPAIN AND THE UNITED STATES, 1776-1977

James W. Cortada

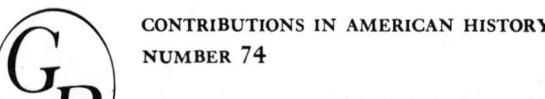

CONTRIBUTIONS IN AMERICAN HISTORY, NUMBER 74

GREENWOOD PRESS
WESTPORT, CONNECTICUT • LONDON, ENGLAND

Library of Congress Cataloging in Publication Data

Cortada, James W.
　Two nations over time.
　(Contributions in American history; no. 74
ISSN 0084-9219)
　Bibliography: p.
　Includes index.
　1. United States—Foreign relations—Spain.
2. Spain—Foreign relations—United States.　I. Title.
E183.8.S7C67　　　　327.73'046　　　　77-94752
ISBN 0-313-20319-9

Copyright © 1978 by James W. Cortada

All rights reserved. No portion of this book may
be reproduced, by any process or technique, without
the express written consent of the publisher.

Library of Congress Catalog Card Number: 77-94752
ISBN: 0-313-20319-9
ISSN: 0084-9219

First published in 1978

Greenwood Press, Inc.
51 Riverside Avenue, Westport, Connecticut 06880

Printed in the United States of America

10 9 8 7 6 5 4 3 2 1

To my father,
James N. Cortada,
American consul general,
Barcelona, 1967–70

CONTENTS

Preface		ix
1.	Birth of a Problem	3
2.	A Continent Conquered	19
3.	An Empire Lost	35
4.	Conflict in the Caribbean	52
5.	Relations at Mid-century	71
6.	Toward the Cuban Vortex	89
7.	The Spanish-American War	110
8.	A Century of Cultural Relations	130
9.	Diplomacy in a New Century	146
10.	A Quiet Interlude	167
11.	Civil War Diplomacy	186
12.	More War, More Friction	205
13.	Diplomacy in Modern Times	223
14.	Recent Cultural Relations	244
15.	Some Conclusions	260
	Appendix A Spanish Envoys to the United States	274
	Appendix B American Envoys to Spain	279
	Bibliographic Essay	284
	Index	299

PREFACE

Since World War I historians have published hundreds of articles and books dealing with various aspects of Spanish-American diplomacy. As a result, scholars today understand these relations better than for many other countries. Their work in European, American, and Latin American archives provided many of the details necessary to formulate a clear picture of how these fitted into the diplomatic history of Europe and the Americas. Yet most dealt with only a portion of the subject and were limited by chronological boundaries, topics, or a writer's abilities. The time has come to consolidate the work of these various researchers into a summary and to indicate the general themes prevailing in Spanish-American relations. Because historians now consider it imperative that diplomatic dispatches be analyzed within the context of domestic history, economics, and international situations, I will survey Spanish-American diplomacy along the lines now considered essential in diplomatic history.

I have purposely avoided writing a day-by-day narrative or a definitive history. The bibliographic essay will guide anyone wishing to study the minutia involved. I limited myself to details illustrating the basic tenets suggesting the directions relations have taken. This seemed appropriate since, with the passage of two hundred years in their relations, Spaniards and Americans have begun to assess this shared aspect of their history and question its future course. The basic purpose of this book is to help clarify the issues involved. But because it is a summary, it is also directed to scholars who may want an introduction to the subject and a guide to sources. Whenever historians left major gaps in this history, I have tried to fill them with my own research in Europe and the United States.

Several preliminary observations occurred to me after studying Spanish-American diplomacy for the better part of a decade. Both Spain and the United States have always recognized that the other wielded an important influence over some of their affairs. Diplomats were the first to admit this, followed by merchants and settlers in the Americas during the eighteenth century. As global politics made the world smaller in the twentieth century, new generations acknowledged what their forefathers already knew. While the impact of one nation on the other changed in many ways over the course of two hundred years, influence remained a fundamental characteristic of their relations. Also, neither could escape the pressure of events in Europe and in the New World on their relationship.

Animosity appeared repeatedly as a theme. Certainly in the nineteenth century, the North Americans and Spanish were openly hostile toward each other. The 1898 war was not an accident but the logical outcome of a century-old competition for control of the Caribbean. This friction was part of their much larger struggle for political and economic hegemony over the New World. In this century, ideologies and cultural conflicts have continued to nurture animosity. Despite this, there have been quiet periods and even some friendliness, but they only concealed nascent difficulties. While the early 1880s or the years between 1899 and 1936 have been considered by some scholars as calm eras, they were merely prologues for such turbulent ones as 1895–98 and 1936–47.

Animosity is an important thread running through the relations between Spain and the United States. The most fundamental questions that Americans and Spaniards can ask about their relationship involves this feature. Why has it been such a critical theme, and can it be aborted in the future? I can answer the first question with some degree of confidence but not the latter. Some of the answers to these and related questions may be found by looking at more than just politics. Historians and diplomats have concentrated too much on political differences and not enough on friction caused by cultural or domestic factors. Americans never fully understood Spanish society, and they totally ignored its impact on Spain's foreign policy. Spaniards failed to appreciate American culture and, more out of ignorance than wisdom, were critical of the manner in which American society functioned, fearing its influences on the foreign policy of the United States and on the Latin American nations.

In order to understand Spanish-American relations, I have found it necessary to discuss economic and cultural factors, along with political issues, in making my evaluation. I will mention domestic Spanish and American history, intuitive feelings of the diplomats involved, and the positions of each nation within international circles.

In the course of this process, many people have shown faith in the project by helping at various stages of its preparation. Although they are too numerous to list, I am grateful to each for his contribution. There are a few individuals, however, whom I would like to mention. The staffs at the National Archives and at the Library of Congress in Washington and those at the Archivo Histórico Nacional, Biblioteca Nacional, and the archive of the Spanish foreign office in Madrid have been of immense help. Dr. J. Leitch Wright, Jr., offered advice on the first three chapters and Dr. Thomas M. Campbell, Jr., also of Florida State University, answered many questions on American diplomacy. Dr. Stanley G. Payne of the University of Wisconsin encouraged my study of Spanish diplomacy for many years. Lawrence S. Kaplan of the history department at Kent State University made suggestions regarding American diplomacy for the entire manuscript, and my father exposed me to some of the realities of a diplomat's craft. Officials of the Spanish and American foreign offices have shared with me their governments' views and kept me informed about contemporary developments. Without their help, the last three chapters would have been more difficult to write. My wife, Dora, also aided me in innumerable ways. To all of them I am grateful. And because my father originally encouraged me to study diplomatic affairs and introduced me to Spain, I have dedicated this volume to him. Any weaknesses or errors in this book, however, are my fault, despite the efforts of my friends to correct them.

J.W.C.
Fords, N. J.
October 1977

Two Nations Over Time

1
BIRTH OF A PROBLEM

From the time Spain began colonizing the New World at the turn of the sixteenth century, other European powers sought to share in the adventure by depriving Spaniards of such a rich monopoly. The European wars of the next two hundred years more than hinted of this. For example, as a result of English diplomatic activity in Europe and piracy in the New World, Spain in 1667 agreed to allow England to trade with Spanish colonies in the West Indies. It was during the same period that Spain allied with England on both sides of the Atlantic against France, which both saw growing as an economic and colonial force of some significance. This situation became manifestly clear during the War of the Spanish Succession (1702–13) when Paris sought to acquire territory in the New World at the expense of Spain. As a result of this war, the British gained increased rights to trade in the Spanish colonies, but more fundamentally, a status quo was established in the New World that reflected French defeats and political realities in Europe. Relating power politics in the New World to those in the Old became a feature of American affairs, which has existed to the present.

This characteristic certainly was evident during the eighteenth century when the British steadily expanded their influence in the Americas, developing colonies along the Atlantic seaboard while expanding their naval and merchant fleets. Paris and Madrid negotiated an alliance directed against London because Britain had damaged French and Spanish commerce, colonial interests, and positions in Europe during the first half of the 1700s. Signing the third Family Compact in 1761 accented the problem that Spain faced in America: Anglo-Spanish competition for hegemony on the North American continent. In fact, the treaty should be called the birth certificate of the rivalry Spain and the United States shared in future years because, as a result of this alliance, colonial events in the next twenty-two years led to the creation of an American government, which replaced Britain as Spain's main rival in the New World.

The Family Compact stipulated that Spain would aid France in its war with Britain. The Seven Years' War of 1756–63, of which the treaty proved to be a significant part, involved fighting both in Europe and in the New World. The British quickly seized Cuba and elsewhere seriously damaged Spanish merchant ships. In 1763 peace finally came to Europe. Madrid surrendered Florida to London, and the British evacuated Cuba. France, also badly injured by Great Britain, turned over Canada and almost all of the territories it claimed or held east of the Mississippi River to its enemy. The British allowed Paris to retain New Orleans as part of the lands France still held near the Mississippi. The Spanish acknowledged that Britain now legally owned areas formerly claimed by France east of the river. And because Britain and Spain had quarreled for years over whether British wood cutters could work in Honduras, London insisted that Madrid allow these men to stay in Central America. In turn, France granted to Spain all its territories west of the Mississippi River, including New Orleans, at the mouth of the waterway.

As a result of this treaty, Spain, France, and Britain agreed that a large, well-defined area in the New World belonged to the English and could be colonized by them, making London master of the North American continent. Behind the eastern banks of the Mississippi and beyond the shore line of the Atlantic, a nation of Anglo-Saxons could grow. (*Anglo-Saxon* had become an important term by this time to both Spain and Britain because it denoted a cultural imperialism that Spain, at least, believed might eventually prove more dangerous to its empire than its political manifestations.) A noted historian on the period argued that the peace treaty led to the creation of the United States because the colonists could spend more time on peaceful pursuits than in war. For this reason, the treaty also continued assaults on Spain by threatening its hegemony in the continent.[1]

---

1. Samuel Flagg Bemis, *The Diplomacy of the American Revolution* (Bloomington, 1957), 8.

Spain consented to this situation for several reasons. The British had defeated Franco-Spanish forces and had seized Havana, the key to Spain's Caribbean holdings. Yet by obtaining from France land west of the Mississippi, Spain created a buffer zone to hold back the Anglo-Saxons from encroaching on its colonies in the Caribbean and in Central America. In order to protect its interests further, Spain decided never to discuss trading privileges or navigation rights on the Mississippi with the British, reasoning that any talks of this sort implied Madrid was granting privileges in its colonies while gaining little or nothing in exchange.[2] Spain's decision to seal off its colonies from Britain's reflected Madrid's determination to meet the challenge of an invigorated enemy. Spain's policy frustrated intercolonial communications, thereby increasing tensions in the New World. Colonial officials and merchants became infuriated with the Spanish. Yet British demands for rights in Spain's lands had the same effect on the Spanish. By the time the United States won its independence, the basic elements of mistrust and misunderstanding had become part of the inheritance burdening future Americans in their dealings with Spain.

Paris and Madrid, smarting from the pain of their defeat in the Seven Years' War, closely watched the deteriorating relations between Britain and its colonies during the next decade. The French realized that British power might be crippled if the English colonies could be encouraged to defy London. In the mid-1770s, Paris secretly sent financial aid to the colonists and soon persuaded Spain to make similar contributions. The Spaniards decided by the spring of 1776 that their assistance might help exhaust the British and their colonists by prolonging the rebellion. This, in turn, would strengthen Madrid's hold on its own possessions in the New World. Both the French and the Spanish also reasoned that a major colonial revolution in America would necessarily draw London's attention away from European affairs, allowing Paris and Madrid to increase their influence closer to home.[3]

---

2. Juan Francisco Yela Utrilla, *España ante la independencia de los Estados Unidos* (Lérida, 1925), vol. 1 passim.

3. Henri Donoiol, *Histoire de la participation de la France à l'établissement des Etats-Unis d'Amérique* (Paris, 1884–1892), 1:370.

Until 1778, when the French signed a treaty of alliance with the American rebels, Paris and Madrid conducted intense negotiations on the British colonial crisis. Each knew that King George's problem could be exploited to their advantage and, being allies, they wanted to coordinate their efforts. Yet each was also influenced by its differing situation in the New World. France owned virtually no property in the Americas other than a few valuable islands in the Caribbean, while Spain held vast tracts spread over two continents. The Spanish wanted to meddle secretly in Britain's colonial predicament because they feared losing their own possessions by setting an example for Spain's colonial subjects. Also Britain might seize land as it had during the last war. Spain did not intend to sacrifice Cuba or even Honduras just for revenge. The Spanish told France they would fight the British if Paris were willing to do so at the same time. Madrid further wanted an agreement on goals in advance: cripple England in Europe, reduce its empire in the New World, ensure Spain's retention of the Latin colonies, and possibly gain possession of Portugal, Gibraltar, and the Floridas. Negotiations between Paris and Madrid on objectives continued throughout 1776 and 1777; at no time did they discuss the welfare of the British colonists as an end in itself.

Spain and France thought mainly of Europe. The Conde de Floridablanca, an intelligent and well-informed politician, became chief minister to Carlos III in 1777. He believed that Britain's troubles should be exploited but not at the risk of another war. He suggested that the British and their colonists settle their differences by negotiation with Spanish mediation because he did not think Spain could gain anything significant in Europe that year. At least by mediation, a chance always existed for Spain to acquire some compensation in the Americas. Relations were improving with Lisbon anyway, causing him to believe that the Portuguese could readily be absorbed by a royal marriage. But he continued to send small amounts of money to the English rebels through French and Spanish channels.

Floridablanca's attitude worried the French, who wanted to implement a more active policy in North America as an extension of their European policies. They searched for ways to include Spain in their plans for weakening the British. A windfall came at the end of the year in the form of news that the British army under General John Burgoyne had surrendered to the American rebels at Saratoga. France now struck out on its own without the Spanish by signing a treaty of alliance with the Americans on February 6, 1778. The treaty stipulated that both would work for the independence of the thirteen colonies and jointly sign any peace treaty negotiated with the British. This major turn of events now made formal and public what had been secret for nearly two years. Moreover France could turn to Spain with new arguments for going to war with Britain. As a result of this alliance, therefore, both London and Paris expected the Spanish to act quickly.

The French did not wait silently for Spain's reaction and tried to push Madrid into the war. First, France attempted to keep Europe quiet in order not to distract the Spanish from American affairs. Second, Paris formally asked Spain to join it in crushing their enemy. Floridablanca, still reluctant to move in this direction, argued that the English could seriously cripple Spain's commerce and aid rebels in the colonies. Spanish diplomats also suspected French motives since Paris had entered into the American alliance without informing Madrid in advance as one ally should to another. The Spanish, however, did not allow their doubts to prevent discussions with the French about the possibility of obtaining Gibraltar as a reward for entering the war against Britain. Both officials and citizens in Spain had little sympathy for the American rebels, who were defying a legitimate authority, but they did want to regain Gibraltar, which England had wrested away earlier that century. Before agreeing to enter the war, however, Floridablanca asked King George III if he would return Gibraltar in exchange for Spanish neutrality. He also offered to mediate London's differences with its colonies. When the British rejected his offer, Floridablanca turned to Paris and signed an alliance in April 1779 in which he endorsed most of the principles laid out in the Franco-American treaty.

The terms of this Franco-Spanish agreement, known as the Treaty of Aranjuez, included a provision that only a joint settlement with London should be concluded. France and Spain agreed to continue the war until Madrid acquired Gibraltar, Minorca, and the Floridas. Spain also wanted to expel Britain from Central America. Yet Gibraltar became the unresolvable point in the pact and later delayed the final peace settlement of 1783. Neither France nor Spain realized in 1779 that Gibraltar would prove so elusive.

Were it not for Gibraltar, France would have been unable to entice the Spanish into the war. The Floridas proved incidental since Georgia, to a great extent, was Indian controlled and thus a ready-made zone for thwarting English expansion. Furthermore Spain already dominated the mouth of the Mississippi. Since the Spanish showed no interest in the welfare of the American rebels, the French could not use the colonials' plight as an inducement. In short, Spanish concerns were almost entirely European.[4] France, aware of this, managed to draw Spain into the fight by simply catering to its European tastes. With that done, Madrid declared war on Britain in June 1779.

Spain now faced a multitude of problems since, from a military point of view, the struggle centered on the fate of the colonies and Gibraltar. Both the Americans and the Spanish realized that the question of what future role the new nation might have in the development of North America had to be answered. This plagued Spain for the next forty years. In fact, almost immediately after entering the war, the Americans began discussing their future boundaries with the French and Spanish. Such issues as western frontiers, navigation of the Mississippi, and expansion into Florida concerned everyone. In order to help the rebels, Spain allowed them limited use of Spanish territory and river—a privilege the Americans wanted to retain after the war. During the 1770s clashes between frontiersmen and Spanish military units in the western lands portended of things to come. Therefore Spain made it standard policy to aid the colonists with occasional supplies of money and keep them from settling in Spanish land while concentrating full energies on acquiring Gibraltar. Fencing the colonists east of the Mississippi River proved as difficult as holding them above the Florida line because, unlike at Gibraltar, there were large tracts of land involved with small groups of men moving uncontrolled in the wilderness. It would have taken thousands of Spanish soldiers to patrol effectively such uncontested areas; at Gibraltar, on the other hand, men concentrated their activities in a small, highly defined area.

---

4. Bemis, *Diplomacy of the American Revolution*, 86.

Americans argued during the Revolution that, by the peace treaty of 1763, Britain had acquired all the land to the Mississippi and the Yazoo River. As heirs of the British empire in North America by right of their war of independence, they claimed the same borders. Floridablanca disagreed, charging that the Americans then would demand rights on the west bank and continue expanding down through the Floridas and into what is today western Louisiana and the Gulf of Mexico. Their conflict over the issue caused heated debates in the colonies. Members of the colonial congress realized, for instance, that a formal position had to be developed long before any peace settlement could be reached, while the Spanish wanted to delay such an eventuality.

Territorial boundaries attracted the attention of the Continental Congress between March and August 1779. Since the rebels did not agree at first on what demands to make regarding borders, the French suggested not asking too much of Spain, Britain, or themselves because if the American position were rejected, then independence might be delayed. Although no proof exists, the Spanish probably asked the French to tell the Americans informally not to ask for too much.[5] By autumn the colonists had a set of requests. They saw the Mississippi, not Canada, as the critical area of concern. This meant that all their future territorial problems would be not with Britain but in the southwest with Spain. They knew the Spanish wanted to keep this region and, counting on French influence in Madrid, asked that the Mississippi River's east bank serve as the American western frontier. To the south, they wanted the English boundary of West Florida running along the 31° north latitude. They were willing to accept Canada as the northern border.

Armed with a set of objectives, the Americans appointed John Jay as their representative to Madrid. Arriving in late 1779, he found the Spanish indifferent to him; they knew he had nothing to offer in exchange for his demands. The Spanish had seized West Florida from the British, and France already had promised to keep fighting until Gibraltar became Spain's. But because the Spanish wanted to continue the colonial war, they gave small amounts of aid to the rebels, and Floridablanca discussed border problems with Jay. The envoy sat in Madrid frustrated until May 1782, feeling useless and

---

5. Yela Utrilla, *España ante la independencia*, 1:305-342.

dejected. His mood was not helped when Floridablanca told him that
the French and Spain could not formally recognize the United States
until after Britain had done so. In fact, while Jay languished in
Madrid, the Spanish secretly communicated with London about ending the war in exchange for Gibraltar. Since the British government
could not agree to this without facing the wrath of outraged politicians and an angry public, London rejected Spain's proposal, a position that hardened the Spanish against King George.[6]

Historians have generally cited Gibraltar as the key issue from
Spain's point of view and the border from America's. Undoubtedly
this was so to the average observer in the 1780s. However, the border question was more important in the long run to both nations. Its
significance to Spain has not been sufficiently emphasized by scholars
who cling to Gibraltar with greater tenacity than the Spanish themselves. Floridablanca always approached the border problem with
great care, fully aware of its significance to Spain. He knew that, if
not properly resolved, the issue might spell the demise of Spain's
empire in the Caribbean. At the same time Gibraltar could not be
ignored. The Spanish public remembered that in 1704 England had
obtained the colony against Spain's wishes. The monarchy, aware of
the public's interest in this small British stronghold, dared not mini-
mize its importance even though it was a strategic and political issue
of lesser significance than the border crisis. Moreover Floridablanca's political position, never secure enough at any time to defy
the public will, bowed to the king's demand that he obtain Gibraltar.

The Americans never fully understood the significance of this
Mediterranean territory to Spain. Jay paid insufficient attention to
Gibraltar, never exploiting it properly. He never admitted that
Spanish intransigence toward him grew in large part out of Spain's
wish to keep all options open as long as a chance remained of gaining
the Mediterranean prize. In addition, Spain believed that the colonial
rebels could not put together a package of concessions equal in public
value to Gibraltar, at least not in the years Jay sat in Madrid.

The Spanish attitude went far to explain why they did little to
help the colonies. The military aid proved negligible, and the money

---

6. Samuel Flagg Bemis, *The Hussey-Cumberland Negotiation Mission and American Independence* (Princeton, 1931), 118 ff.

involved was hardly influential.[7] Spaniards felt annoyed by Americans such as Jay who continually asked for more assistance, money, or land. Dashed hopes made Americans criticize Spain, while Floridablanca and the king adopted a similar attitude toward the colonists. Yet Spain continued negotiating with them in 1781 and 1782, mainly because of the possibility that a general settlement might lead to the acquisition of Gibraltar and protection of its borders in North America. Moreover the French insisted that her ally negotiate with the rebels. But by late 1782, these talks had virtually created the impression that Americans and Spaniards were at greater odds than the rebels with Britain.

Spain's policies toward France, Britain, and the North American rebels were also stiffened by Spanish military successes in the Caribbean and in the Gulf of Mexico. Using Cuba and Puerto Rico as bases of operations, the Spanish seriously damaged British naval power in the area, practically eliminated Anglo-Saxon commerce in the region, and reinforced their claims to Louisiana and the Floridas. The governor of Louisiana, Bernardo de Gálvez, commanding an army of nearly 7,000 men at one point, seized Baton Rouge and several communities in Mississippi, and occupied Mobile and Pensacola. Such successes against the British made Spain reluctant to participate in negotiations that seemed to threaten the loss of these prizes— areas that could serve as buffers against North American encroachment on Spanish colonies.

In 1782 the French concluded that if the parties involved continued to negotiate with each other jointly, little could be accomplished. Changing tactics, they maneuvered all diplomatic conversations into two channels: one with France, Spain, and Britain discussing European problems and another with the British and Americans talking about the New World. The rate of progress established by each set of negotiators advanced rapidly during 1782. Spanish-American bargaining continued independently of the other negotiations in a ponderous fashion because neither side would compromise. Floridablanca, for example, said in August that he did not believe Madrid should recognize the United States until Britain had done so first, still fearing the precedent for Spain's colonies. He also did not want

---

7. Bemis, *Diplomacy of the American Revolution*, 111.

to recognize the Americans until the British had surrendered Gibraltar.

Jay felt Spain would not hesitate to sabotage his nation's independence if it believed such a move would secure holdings in the New World and win land in the Mediterranean, a fact confirmed by Gérard de Rayneval, a well-informed French official of the time. It took Jay over eighteen months, however, to realize the importance of Gibraltar to Madrid. By then he knew there was little he could do in Spain, so he left for Paris where, he believed, the key decisions would be made. After moving, Jay continued talking to the Spanish through their local representative, Pedro de Aranda. Both men concentrated on boundary problems. Jay still wanted the Mississippi line and the 31° north latitude. Aranda claimed West Florida up to what today is Vicksburg, Mississippi, and over to the Chattahoochee in Florida. Aranda offered to concede a border running north to south, east of the Mississippi, and winding from around the west side of Lake Superior down to St. Mary's River in eastern Florida. Both men suggested various alternatives to these borders but could not agree upon one.

During the fall of 1782, a turning point was reached in America's negotiations with Britain. Frustrated with the Spanish, Jay decided to settle with London. He offered the British part of West Florida, which would be contrary to Spanish wishes, because he concluded that in the long run Englishmen would make better neighbors than Spaniards. He understood them and their goals for North America, which could include a large United States; he knew the Spanish felt differently. Also, the Spanish had refused to treat him with the same seriousness as the British. The Florida proposal never made it into the final settlement, but in the process of discussing it, the British agreed to recognize the Mississippi River as the western frontier and acknowledged that the new nation should have free navigation on it. Jay believed that, armed with this British understanding, Spanish claims to land east of the river could be blunted since London might change Spain's attitude toward the boundary by exerting pressure on Madrid in Europe. In order to gain British cooperation, he sacrificed American claims to Canada and was willing to let Britain have part of Florida. The western line drew the greatest attention from the Americans, who already knew their future lay in that direction.

In September Paris and London learned that the major Franco-Spanish military offensive against Gibraltar had failed. The French and English quickly recognized the change this caused in all negotiations, and from late October to early November, they held intense discussions on peace terms. On November 3 they signed a preliminary peace treaty with the Americans. The British promised to recognize American independence and acknowledge the Mississippi River as part of the western boundary. Gibraltar remained the only real problem since Spain refused to conclude peace without gaining it. This stubborn attitude also meant France could not agree to a badly wanted peace since, by the Treaty of Aranjuez, Paris had agreed to keep fighting until London lost the colony. Americans, Frenchmen, and the English, therefore, looked toward Madrid for real peace.

Officials in Paris saw the need to turn their full attention to Spain in search for other concessions to offer their Spanish ally in lieu of Gibraltar. The United States could not do this and since the British refused to give up Gibraltar, France had to take the initiative. French efforts were energetic because French officials saw the need for peace. The war had cost the government more than it could afford, the nation had won no land, and public support for the fight was virtually dead by late 1782.[8] French authorities thought of granting Spain Florida and some islands in the Caribbean, but they learned that the Spanish did not want these alone. The French explained to Madrid that any British government that dared to surrender Gibraltar would fall before a public outcry. The British helped by expressing their willingness to curtail their activities in Honduras and give up Minorca to Spain. In the face of British and French firmness, the Spanish were forced to take less than Gibraltar. After the negotiations ended, Floridablanca and Carlos III concluded that Spain had not done too badly even though Gibraltar remained in British hands.[9] This would lead one to suspect that they continued the talks long after they realized Spain could not obtain Gibraltar in order to gain numerous other concessions and at least be able to tell the Spanish public they tried. Spain had the satisfaction of seeing the Americans caged east of the Mississippi River and above Florida. More impor-

---

8. Manuel Dánvila y Collado, *Reinado de Carlos III* (Madrid, 1893–1896), 5:381.

9. Charles Petrie, *King Charles III of Spain* (London, 1971), 183–203.

tant in the long run for both Spain and the United States were the legacies of the Revolution, which influenced their relations for decades.

The colonial war was less important to Spain than the broader problem of European politics or, more specifically, Anglo-Saxon expansion in North America. In fact, Spain never really wanted an independent United States. Land, therefore, became the real issue between them. Each recognized that the other wanted to restrict its growth while seizing more territory. Spain bottled up the new nation behind the Mississippi, but the Americans leaned hard against the closed door to the west. Their conversations invariably concerned borders, focusing less on recognition and foreign aid. Even commercial questions, always linked to territorial problems, became complex. Each side became jealous and frustrated, mistrusting the other and following the same pattern of distrust that had marked Anglo-Spanish relations in the previous 270 years. The Americans inherited these difficulties from the British in 1783; frontiersmen and diplomats, merchants and soldiers all knew this. Events in the 1770s and 1780s simply exacerbated these problems. Since the peace settlement did not lay to rest territorial conflicts, 1783 cannot be considered the end of a historical period in Spanish-American diplomacy. Instead rivalry in North America continued unabated for years.

Soon after signing the peace treaty, Spanish and American diplomats met to discuss navigational rights on the Mississippi. The new nation considered the question an urgent one because American traders and frontiersmen were demanding an open river and the Spanish were prohibiting traffic on the Mississippi. At the same time, both governments knew that more American settlers were moving closer to the Mississippi each day. Spain thus had added reason to close the river while Americans demanded its opening. Along with disagreements regarding the exact borders in present-day Louisiana, Alabama, and Mississippi, the Spanish policy led to enormous difficulties between 1783 and 1795. During these twelve years, a tradition of hostility nurtured by the two nations solidified, infecting frontiersmen, Indians, and Spanish and American officials, and even involving the publics in Spain and along the Atlantic coast of the United States.

Spaniards learned that they could not simply claim an area; they would have to control it by force. Consequently they increased their penetration in such contested regions as a wide strip east of the Mississippi. Like the British farther north, they maintained forts, traded and plotted with the Indians, and tried to pit frontiersmen against each other by exploiting their grievances with the new republic. American discomforts steadily increased. When Spain closed the Mississippi to all non-Spanish traffic, over 50,000 Americans were restricted in their business affairs. Even the British could not escape the ill effects of this ruling and wanted access to the river for their traders. In fact, the British and Americans, independent of each other, worked to open Spanish lands by both negotiations and force.

The new American government thought that the navigational problem could be solved by signing a comprehensive trade agreement with the Spanish, but the negotiations they conducted during 1785 and 1786 revealed the extent of their differences. John Jay, representing the United States, demanded that the Mississippi River be opened to free navigation and that the United States have the right to deposit goods at New Orleans; Diego de Gardoqui, speaking for Spain, refused. The two men, however, in 1786 did draft a treaty agreeable to both sides covering commerce on the Mississippi in which they acknowledged free trade on the river for thirty years. The United States rejected the draft proposal. Meanwhile western frontiersmen threatened to open the Mississippi by attacking New Orleans. The Spanish, aware that their hold on Florida, Louisiana, and New Orleans was weak, worried that such an effort might succeed. They wisely decided in 1788 to allow the Americans use of the river for a fee.[10] Simultaneously British negotiators insisted that Spain grant London rights around Nootka Sound at Vancouver Island. The British demand led to a treaty, signaling a further Spanish retreat from the North American continent.[11]

The United States, encouraged by these Spanish setbacks, raised the issue of frontiers around Florida, again claiming 31° north latitude; the Spanish held that their border ran at least one hundred miles farther north. American merchants, who wanted to use New Or-

---

10. J. Leitch Wright, Jr., *Anglo-Spanish Rivalry in North America* (Athens, 1971), 150.
11. Warren L. Cook, *Flood Tide of Empire: Spain and the Pacific Northwest, 1543–1819* (New Haven, 1973), 524–532.

leans, insisted on a fast settlement. U.S. diplomats thought that by pushing the border to Florida, the port might be opened. Meanwhile traders arrived in New Orleans, and American settlers slowly worked their way south. The British respected American prowess in this area as a result of these developments. Yet the problems were serious, even leading to sporadic fighting between Spanish and American soldiers and settlers. Furthermore with Anglo-Spanish relations improving in the 1790s (as a result of their settling the Nootka Sound dispute and because of the events engulfing France in revolution and war), Americans felt a sense of urgency in obtaining a settlement to the south.

By 1794 these territorial problems were seriously damaging diplomatic relations. Britain and the United States balanced precariously on the brink of war over control of the Northwest Territory. Other Americans talked of seizing Louisiana and Florida. In Europe, France forced Spain to join in an alliance directed against the English. Britain and the United States still objected to Spanish attempts at restricting use of the Mississippi. London also worried about its holdings in the Caribbean since Madrid had just ceded Santo Domingo to France. Most Americans found developments in Europe sufficiently disturbing to avoid involvement there. This feeling of isolationism encouraged their conscious efforts to expel Spain and England from North America.

Madrid decided to placate the Americans in order to reduce pressure in the New World, while concentrating on the more important problems in Europe. Calling in the American envoy, Thomas Pinckney, the government negotiated some differences. Their agreement, signed on October 27, 1795, opened the Mississippi River to free use and in effect pushed forward the conversations held between Jay and Gardoqui in the 1780s. For the following three years, goods brought to New Orleans would not be taxed. Spain promised to control the Indians and not foment unrest on the frontier. It also surrendered all claims to land connected to Florida above the 31° north latitude. By this instrument the United States gained everything it had asked for in 1783 without cost. Relative peace now settled on the frontier, and the West slowly opened to commerce and settlement.

Spain's concessions reflected the country's list of priorities. Europe remained more significant than North America or the Gulf of Mexico. Spain was again reminded (for example during the Nootka Sound controversy) that actual possession rather than claims determined who would own territory in North America. Clearly this principle also applied to the Southwest. Spain's retreat from Nootka momentarily improved relations with Britain, and a similar improvement with the United States seemed reasonable. Spain needed peace in the New World because of the problems posed by the Anglo-French wars—conflicts that were upsetting Europe's balance of power and the Spanish position within it. Authorities in Madrid knew it would only be a question of time before they went to war against London, and none of them wanted their enemy to ally with England's cousins in America for a massive assault on Spanish property.

The influence of Anglo-Spanish rivalry on Spanish-American relations has long been an issue improperly examined by historians. Recently J. Leitch Wright, Jr., addressed himself to the issue, discovering that this rivalry contributed generously to American successes. By the end of the 1790s, the United States controlled all territories that it had asked of Britain and Spain in the 1780s. He credited Europe's wars of the 1790s for much of this change. Moreover European withdrawal from North America made it almost inevitable that Florida and Louisiana would next fall into the hands of the United States.[12]

The years between 1795 and 1800 illustrated several patterns of behavior in relations between Spain and the United States that both governments virtually institutionalized. It became obvious to Europeans and Americans alike that the new republic wanted to extend its control over North America by either accident or intent and, because of its geographical proximity to Spanish lands, at Spain's expense. Europe learned to respect the skill developed by the new government in dealing with border disputes. In the process, Spaniards became irritated with the lack of respect Americans showed for their interests in the New World.

Spaniards began formulating strong opinions about American diplomacy. They increasingly became convinced, for example, that

---

12. Wright, *Anglo-Spanish Rivalry*, 160.

the new republic might align itself with the British. One Spanish official, the Marqués de Castejon, reflected their common concern that "the English and American powers would still be of one nation, one character and one religion, and would so form their treaties and compacts as to obtain the objectives they both desire."[13] Events fortified this view. The American Revolution, wars in Europe, and economic realities in the Southwest suggested that uncomfortable relations would continue for years to come. Indeed there remained problems to solve: establishing peaceful diplomatic and economic relations, and American expansion into Florida, Louisiana, and, later, into the Caribbean and Gulf of Mexico. These conflicting interests led both nations to mistrust each other intensely. Hampered by two centuries of animosity between Spaniards and Americans (Englishmen), diplomats on both sides of the Atlantic believed that Anglo-Saxon society competed with Hispanic civilization. Spaniards, at least, began to talk of a cultural or racial (*raza*) conflict in the New World, one in which both political and cultural hegemony of the Americas meant a massive struggle between two ways of life. Americans concurred but never to the same degree of consciousness as their Spanish competitors.

The Americans also carried grudges with them into their new experience in nationhood. They strongly believed Spain would be their most important enemy for years to come. Their accusations that Spaniards wanted to sabotage American independence for the sake of much unsettled territory in the New World or for European objectives clearly illustrated a future course of events. Not allowing them to use the Mississippi, which seemed large enough for both, angered many in the United States. The Spanish policy of encouraging Indian uprisings disgusted frontiersmen and citizens along the Atlantic seaboard. As a nation, Americans realized that to protect themselves from Spain, it might be necessary to push Spain completely off the North American continent.

---

13. Quoted in Edward S. Corwin, *French Policy and the American Alliance of 1778* (1916; reprint ed., Hamden, 1962), 109.

2
A CONTINENT CONQUERED

By 1820 the United States had more than doubled the size of its territory, and mostly at Spain's expense. These years were scarred by bitterness, confusion, and complicated diplomacy while Spain tried to preserve its empire. Both nations clashed at the conference table and in the wilderness in an attempt to protect their respective interests. Virtually bringing them to the brink of war, their competition for mastery over North America reinforced and augmented the mistrust they felt for each other. These uncomfortable events took place in a volatile era in European and American history. Napoleon Bonaparte had disrupted the very fabric of European life by wars of conquest and, specifically, by his invasion of Spain in 1807. American infiltration into Florida, Mississippi, Alabama, Arkansas, and Missouri further complicated relations with Spain. The republic's expansion and Spain's continued withdrawal from North America in turn threw Madrid's colonial policies into chaos and inevitably drew Europe's problems into the vortex of American politics. Fundamental changes affecting the future of Spain's colonial holdings permanently influenced the nature of nineteenth-century American history.

Their contacts obviously dictated that quarrels, discussions, and animosities would involve three general tracts of land. The first concerned the Louisiana Territory with its poorly defined borders. Spanish claims in the Pacific Northwest in what today is Oregon became a second issue. The third and most heatedly contested struggle came over Florida. In each region, Spain faced threats from the United States and such rival European powers as France and England. As the years passed, Spain retreated from North America, but never without a long struggle. Each time, as the contested property fell into the hands of the United States, Spain worried about American power in the New World, an irritation that hurt Spanish relations with France and Britain as well. Americans in turn learned to despise Spaniards, whom they thought wanted to abort their natural destiny, which they defined as possessing the entire continent of North America.

The first area to cause problems lay beyond Florida around New Orleans and west of the Mississippi River. Spain sought to maintain control over this region, known as the Louisiana Territory, as a large buffer zone between the United States and Mexico. Americans, still wishing to use the river for moving westward or transporting goods to the Gulf of Mexico, criticized Spain's policies regarding the waterway and New Orleans. Frustrated, they wanted to acquire the port and land around it to ensure the smooth flow of traffic. This rivalry increased bitterness along the frontier, worried Washington and Madrid, and led to numerous ugly incidents in the region.

To complicate matters further, France also became interested in regaining this area by the end of the eighteenth century. Despite the fact that Paris had surrendered Louisiana to Spain in 1763, the Directory (which superseded the monarchical and republican governments between 1795 and 1799 in France) believed it could be made into the cornerstone of a great empire in the New World. Carving it out at the expense of Spain and Britain posed no problem since military victories in Europe would provide the necessary conditions for such an acquisition. French officials knew that Spain's grip on Louisiana remained tenuous at best. The colony cost Madrid enormous sums and increased Spain's national debt. American encroachment into the area also highlighted Spain's weak defensive posture in Louisiana. Administratively the colony proved difficult for Spaniards to control. Therefore the French felt that Spain might be persuaded to surrender the colony with a minimum of diplomatic or military pressure. The chief Spanish minister, Manuel Godoy, found Louisiana enough of a burden for French diplomats to report that he would not object to Paris's obtaining it. He stipulated, however, that Napoleon had to guarantee never to allow Britain or the United States to acquire Louisiana. In fact, Godoy went to some lengths to discuss with the French how important that buffer zone was in protecting the Mexican silver mines.[1]

Godoy expected the United States to continue pressing for concessions along the Mississippi River down to the Gulf of Mexico. The United States threatened his nation's precarious situation in the New World by giving encouragement to Latin Americans critical of Madrid's colonial policies. As early as December 1795, the Spanish had explored with France the possibility of exchanging Louisiana for French Santo Domingo, which, more readily than the former, could be protected from European or American encroachment and was already an economically productive region. The tendency of Spanish officials to shorten their lines of defense in the New World reflected the increased demand for soldiers and money with which to protect the homeland once Napoleon came to power. This pattern continued until the British exiled the emperor to Saint Helena in 1815.

In the late 1790s France did not want to make such an exchange becaused it was involved in an undeclared war with the United States (1797–1800). The French feared the Americans might seize the newly acquired territory. Yet the quasi-war threatened to draw Spain into it since France wanted Spanish support in the Americas, while at the same time the United States demanded concessions from Madrid. If anything, the Franco-American conflict further accented Spain's exposed position, forcing Spanish officials to look upon Louisiana as a liability. Thus when Napoleon became first consul of France and suggested that Spain turn Louisiana over to him, Madrid seriously considered the proposal. The Spanish concluded that their French neighbor could maintain the area as a buffer zone better than they.

By the Treaty of La Granja, signed on October 1, 1800, Napoleon promised to give the duke of Parma (King Carlos IV's brother-in-law) the kingdom of Etruria, made up of Parma, Tuscany, and possibly other Italian territories belonging to the Catholic church. Six months after the establishment of this monarchy, Spain would sur-

---

1. Thomas M. Marshall, *A History of the Western Boundary of the Louisiana Purchase, 1819–1841* (Berkeley, 1914), 17–38.

render Louisiana to France. The arrangement was a good one for Madrid. On paper at least, France took over the protection of this important buffer zone at no expense to Spain. Also the Spanish traded an unknown number of non-Europeans for nearly one million new citizens in Europe who were taxable and could serve in Spanish armies. The strategic balance of power in the New World and the international situation in Italy did not appear to have been radically altered. Moreover Spain had the French agreement never to turn Louisiana over to a third power (such as Britain or the United States). The Spanish, not yet having become aware of Napoleon's penchant for violating treaties, believed this third-power clause ensured Mexico's security from further American threats.

A good test of the real implications of this trade could be found in London's reaction. From Spain's point of view, Madrid's major concerns were European. The British saw that Spain wanted to freeze problems in the New World until those in Europe were resolved. The United States appreciated this thinking and was thus wary of the British, French, and Spanish. London's attitude illustrated the problem more precisely. During the 1790s, Britain worried that France might obtain Louisiana and thereby threaten British interests because on the one hand, the United States, a potential ally, might find itself involved in controversies with London if the Americans fell into the French orbit; on the other hand, Spain could be drawn further into the French camp against England. Therefore the British attempted to improve relations with the United States. They clearly discouraged the French from thinking they could hold on to such a vast territory without fighting the Americans. The British even considered seizing this land.[2]

Events in Europe further complicated Spanish-American competition in the Mississippi Valley. By the convention of Aranjuez of 1801, Spain again allied with France to fight the second European coalition composed of Britain, Austria, and Russia. Napoleon's armies proved successful against this alliance, leading to the Treaty of Amiens in 1802. By its terms, peace came to Europe, Britain received

---

2. J. Leitch Wright, *Britain and American Frontier, 1783–1815* (Athens, 1974), chap. 7.

Trinidad, and Spain was given the Mediterranean island of Minorca. But Spain already mistrusted Napoleon by this time. The Italian kingdom for Carlos's relative did not come into being as quickly as agreed to in 1800, and the emperor's increased interest in America led the Spanish to think he might try to conquer their Mexican properties instead of the United States. The Treaty of Amiens proved to be the final convincing factor: Napoleon failed to respect Spanish rights, keeping them at bay without consulting them as equals during its negotiation. The French repeatedly assured Spain that the Tuscan kingdom would be established and that no power, especially the United States, would ever be sold or given Louisiana. With no other option open to them (since the French could always attack Spain), Madrid announced the return of this colony to France on October 13, 1802.[3]

Americans had heard rumors concerning the transfer of Louisiana to any number of powers. By 1800 officials had learned about the possibility of Spain's selling or trading it to either France or the United States. During 1801 and 1802, Americans believed it would go to France and worried about French imperialism in the New World. By 1802 problems related to Louisiana grew because Spain suspended the American right of deposit at New Orleans, citing numerous violations of customs regulations by the frontiersmen. The territory's future status also made settlers along the Mississippi as nervous as President Thomas Jefferson's government. Frontiersmen again wanted to use force in opening the Mississippi and New Orleans. In order to reduce tensions along the frontier, Jefferson notified France that he could not approve of Paris's acquiring Louisiana. Then he turned to the Spanish, threatening to open New Orleans with an army if Madrid did not voluntarily allow Americans to use the river and its port facilities. Spain reopened New Orleans, but the president went further by flirting with the British in order to reduce French interest in repossessing the Spanish colony.[4]

---

3. Jerónimo Becker, *Historia de las relaciones exteriores de España durante el siglo XIX* (Madrid, 1924), 1:71–84.

4. Mary P. Adams, "Jefferson's Reaction to the Treaty of San Ildefonso," *Journal of Southern History* 21 (1955): 173–188.

Once the United States learned that Spain had transferred Louisiana to the French, the Americans immediately moved to protect their interests. James Monroe left for Paris, hoping to buy New Orleans and some surrounding land. He carried instructions to purchase West Florida, New Orleans, and portions of Louisiana for about $10 million. By the time he arrived in Paris (1803), Napoleon's interest in the newly acquired land had dwindled. The bulk of his forces in the New World had been decimated in a Dominican revolt led by Toussait L'Ouverture. The men lost in this campaign originally had been slated for use in Louisiana, but now France could hardly defend its Caribbean holdings, let alone the vast new colony in North America. Further, if Britain and the United States should decide to unite against him, Napoleon could lose all of his holdings and influence in the New World. London controlled the oceans, making any communication with far-away Louisiana risky at best, not to mention expensive. Napoleon also needed funds with which to fight in Europe. At this uncomfortable moment, Monroe arrived in Paris with an offer to buy some of the unwanted land for a sizable sum, so Napoleon decided to sell Louisiana to him. Britain would be crippled in the New World, while the United States might be drawn into the French orbit at no expense to Paris.

The negotiations went quickly. When Monroe arrived in Paris on April 13, 1803, he and the regular American envoy there, Robert Livingston, immediately began discussions with the French. The final agreement stipulated that the United States would pay $15 million for the entire Louisiana Territory, which ran up the spine of the North American continent and deep into the western reaches. The boundaries were vague since neither government had any precise knowledge of them. Napoleon had insisted that the United States buy all the territory. The American negotiators soon realized that they would have to discard their instructions and purchase the entire territory if they were to acquire New Orleans.

The sale obviously pleased Napoleon, who saw the future benefits of it. He gambled on the United States and Spain quarreling over the arrangement since France had been forbidden, by his agreement with Madrid, to surrender this land to a third power. He hoped that Spain and the United States might go to war, allowing France to play one side off the other and even gain Spanish cooperation in Europe in return for supporting Madrid in America. If Spain refused to conform to his plans, then the United States might be used to neutralize the Spanish. Predictably when the sale became public, Spain protested loudly to the French and Americans.

Hardly wasting any time, Spanish diplomats informed Paris and Washington that this sale violated the previous treaty between Spain and France. Both the French and Americans ignored this protest since Madrid could do little to change the situation. Spain, however, could at least irritate the United States. Godoy instructed his representative in Washington to restrict the new territory's borders as much as possible by formal agreement. He had in mind confining the Louisiana Purchase to present-day Louisiana and Arkansas and denying the United States land from western Missouri north and west. Not relying solely on diplomacy, which Godoy believed would not work anyway, he developed military plans to block any physical penetration by the Americans into the lands Spain wished to retain. In 1803 Spain saw the purchase as a serious threat to Mexico. What made the situation painful was the fact that an ally, France, had robbed Madrid of the buffer zone that had so long protected Spanish possessions.[5]

Spain sent out four small military expeditions to prevent the exploration of the new territory by Meriwether Lewis and William Clark between 1804 and 1806, but all four failed to find and stop the team. That Spain initiated these complex maneuvers in virtually uncharted country indicated how serious Spanish leaders viewed the threat to Mexico. By the fall of 1806, Spain knew that Lewis and Clark had completed their trip to St. Louis. To the Spanish their work meant that the United States would challenge their holdings in the Far West from Mexico to Oregon. Still hoping to hold onto the West as a last buffer zone, Spain loudly renewed its claims to the area, yet it could do little in the face of expected assaults on this region and in Texas and Florida.

The penetration of Louisiana by the United States and Spain's attempts to thwart this almost led to war between the countries in 1806–07. Spain wanted to send other expeditions into North America but could not; during this period it became far too involved in Eu-

---

5. Becker, *Historia de las relaciones exteriores*, 1:85–103.

rope's wars to divert attention or resources. The United States focused on taming the newly acquired land. Almost the only European complication directly affecting the United States grew out of Anglo-Spanish rivalry during 1807, which reached fever pitch. Briefly, Spain expected Britain to invade its Caribbean holdings. Instead the British decided to fight with the Spanish against Napoleon on the Iberian peninsula. At the same time, Napoleon's invasion of Spain and Portugal and his establishment of a new government in Madrid minimized Anglo-Spanish complications in the New World, leading to a lessening of tensions in America, which provided the United States with a series of opportunities to strengthen its grip on the continent. Through 1814 European influence near the United States declined steadily, while that of the young republic grew. By 1815 Louisiana had become a clearly defined territory of the United States, filling with settlers and American officials.[6]

The United States was not completely oblivious to Europe while firming control on the continent. In fact, events on the other side of the Atlantic cramped relations between Spain and the United States. While the French invaded Spain (and finally were expulsed), the United States maintained neutrality. Conflicts over the violated rights of American citizens led to some heated discussions with the French, Spanish, and British during the years from 1808 through 1814. The United States challenged Britain's claims to the Oregon territory and Spain's to the far southwest. Increasingly, the young nation focused attention on Florida where frontiersmen demanded the extension of American authority. Yet the United States remained less aggressive than Spain had expected. Spaniards simply overestimated American hostility toward them during these years, fearing that the United States or Britain would seize Florida, Mexico, or other lands during the Spanish struggle with the French. During 1810–11 they believed French agents were working with the United States to steal Spanish possessions. This never happened because Paris and Washington remained on poor diplomatic terms due to French infringements on the rights of American citizens. Spain's inability to protect colonial interests continued during 1812–14 when the United States and Britain were at war. Still involved with fight-

---

6. Warren L. Cook, *Flood Tide of Empire: Spain and the Pacific Northwest, 1543–1819* (New Haven, 1973), 460–483.

ing at home, Spain helplessly stood by without being able to reinforce garrisons in Florida or Mexico.

Spain's weakness, obvious to the United States and Britain, could not be hidden from the Spanish colonists in the New World either. During these years (1808–15) the majority of them revolted from Spain, bursting the bonds of colonial authority one by one. The Spanish public and their authorities quickly blamed the United States for setting the example, a situation that aggravated relations with the United States for decades. Yet Latin America supplied only a few of the complex influences on Spanish-American diplomacy, most of which still centered on unresolved territorial problems in North America.[7] In fact Latin America's impact on relations between Spain and the United States was not as decisive prior to the Congress of Vienna as competition over Florida.

Since the late eighteenth century, when Americans had begun pushing into Louisiana and across the Mississippi River, they had also moved into Florida to trade with Indians and Englishmen and to settle or suppress Indian disturbances affecting Georgia. As with other parts of North America, Spain eventually lost Florida. The Spanish had established two administrative districts there, East and West Florida, to use as bases for encouraging Indian unrest directed against the American settlers in contested land north of Florida during the 1780s and 1790s. English traders also did a brisk business there, so much, in fact, that one of London's primary reasons for being concerned with the Floridas grew out of this commerce. The area also played a major role in Anglo-Spanish-American rivalry. For example, before France regained Louisiana, Britain sought to expand control over the Floridas. After France acquired Louisiana, which, in fact, the English thought of seizing or at least using in order to push Canada's borders south to the Missouri in 1802–03, London decided to support the Spanish there to help erode even further French power in the New World. This was made possible because the boundary between Louisiana and West Florida never had clearly defined lines accepted by any nation.[8]

The border confusion increased during 1803 after the United States purchased Louisiana, when many frontier Americans believed

---

7. See chapter 3 for details.
8. Wright, *Britain and American Frontier*, chaps. 8–9.

that West Florida belonged in their new territory. Others, like President Jefferson, thought it continued to be Spanish, and he formally offered to buy it. Borrowing an idea from Spain, he wanted to develop a wide buffer zone around New Orleans for its security. The land dominated the nearby Gulf of Mexico's coastline, running from the Mississippi River to Apalachicola. But fully aware of the president's intent, the Spanish refused to sell the land. He next threatened to seize it by force in 1805. Spain remained stubborn, no doubt because Britain continued to lend support in this crisis. American and British concern for Florida grew over the next few years as English traders and American settlers expanded their business interests there and established homes. The Spanish repeatedly rankled local Americans with their laws and policies, and the settlers complained to Washington.

By 1810 President James Madison began encouraging the Americans in Florida to revolt against the Spanish in the belief that Spain could do nothing at the moment to assert authority. To help matters, he announced in October that American jurisdiction now extended to West Florida as far as the Perdido River, justifying his position by declaring that the land in question was part of the Louisiana Purchase. Both Britain and Spain protested what they termed Madison's illegal conduct, but they could do little since they still faced Napoleon in Europe and lacked sufficient troops in Florida to expel American officials.

The War of 1812 between Britain and the United States weakened Spanish control over Florida, and Americans resolved to take advantage of the fluid conditions by seizing the colony. Spain counted on British naval power to help preserve authority there, but London could hardly do more than promise aid. Spain maintained neutrality in the Anglo-American war because of its own domestic problems and in order not to irritate the United States any further. Behind the scenes Spain encouraged the British, hoping they could weaken the United States. After Napoleon's defeat at Leipzig in 1813, Americans generally believed that Britain and Spain would devote more attention to Florida. The Spanish wanted to recover West Florida and push the Americans out of Louisiana. The British still had considerable economic interests in the area that they wanted to maintain. During the same year peace in Florida deteriorated when General James northeast as possible. Adams claimed that Louisiana's line ran to the Rio Grande River in Texas; Spain called the Mississippi the correct border.[11]

Unable to gain any European support, finding the Americans stubborn and willing to take by force whatever land they wanted, and faced with major revolts southward, Spain finally agreed to compromise. The United States helped turn Spanish thinking by threatening to seize Florida and, by implication, to help the Latin American rebels. The Americans agreed to compromise also because settlers, traders, and frontiersmen were demanding a resolution of the boundary problem. The American government, pressured to open the West for further trade and settlement during 1817 and 1818, found it politically expedient to reach agreement with Spain. Although it was a complicated treaty, many basic issues were settled by it.[12]

The new boundary between Spanish and American territories began at the Gulf of Mexico and worked its way up the Sabine River to 32° north and then across to the Red River. From there the line ran to the one hundredth meridian and pushed up to the Arkansas River and its source; then at 42° it went west to the Pacific. In effect, the United States surrendered claims to Texas and land south of California's northern border. These southern lands did not stay in Spanish hands long, because in 1833 Mexico declared independence from Spain and absorbed them. The United States ultimately gained possession of the Southwest in 1848 as a result of the war with Mexico. Beyond this area, to the Far West, Spain gave up claims to lands north of California and east of the western line of the Louisiana Purchase. Thus the nearly three-hundred-year-old Spanish claim to the Oregon territory finally melted away. By the same treaty, the United States acquired Florida and agreed to pay up to $5 million in claims lodged by Americans there against the Spanish for damages accumulating over the past thirty-seven years.

The treaty, known as the Transcontinental Treaty of 1819, dealt with vast territories and major issues. Spain finally recognized the acquisition of Louisiana by the United States from France while surrendering claims to the northwest. The United States gave up de-

---

11. Philip C. Brooks, *Diplomacy in the Borderlands: The Adams-Onis Treaty of 1819* (Berkeley, 1939), 85.
12. Ibid., passim.

mands for land in what is today Texas, New Mexico, Nevada, and California in return for the much desired Florida. More comforting to both was the formal, rather than implicit, recognition of each other's property. Unquestionably the United States gained more from the exchange than Spain did. In return for poorly justifiable claims to the Pacific Northwest, the republic obtained actual control of new lands and the prospect of peace during a future thrust toward Oregon. Moreover Florida fell into American hands.

Spain preserved a large southwestern buffer zone to protect Mexico while divesting itself of troublesome Florida. Peace came to North America, allowing Spain to concentrate on problems to the south. In the long run, the settlement was not favorable. Spain later lost Mexico, plus the Southwest and all of South America. But there was little Madrid could do to protect its holdings. The United States would have seized Florida and eventually occupied other parts of North America. An embarrassing defeat of this nature carried great political danger at home and expense abroad since some military defense would have had to be made for the sake of Spain's national honor. Yet King Fernando VII criticized the agreement and delayed ratifying the document since Washington had refused to promise not to recognize the new Latin American governments. Finally in 1821, long after the U.S. Senate had approved the treaty and belated attempts to gain some European support for continuing a struggle by Spain against the Americans failed, Fernando consented. By his action Spain admitted defeat at the hands of its Anglo-American competitors who had nibbled at the Spanish empire since the early 1500s.

The activities of both governments during the years between 1815 and 1821 were important because they reinforced images of each other that persisted in one degree or another for the rest of the century. The United States found Spanish intrigues with European powers frustrating and even malicious. Americans believed Spain wanted to weaken their power and abort America's destiny by crippling the republic's position in North America. Sympathetic with the Latin rebels, then fighting for independence from Spain, Americans could hardly help but see in Madrid's efforts to squash such revolts a sinister struggle to prevent the pure winds of freedom from blowing across the American continents.

Spain was injured by the United States in much the same manner.

Wilkinson seized Mobile from the Spanish. Americans now became more confident that East Florida, which occupied part of the territory making up present-day Florida, would soon fall into their hands.

At the Congress of Vienna, the question of who would ultimately retain Louisiana and Florida surfaced as a secondary issue. Britain still coveted it and certainly did not want France to regain control of Louisiana. Both Britain and Spain hoped the United States could be prevented from regaining control of East Florida. Spain still felt confident it could hold on to the colony, but most delegates at Vienna thought otherwise.[9] Spanish diplomats sought support for its claims by arguing that Napoleon could not legally sell Louisiana to the Americans. Earlier in 1814 the British had liquidated their war with the United States by the Treaty of Ghent. According to this settlement, the British recognized Washington's dominance over North America. Therefore as of 1815, the United States owned or controlled all of Louisiana and much of West Florida, but none of East Florida or Canada.[10]

Because Spain did not accept American hegemony over the continent and abandon Florida, friction inevitably remained. In 1817 Andrew Jackson went into Florida to punish Indians who were raiding American territory. In carrying out his orders, he invaded Spain's portion, seizing a fort at St. Marks, West Florida, in the spring of 1818. He then captured Pensacola, dismissed the local Spanish governor, confiscated other property and official records, and established American authority. Although he probably exceeded his authority—a subject still in controversy—his actions reflected how weak Spain's hold on Florida proved to be. Spain could neither control the Indians nor resist Jackson's small force. The United States defended his actions by saying that if Spain could not restrain the Indians from raiding American territory, then U.S. soldiers would have to protect American interests.

Like Madrid, London knew that the tense situation there could lead to another war with the United States—something the country wished to avoid. In previous years, Spanish, British, and American

---

9. Ibid., chap. 11.
10. J. Leitch Wright, Jr., *Anglo-Spanish Rivalry in North America* (Athens, 1971), 184.

troops clashed in Florida, and any further involvement there by London spelled trouble. Moreover the British still wanted Spain to retain Florida since this would keep the United States distracted enough from coveting Canada. But Spanish authorities decided that they could not properly govern Florida and surrendered to the inevitable by allowing the United States to have it in return for a collection of concessions. By giving up the colony in such an honorable manner as a treaty would prove less rankling to the Spanish public than having it brutally seized. The negotiations, which led to the Adams-Onís Treaty of 1819, reflected the much broader issues of Spanish-American competition for control of various parts of North America and not merely for Florida. They discussed specific issues, such as borders in the Southwest, Northwest, and along the coastline of the Gulf of Mexico before determining the final terms of the treaty. This agreement proved to be the last major formal diplomatic instrument to emerge from Spanish-American rivalry in the New World before their war in 1898, which heralded Spain's final retirement from that half of the New World.

Fernando VII (who came to power in Spain during 1814) and his cabinet decided that East Florida could be formally turned over to the United States in exchange for a clearly defined set of boundaries in North America. The troops then stationed in Florida would be transferred to Latin America to suppress revolutions. Mexico still worried the Spanish since they feared the United States might want this area next. Troops in Florida could be moved over to protect Mexico. The Spanish wanted to wrestle from the United States a written promise not to recognize any of the rebel governments being established in Latin America. In fact, this goal ranked with that of protecting Mexico with a buffer zone.

In the fall of 1817, Luis de Onís, the Spanish representative in the United States, first broached the subject of a treaty with Secretary of State John Quincy Adams. Adams believed that the United States would eventually dominate the entire North American continent, and Spain's offer to settle boundary disputes appeared to him to be an excellent step in the right direction and an opportunity for him to contribute to the fulfillment of his country's destiny. Specifically he wanted East and West Florida and Spanish recognition of American borders in the Southwest. Spain hoped to push the frontier as far

Americans brashly marched into Florida, attacked Spanish fortifications, and claimed lands Spain had coveted for several hundred years. They eyed Mexico and its buffer regions with almost the same fervor with which they went after Florida and the Mississippi Valley. Pretentiously and with a rude manner irritating to self-styled genteel Spanish diplomats, Americans demanded the Pacific Northwest over which Spain and Britain had been haggling for centuries. Helpless in the face of geopolitical realities, Spaniards accused the United States of being recalcitrant and one of their worst enemies.

From 1795, when the first territorial treaty went into effect, to 1821, after the second agreement became operative, relations were difficult and fraught with miscalculations, complex problems, and accidents. Force and persistence, fighting in Europe and in America all contributed to Washington's ability to acquire vast territories. Spain, crippled and bound by European wars, confused and changed by the forces released during the French Revolution, Napoleon's wars, and the invasion of their peninsula and later by revolutions in Latin America, could hardly deal with the challenge posed by the United States. If anything, it is a surprise that Spain held on to its North American property as long as it did. Without convulsions in Europe, it would have been difficult for the United States to dislodge Spain from Florida, Louisiana, and the Southwest as quickly as it did.

American society and culture withstood the test of these years more successfully than did Spain by exhibiting greater degrees of flexibility, strength, and determination. Concentrating the vast resources of the nation on the goal of protecting itself by expansion, the United States did not to have to waste men and dollars on wars defending the homeland from European armies. Barricaded behind the Atlantic, Americans were more secure in their belief that they had a right to own the continent and inevitably would than Spain in its conviction that it legally held claim to lands thousands of miles away from Iberia. After the American Revolution Spain's military might clearly declined, a fact not lost on the United States. Such beliefs and facts inspired the American nation while self-doubts confused Spain. Coupled with the United States's proximity to the contested territories, it is hard to see how Spain could have justified a presence in North America much past the Napoleonic era.

By the early 1820s a turning point was discernible in relations between Spain and the United States. The main battle for control of North America had been fought and won by the United States. The southwestern lands that Spain still owned (until they were lost to Mexico) were momentarily unimportant to the United States since they were uninhabitated, uncharted, and difficult to reach. Americans still owned more than enough territory eastward to occupy their time for years to come. Consequently Spanish-American relations dealt with new problems during the following years, essentially the competition for hegemony of the Caribbean Sea. This new phase did not neatly begin in 1821; it was presaged by Spanish-American bitterness over the fate of Latin America during the various colonies' revolutions against Spain at the same time that the United States struggled for domination over Louisiana and Florida.

3
AN EMPIRE LOST

The colonial revolutions against Spain in Hispanic America, which began during the years Napoleon occupied the Iberian peninsula and culminated in the complete independence of Central and South America by the early 1820s, profoundly affected diplomatic relations between Madrid and Washington. The balance of power in the New World altered as Spain's influence receded and that of the United States filled the political and economic void. The process was not quick, but observers of the day clearly noticed a changing of the guard. The power vacuum created took nearly 150 years to be filled by the United States and even then never to the extent that Madrid had had prior to 1808. Because independence so profoundly affected the foreign policy of the United States to the present day while modifying the size and nature of Spain's overseas possessions, the Latin American revolutions occupied a major portion of the early diplomacy between Madrid and Washington. Reflecting Spain's and the United States' previous experiences on the North American continent, developments in Latin America further complicated and irritated both nations.

Guided by Napoleon's dreams for a French-dominated Europe, France extended its political and military influence into the Iberian peninsula in 1807. In the following year, Napoleon placed his brother Joseph on the Spanish throne. The Spanish people rose in rebellion against the French and over the next several years slowly expulsed Napoleon's armies, officials, and brother from Spain. The fighting at home seriously interrupted the normal administration of the empire. Moreover French authorities could hardly communicate with the Spanish colonies, let alone conquer them, because in 1805 the British had destroyed virtually all the French navy at the battle of Trafalgar.

In effect, the Spanish colonies drifted alone with minimal control from Madrid. This fluid situation led Europeans, the colonists, and North Americans to speculate on who would control the empire. Because they ruled the Atlantic Ocean, the British thought they might win Spain's colonies. France hoped to seize them in order to augment its strength in Europe. The United States wanted to increase its own influence in the Hispanic world by keeping the Europeans bottled up in Europe. European and American interest in Spain's colonies obviously predated Napoleon's invasion, but their concern heightened as a result of Madrid's crippled condition after 1807.

The Spanish colonies also found the international situation bewildering. The lack of effective colonial government had always irritated them and with the added confusion of the early 1800s, they thought about independence. Many believed Spain could never govern them properly or provide the commercial life they sought. When Napoleon's army marched into Spain, colonial officials and colonists were forced to govern themselves, relying on their own initiative and talents. Although colonists took sides in Spain's troubles, they questioned Madrid's authority over them. All over Latin America colonists thought of independence, and the opportunity seemed at hand to wrestle it from Spain. Obvious advantages existed at the moment. Prostrated by fighting at home, Spain could hardly suppress such revolts. Britain and the United States also promised to develop broader commercial relations with the colonists. Thus the Latin rebels thought London and Washington would help them in their struggles.

Indeed the United States had expressed an economic interest in South America. Early in the 1790s American traders had penetrated Latin America, slowly overcoming Spain's restrictive laws and policies. These commercial relations increased in 1797 when Spain implemented a series of laws that permitted expanded trade with the United States. American appetites were thus whetted, but North American traders were frustrated by the remaining trade restrictions, so Washington complained vociferously as it had over similar rules existing in the Mississippi Valley. Spain's reaction was to restrict

---

1. Arthur P. Whitaker, *The United States and the Independence of Latin America, 1800–1830* (Baltimore, 1941), 23.

trade even more by regulations promulgated in 1799, 1801, and 1804. Despite these handicaps, the United States exported twice as much to Spain's colonies by 1805 as to the rest of the world.[1] Americans saw the south as an unlimited commercial frontier rich in natural resources and populated by eager customers.

Washington officially maintained its neutrality in Spain's conflict with France. Theoretically this policy applied to the New World as a whole. Unofficially the United States sympathized strongly with the Latin rebels but decided not to help them. Each president encouraged expanded trade with Latin America but never at the expense of political involvement in European affairs. Washington's formal neutrality afforded an advantage to its citizens because, having taken no sides, Americans could trade with the Spanish, French, English, and other European countries so long as a naval blockade did not exist at any particular port. This meant that the economic gap created by Spain's inability to sell goods and services to its own colonies, London's requirement that its own products be used in the wars against France, and Napoleon's primary commitment to fight in Europe left U.S. businessmen almost completely free to conduct commerce in the New World.

By 1810 the colonies had been left to their own resources completely. Civil war raged in Spain where juntas competed with France for power, and poor communications confused colonists and Spaniards alike. Each colony, therefore, began making its own administrative and political decisions. For example, Mexico proved loyal to the Bourbon family, while Chile declared independence from Madrid. Revolutions all over Latin America broke out against Spanish authority, and little could be done to stop them. Every available soldier in Spain had to be kept at home. At most, colonial officials tried to delay American independence until such time as Spain could send more troops to suppress the rebels. Although between 1810 and 1812 these rebellious subjects hoped that the United States would help them, Washington refused, fearing European powers would react by intervening in Latin America and reestablishing Spanish authority and even some of their own.

Understandably the Spanish viewed the United States with suspicion, firmly believing that Washington had helped the rebels with the blessings of the American public. Spanish diplomats, knowing the

United States wanted to control all of North America and aware of the extensive economic penetration by that republic into Latin America, could hardly be expected to think otherwise. Evidence for their suspicions lay everywhere. In 1810 the North Americans seized Mobile; American newspapers encouraged Spanish rebels and blasted Spain's colonial policies; and Madrid's legation cataloged various types of local aid to the revolutionaries. Spain remained moribund and frustrated, unable to assert authority in the New World or prevent the United States from encouraging the rebellions. Yet the Americans served as a convenient scapegoat in Spain for officials who shifted the blame for their nation's troubles to the United States, using existing latent anti-Americanism to their advantage.

During the war between Britain and the United States (1812–14), Americans experienced the same debilitating difficulties that Spaniards had faced for the past several years. Combat at home coupled with British control of the seas made it virtually impossible for Washington's influence to grow in Latin America. Trade declined. The British improved their commercial relations with Hispanic America, thereby reviving and expanding the traditional theater of Franco-Anglo-Spanish rivalry, which, in recent years, had been concentrated in North America. This was also, however, the period during which the border incidents in North America and economic rivalry in Florida also took place. Thus the diplomatic environment was both complex and serious.

In 1812 Latin America attracted considerable international attention. Europeans viewed the various rebel governments as one unit, a single mass on the map, and they considered the revolutions almost as one rather than many separate ones. They knew the fighting persisted to the detriment of Spanish, European, and North American political and economic interests, and there was no end in sight. The governments that had overthrown Napoleon—Austria, Russia, Prussia, Britain, Portugal, Sweden, and Spain—known as the Concert of Europe, viewed the Latin American situation as a grave international crisis. The allies believed that unsettled conditions there threatened monarchical authority since the rebels were challenging a monarchy and establishing republics. Moreover the southern hemisphere caused some members of the concert to compete among themselves for economic privileges, which threatened to disrupt the unity each believed they shared in Europe. Therefore in order to preserve the status quo in Europe, they sought to end the rebellions in the Americas.

The United States understood Europe's concern since Washington provided many problems for the concert, competing with this block in the Hispanic world rather than bilaterally on a country-by-country basis. American officials knew they did not struggle merely with the British, French, or Spanish; they faced what appeared to them to be a united alliance of powerful nations bent on crippling the growth of American power in the south while reducing its vitality to the north. To protect itself, the United States attempted to convince Europeans it did not threaten them either in Latin America or elsewhere; at the same time, it encouraged the rebels in the south. Europe saw through this subterfuge quickly enough. Yet because Spain's control over the colonies remained an open question, it was difficult for European and American diplomats to analyze Latin American conditions, let alone influence them effectively.

Despite this confusion, Spain stood in a better position to resist the United States and subdue the rebels in 1814 and 1815 than it had earlier. Officials faced Spanish problems confidently after expelling Napoleon and his brother Joseph. Fernando VII had an alliance with the British, which he hoped might bring assistance in restoring his authority. Spain felt spiritually renewed by its recent experiences, and its king resolved to block the expansion of American power into the colonies, even though he knew his influence in North America could hardly be broadened. By 1815 this determination had hardened both nations against each other in the Hispanic world. John Quincy Adams led the country in believing Spain harshly ruled the colonies. Yet he admitted that the colonists were Spaniards and therefore shared similar cultural and political views. Americans knew little about Latin America, acknowledging only that the unknown lands to the south were a potentially vast market and possibly the future home of more republican governments.[2] The Spanish envoy to the United States, Luis de Onís, thought Americans wanted to plant republican regimes all over South America, and unquestionably many thought this should be a task for their nation.[3]

---

2. Ibid., 148–149.
3. Ibid., 184.

While the Spanish were sending troops to America, the United States helped the rebels by continued neutrality. This way, as stipulated by international law and long-standing custom, the colonists could use American ports on a limited basis. Aware of the feelings U.S. citizens entertained toward Spain, most Spaniards concluded that Washington was anything but neutral. Yet each country respected the military might of the other, at least enough to worry about the ramifications of a clash, not to complain too vociferously.[4] European governments wished Spain luck in ending the revolts and at the Congress of Vienna even considered how they might help the country. After a few discussions among themselves, however, they realized that no government wanted to commit troops to Latin America, which is what Madrid really needed from them. Yet their talk of concerted action in 1815 proved serious enough to slow any desire by the United States in considering too active an intervention in Latin America.

American public interest in the revolts never waned. In fact, by 1818 this concern affected domestic politics as public clamor to help the rebels increased, while small filibustering groups launched irritating expeditions against Spanish authorities. Congress passed a neutrality act in 1818 preventing filibusters from using American territory. Done to keep Europe away from U.S. problems, it indicated some degree of concern in the United States for the Latin revolutions, while further signaling to Spain North American hostility. Public interest in America more than offset its government's caution to Spaniards because the president could hardly ignore the majority's will too long. In short, Spanish officials thought it only a question of time before Washington would extend open assistance to the rebels. Quite correctly they saw that the neutrality legislation served merely to curb the public's enthusiasm at a time when negotiations were underway for Florida's purchase.[5]

With the Napoleonic wars several years behind them, European governments in 1818 and 1819 took a fresh look at the Latin Ameri-

---

4. William Spence Robertson, *Hispanic-American Relations with the United States* (New York, 1923), 196.

5. Charles G. Fenwick, *The Neutrality Laws of the United States* (Baltimore, 1912), 40–41.

can situation. By 1818 the concert, well organized and representing the forces of order as symbolized by monarchism, alliances, and peace in Europe, stood ready to use military force to suppress any disturbances threatening their status quo. The series of congresses and military interventions in various parts of the continent proved to all in the next several years how real their determination could be. These efforts at restoring order consequently involved Latin America, which affronted Spanish authority and encouraged dissident groups in Europe by its continued instability.

It appeared obvious to most Europeans that Spain could not suppress the revolts alone. Nevertheless the colonists failed to muster sufficient strength to expel the Spanish. It was evident that unless one side or the other received outside help, the unsettled state of affairs would continue indefinitely. This warfare damaged trade, and the Americans took advantage of the situation by making Spain feel they would aid the rebels more actively. The war taxed Spain's strength by absorbing so much energy that the country could not fully participate in European affairs. When the allies met at the Congress of Aix-la-Chapelle, France and Russia proposed that Europe intervene in Latin America to restore Spanish authority so that republicanism would not spread to all of Latin America and possibly to Europe. They reasoned that if this threat to monarchism were not met, every monarchy in Europe stood to fall eventually. French and Russian diplomats suggested that the Europeans first agree to a set of terms to offer the rebels, one of which would be their return to Spanish control. If the terms were rejected, then they could impose economic sanctions against the colonists while lending Spain full diplomatic support. These proposals, at a minimum, would have to be implemented if the balance of power in Hispanic America were to be tipped in favor of Europe.[6]

Britain rejected the plan, mainly because it hesitated to use military force in the Americas, which would be inevitable if these proposals went into effect. Moreover since British trade with the Latins proved far greater than that of the other European nations, economic sanctions would be expensive for London. Yet Spain still campaigned

---

6. French Ensor Chadwick, *The Relations of the United States and Spain* (New York, 1909–11), 1:163–165.

for intervention of some sort. The British stand encouraged President Monroe to seek closer cooperation with London regarding Hispanic affairs, reasoning that it would be better to compete with Britain for influence than with all of Europe. He believed England's stand at Aix-la-Chapelle suggested that London would support the United States in Latin America. Unknown to Madrid, the results of the congress indicated to Washington that it could not yet become too aggressive in supporting the rebels because Europe was still interested in intervention.[7]

Europe's concern for the worldwide threat of republicanism did not cease in 1818. In fact, fear of this menace affected the Latin American situation for several years. In 1820 liberals in Spain revolted against King Fernando. Others, not necessarily liberal or republican, protested his rule as well. Soldiers, for instance, did not want to be sent to Latin America, believing their lives were more important than the empire. Some objected to high taxes and were tired of fighting for so many years. Many civilians and soldiers felt the empire could not be saved anyway. In combination with other irritated segments of Spanish society, confusion reigned in Spain as local governments, often with liberal leaders, sprang up in opposition to Fernando. Between the spring of 1820 and early 1822, liberal politicians ruled Spain virtually uncontested while negotiating with the king for concessions that would permanently institutionalize their programs within the framework of monarchical rule. The king promised them what they wanted, but in 1822, he turned to the French for help in suppressing the liberals. After gaining the approval of Europe, France marched 10,000 men into Spain on April 7, 1823, and within six months restored Fernando to his throne. The king reasserted his conservative, autocratic authority by imprisoning and executing liberals and announcing a renewed campaign to establish control over Latin America. However, he did not fully realize that between 1820 and 1823, the Latin Americans had moved closer to permanent independence.[8]

Several situations governed life in the New World by 1818–19 that would affect all Americans after 1820. There were not enough

---

7. Whitaker, *United States and the Independence of Latin America*, 260–261.
8. Raymond Carr, *Spain, 1808–1939* (Oxford, 1966), 129–143.

soldiers and well-instructed and skilled officials either to suppress revolts or to provide good local leadership. The king also refused to compromise by satisfying colonial grievances, which included representation in the cortés (Spanish parliament), local taxation and administrative rights, and expanded trade with non-Spanish areas. The rebels therefore continued their revolutions. In 1819 New Granada shook off Spanish rule and in 1821, Venezuela. During the following year, Mexico broke from Spain. These revolts indicated that ideological and political confusion, along with other local concerns, went far to explain Fernando's reluctance to compromise. For example, Mexico's revolution resulted in the establishment of an ultraconservative government, in part as a reaction against the liberal regime then ruling Spain. In other Latin colonies, the opposite took place. Generally they advocated independence under liberal administrations. These Latin Americans usually fought for freedom in the belief that the Spanish government, characterized by an almost arthritic conservatism, could not provide the dynamic leadership they then wanted.

During these critical years (1818–23) the United States watched the revolutions and the convulsions in Spain, playing a low-keyed yet nonetheless active role. Spain's inability to govern the colonies dictated such a policy. The United States, still fearing possible European intervention if the rebels were aided, felt that the best course to follow would be to see if the American revolutionaries could break from Spain alone. Officials in Washington, more concerned than complacent, envisioned conservative Europeans restoring autocratic rule in Spain and Madrid in turn extending its control over Latin America. In fact, the European concert easily suppressed liberal revolutions in Spain, Portugal, Naples, and Greece. Americans thought it might only be a question of time before the same happened in the New World. The last thing Washington wanted was to clash with European troops in South America. The Spanish hoped for such a conflict; otherwise they would lose economic, political, and possibly cultural hegemony in the Hispanic world.

In addition to these external pressures, the Monroe administration faced serious domestic problems related to Latin America. Merchants, politicians, expansionists, and others bombarded the government with requests to help the rebels. Finally Washington decided that it could move in this direction without great risk. The president asked Congress in March 1822 for funds with which to open legations in La Plata (Argentina), Chile, Peru, Colombia, and Mexico. This request represented the first significant change in Washington's Latin American policy in years and reflected the government's opinion that Spain would not long rule in the southern hemisphere. Washington concluded, therefore, that it could no longer delay recognizing these governments for fear of losing any influence, especially economic, that the country held in Latin America because the rebels, who had been demanding recognition for many years, might turn their backs on the northern republic once they were completely free of Spain.

The Spanish were furious. Joaquín de Anduaga, Madrid's envoy in Washington, lodged a formal protest, calling recognition of his country's colonies a breach of international law. American officials responded that the regimes in question had proven their ability to maintain their independence in the face of Spanish military pressure. Therefore they could be recognized.[9] Since Spain understood the dilemma the United States faced if the new governments were not acknowledged, Madrid saw in the American move further erosion of its influence in Central and South America.

Spain apparently did not fully understand the United States because in 1823 its diplomats failed to appreciate the dual influence that the threat of European intervention and the pressure of domestic presidential politics had on American foreign policy. Some Americans still worried that the Holy Alliance would interfere even though an increasing number, encouraged by Britain's reluctance to support intervention with troops, felt that the problem was going away. Many in Washington were never sure but that Paris or London might wrestle important concessions from the Spanish in the New World—for example, Cuba—without resorting to arms. When the French invaded Spain, Cuba lay vulnerable to British seizure. From an early time the legation in Madrid received instructions to thwart any attempt to negotiate Cuba out of Spanish control. In fact,

---

9. Whitaker, *United States and the Independence of Latin America*, 334.

10. The first part of chapter 4 explains the reasons for Washington's Cuban policy.

the United States wanted to ensure that the island remain in Spain's hands for the time being.[10]

By late 1823, however, European intervention in Latin America seemed less imminent than before. The only danger spot remained off Florida—Cuba—which Washington closely watched. The government by now had come to the conclusion that its interests could better be protected and expanded by establishing diplomatic missions in each of the new Latin countries while developing an international policy directed at keeping Europe out of the American hemisphere. Their need for a bold diplomatic offensive against European encroachment became painfully obvious after news arrived in late 1823 that France had restored Fernando to power.

The way became clearer in August 1823 when the British decided to curtail France's new-found influence in the New World, which had come with its success in Spain. London worried that its own interests might be compromised by the French obtaining concessions from a grateful Spanish king. George Canning, the British foreign minister, suggested to the United States that they issue a joint statement designed to discourage European intervention in the Americas. Essentially Canning proposed that no European power be allowed to conquer Hispanic territory. He even offered to declare that neither Britain nor the United States would attempt to acquire any. This pledge would appease Europe (and England), which feared if other nations were kept out of the New World that the United States might overrun it eventually. The Americans rejected his proposals since they limited their options in the future, especially in the Caribbean and in commercial relations with Latin America, and with presidential elections coming up, no one in the government wanted to agree to an unpopular restriction. But Canning's suggestions indicated to President Monroe that the British would not object to some statement limiting European expansion by preserving the status quo in the Americas. Encouraged, he decided to issue his own declaration, which would not compromise American options on the one hand and more important on the other, would not harm his domestic political aspirations.

What he implemented became a basic tenet of American foreign policy toward the Americas: the Monroe Doctrine. In general, Monroe aimed it at all Europe and not just toward Spain. Leaving aside domestic considerations, which were dominant in his decision to issue the statement, let us simply examine its diplomatic features. Monroe understood that Russia, for instance, still claimed territory along the northwest coast south of present-day Alaska, an area he did not want reinforced by Moscow, although Monroe knew that in contrast, Madrid's claims to the New World were weakening. As the century aged, his doctrine provided some of the inspiration for Washington's Latin American policies, which always clashed with those of Spain. Diplomatic relations between the two nations came under the influence of the doctrine, but at the same time their competition affected its meaning and role in international affairs.

President Monroe announced his important policy on December 2, 1823, as part of his annual message to Congress. In his address, he held that governments in the New World could not "be considered as subjects for future colonization by any European powers." Moreover, any extension of monarchism to Latin America would be considered "dangerous to our peace and safety." Anyone who threatened to destroy an existing regime in this part of the world would be treated as an enemy of the United States.[11] He announced that his country did not attempt to interfere in Europe's affairs; therefore Europeans should not bother America's. In short, his message made clear that the United States would not allow Europeans to trespass on what he considered to be his nation's private preserve. Monroe avoided the suggestion that European-owned territory be freed; rather his remarks reflected his willingness to maintain a certain status quo.

The public in the United States took notice of his statement immediately. They generally approved of it since the doctrine reaffirmed their government's intention of protecting their commercial interests in the New World while promising to expand Washington's political influence. Latin Americans reacted in various ways. Some approved since it meant they had an ally against Europe. Others felt that the United States had simply stepped into their hemisphere, posing the same problems experienced with the Old World. More conservative elements usually drowned such doubts with

---

11. James D. Richardson, ed., *Messages and Papers of the Presidents, 1789–1892* (Washington, D.C., 1896–1903), 2:209, 218.

praise for the president. Colombia and Brazil, for example, made Americans and Europeans feel that the Latin countries supported the United States wholeheartedly.[12]

Of greater importance than Latin America's views were those of Europe. British diplomats realized that Monroe's statements meant England would be limited in its plans for the New World much like any other European country. The British public, slower to realize this, at first thought the doctrine a good one, although it posed some problems for their government, which wanted to voice an objection. Canning protested, knowing the effects it could have on British diplomacy and commerce. It galled him that the United States had acted in the belief that Britain would not contest such a declaration. In short, Monroe stole a march on Canning, and there was little he could do about it. Even more irritating to Canning, although completely unknown to Monroe, was the fact that he had asked the French back in October not to invade Spanish America. The French had assured him they would not, frustrating Canning after news of the doctrine arrived in London, since he could not easily change his position in light of the French stance.

The reaction on the European continent was predictably hostile. The monarchies, particularly France, Russia, Prussia, and Austria, refused to accept the doctrine as a guide for international behavior or binding on their foreign policies. Their diplomats generally laughed at its pretentiousness and thought the United States could never enforce it. Austrian Chancellor Clemens Metternich, the architect of Europe's post-Napoleonic political structure and very much its dominating figure in the 1820s, condemned the message in no uncertain terms, calling it "indecent."

The doctrine infuriated Spaniards. Since they believed the United States had continually helped the Latin Americans, this message merely confirmed what they already considered as fact, representing another, more overt act directed against Spain's interests. Therefore they did not hesitate to call it piratical. Spaniards found it wrong because the policy excluded Europeans from helping Madrid to restore legal authority in the Americas while allowing filibustering groups to continue operating from such places as New Orleans and

---

12. Whitaker, *United States and the Independence of Latin America*, 535–538.

New York. Since they billed this as a patently unfair discrepancy throughout the 1820s, Spaniards never considered Washington's policy of proclaimed neutrality as anything but a farce. Officially the Spanish called the doctrine false international law.

Spain knew Monroe's timing would prove harmful to it because Britain, France, and Russia could not aid in meeting this challenge. Britain had already committed itself to peace in the New World, and a similar pledge for the status quo from Paris lay on Canning's desk. Austria worried about its own domestic problems, and Portugal could not muster sufficient strength to interest Spain. Russia considered some independent action to strike down the Monroe Doctrine since it threatened monarchism and European authority in the New World but eventually concluded that any unilateral effort would be futile and, worse, might jeopardize its own interests in Eastern and Western Europe.

Spain wanted to destroy the Monroe Doctrine by having all powers repudiate it as international reality, but a combination of lagging European interest, successful liberation of the colonies, and the growing strength of the United States in the Caribbean led most Americans and Spaniards to acknowledge its permanency in Washington's Latin American policy. Proof came in the actions of all concerned. The British openly advocated independence for the colonies, and in January 1825, France, although a staunch supporter of the Spanish, announced it would recognize some Latin governments. Spain formally protested to each power that extended diplomatic recognition to the Americans, but to no avail. It still officially refused to acknowledge the independence of these new governments. Mainly for domestic political reasons, Spain felt formal, public protests should be lodged each time a new legation opened in the Hispanic hemisphere.[13] By the end of the 1820s, however, even the stubborn Spanish king could not ignore the reality of Washington's rising star or deny the success with which his ex-colonies held onto their independence.

The Spanish were suffering setbacks in the Americas despite all their efforts. On the heels of the Monroe Doctrine, the majority of the Latin American states decided to have a conference to promote

---

13. Jerónimo Becker, *Historia de relaciones exteriores de España durante el siglo XIX* (Madrid, 1924), 1:535–545.

hemispheric unity. Guided by Simón Bolívar, delegates attended such a meeting at Panamá in June 1826. Some American governments wanted Washington's help in convincing the Spanish to accept their independence. The Department of State asked to send delegates in order to protect American interests there. Reluctantly Congress approved but so slowly that the envoys failed to arrive in time for the conference (and one even died on his way there). Although Washington's first important attempt at hemispheric diplomacy failed from its viewpoint, Spain thought otherwise; such incidents led it to believe that Madrid's position in the New World was rapidly deteriorating.

Spanish newspapers of the time pictured the North Americans as a cocky, rude nation, armed with the Monroe Doctrine bursting into Spain's compound to steal what rightfully belonged to Madrid. The Foreign Office shared this view and worried about Cuba's security now as a result. In fact, at about the same time, Washington's interest turned to concentrate on the Caribbean, where trade in Cuba appeared more appealing, to the consternation of the Spanish. Many believed the United States would initiate an aggressive policy against the remaining colonies with, as usual, no regard for Spain's rights.

Spanish and American rivalry over Hispanic America from the time Napoleon invaded Spain to the mid-1820s wound a twisted path through the histories and prejudices of both, bruising each and violating each one's rights. Spaniards, especially Spanish officials who could not publicly accept responsibility for their shortcomings if they hoped to continue their political careers, used the United States as a whipping boy for many of their problems. The majority at the Foreign Office sincerely believed Washington worked incessantly against Spain's interests.

Because of conflicting political currents and the wavering military situation in Latin America, Spain dreamed of reconquering its empire over at least the next thirty or forty years. Some Hispanic states supported liberal governments, while others maintained conservative ones. They were all volatile, insecure institutions, which could offer only political instability to the New World. Spain's conviction that the cultural or racial bond it shared with Latin Americans would draw them naturally closer together further raised hopes. Spain considered this a fundamental advantage over the United States, which drew its cultural nourishment from Anglo-Saxon institutions. Spaniards knew their Latin cousins did not like or understand the North Americans, encouraging Madrid to battle Washington in the Americas. This view changed by the mid-1830s when Spaniards realized that the struggle also had cultural fronts. By then the issues between Spain and the United States included competition for cultural hegemony in the New World, for the survival of hispanic culture (*hispanismo*).

The colonists were bitter after long years of fighting Spain. Even conservative Mexico refused to establish intimate relations with the former mother country. Throughout this period, Spain repeatedly underestimated the growth of North American political and economic influence in Central and South America, which, in the long run, replaced Spain's connections, leaving only the cultural bond. And even this thread appeared threatened as the century grew older. Spain failed to appreciate in the 1820s and 1830s that the blame for losing these colonies rested squarely on itself; perhaps the events of these years made such a realization difficult, if not impossible, to face.[14]

Spain's shortcomings were not Washington's victories. The United States followed a cautious policy of virtual nonintervention and, to a degree, even of noninvolvement. This attitude, however, offered American rebels the fruits of North America's nonbelligerency.[15] Inherent weaknesses in Spain's colonial administration in the late eighteenth and early nineteenth centuries initially encouraged the colonists to revolt. Europe's total occupation with the Napoleonic wars, which placed a premium on Spain's participation by making it a center stage for the fighting between 1807 and 1812, limited Madrid's capability for retaining possession of its colonies. Consequently Spain should have shared its defeats in the Americas more with Europe than with the United States.

It is a well-accepted political maxim that all power vacuums fill quickly. What happened in Latin America confirms the validity of this law. Left to their own resources, the colonists conducted their political lives almost independent of Spain. They saw their oppor-

---

14. Carr, *Spain*, 144.
15. Whitaker, *United States and the Independence of Latin America*, vii–ix.

tunity to redress serious difficulties by rebellion. The United States watched as a crippled Europe failed to help Spain preserve the old empire. In the 1820s the United States encouraged the demise of Spanish influence. The Monroe Doctrine and other warnings to Europe reflected Washington's views clearly. Leaving aside the few filibustering expeditions (which were exceptions to the pattern of nonintervention), the United States did not feel the need to be too active. It wanted to expand its commercial interests southward yet avoid open warfare with Europe.

With Spain's empire virtually lost except for Cuba, Puerto Rico, and a few small islands in the Caribbean Sea, the reality of the recent change in Latin America's status reinforced each other's views and policies. Desperately Spain held on to its remaining possessions. Because United States-Spanish problems now focused on the Caribbean for the rest of the century, rivalry over Cuba opened a new phase in Spanish-American relations.

4
CONFLICT IN THE CARIBBEAN

The Caribbean Sea, tucked under North America, governed the sailing routes from North to South America, between Europe and the southern United States facing on the Gulf of Mexico, and portions of the Atlantic side of Latin America. Whichever nation controlled the Caribbean influenced the course of diplomatic events in the Gulf of Mexico and Central America and held Florida and Louisiana as potential hostages in peace while threatening them in war. Cuba, less than one hundred miles off the North American coast, played a major role in North American seaborne trade from Latin America. Much of the commercial traffic in the Caribbean sailed between the narrow division separating Florida from Cuba's northern coast. The island shares the sea with Santo Domingo and Haiti. These islands lie off Cuba to the south, but from a strategic point they encircled her when the United States could use them as bases of operations. The British Bahamas north of Cuba in the Atlantic stood as a gateway to the Caribbean for most sailing ships. The small French and Danish possessions acted as anchor points at the lower end of the Caribbean. In short, the political and diplomatic importance of the Caribbean clearly marked it for constant attention from European and American governments.

By the late 1700s, France, Britain, and Spain occupied various islands and also claimed land in Central America. Over the years they had struck a balance of power, which, although not perfect, prevented any other nation from dominating the region. When the United States came into existence, its officials recognized that the security of their nation depended on preserving this balance until they could control the Caribbean. Therefore they participated early in the complex diplomacy of the Caribbean.

Various nations conducted business in the Caribbean. Britain's commercial ties with Florida and concern for its woodcutters in Honduras, Spain's economic relations with Cuba, and French sugar trade with the Dominicans and Haitians all attested to this. Consequently economic factors often influenced international talks regarding the Caribbean, especially in the eighteenth century when British merchants penetrated deeply into its commercial life. The United States also participated by the mid-nineteenth century and virtually dominated the local trade. Yet although economics affected diplomacy in Spanish America, the political and military importance of the area superseded commercial considerations.

Spain and the United States increasingly turned their attention to the Caribbean as the Latin colonies gained independence. Even the Spanish colonies wanted to participate in the politics of the Caribbean. Spain, of course, attempted to protect the last vestiges of its American empire in Cuba and Puerto Rico. Thus the rivalry characterizing relations between Spain and the United States in the nineteenth century slowly shifted from concerns in North and South America to the Caribbean. During the reign of Fernando VII (1814–33) attention focused on Cuba, the largest and richest colony, following the end of the Latin American wars. Both nations cast Puerto Rico, Santo Domingo, and the Gulf of Mexico in support roles around Cuba. Since Spain and the United States considered the Caribbean as a single political unit, their competition ranged widely over the islands and even Central America, involving all Spanish possessions and even those of France, Britain, and Denmark.

Most historians argue that Cuba dominated Spanish-American diplomacy in the nineteenth century, ignoring the smaller islands. They are generally correct, because Cuba became the focal point of much concern. But this interpretation does little justice to the reality of power politics and minimizes the historical role of the Caribbean because Spain and the United States competed for control of the entire area, not just for Cuba. An understanding of Cuba's impact on Spanish-American relations must include an acknowledgment of the roles played by other parts of the Caribbean. Cuba was the grand prize, but other awards awaited any victor.

During the 1820s, economic, political, and cultural considerations weighed heavily on Spanish and American minds, creating a flurry of diplomatic activity and making Cuba's welfare of paramount importance. Yet their rivalry gestated quietly during the late eighteenth century while North America and Europe claimed attention. The attitudes and behavior that evolved to meet the problems of Latin American independence were next employed in the Caribbean. By the 1820s, this became clear to both nations. Americans and Spaniards took a new look at the military and economic significance of the Caribbean. Each explained to the other the vital role it played in national security and future prosperity. Both warned rivals not to expand into the area on penalty of economic, diplomatic, and even military sanctions.

Spain told Americans it would never surrender its remaining colonies. Spaniards wanted the colonial revenues, recognized their impact on its own international trade, and saw the convenience of using them for regaining control of Latin America. Most believed their nation's honor would be sullied if they lost them. The United States spoke of the military threat Cuba posed to the southern United States, of the economic importance of Cuban and Puerto Rican trade, and by the 1820s, of the relationship between Cuba's slavery to slave politics at home. Cuba even affected relations with Britain and France by repeatedly forcing London and Paris to interfere in Spanish-American rivalry throughout the nineteenth century.

The Caribbean first became an issue during the American Revolution when Spain developed broad lines of military and diplomatic strategy to combat the British. In order to help the English rebels, Spain granted them permission to trade with its Caribbean colonies, waiving many of the economic regulations carefully established over the centuries to protect its interests from the constant threat of British seizure. During the war, a considerable trade developed between these colonies and North America over Cuban sugar and molasses for food, lumber, and some manufactured products in quantities Spanish merchants could not always match prior to the Revolution. This commerce grew large enough to affect American foreign trade adversely when, at the end of the war, Spain closed these ports to non-Spanish business. This act raised protests in the halls of the new government. Yet Spain had simply implemented in Cuba and Puerto Rico the same policies prevailing in the Mississippi Valley—and with similar results.[1] Officials feared American expansion into the Caribbean as much as into the heartland of North America. Using what Americans considered an unfair policy, Spain sought to protect its interests with economic weapons at a time when it could not use large armies.

Although Spain understandably overreacted to what it considered a threat to its Caribbean possessions, North Americans held a different view. Early administrations ruled out any attempt to seize these islands or help them gain independence. Leaving aside their various obvious inability to mount any military offensive against Spain, the horror Americans felt when the Haitians revolted at various times from 1801 through 1809 convinced them that it would be better for Spain to rule Cuba and Puerto Rico. Few wanted to face the problems of bloody revolutions or black governments (with all that implied for American slavery) or risk an unrest that threatened the political balance of power so close to home. American officials thought it was bad enough that Europeans considered helping Spain suppress revolts in Latin America; it would be worse if they invaded the Caribbean. At least Spanish rule kept the colonies quiet.

The issue of slavery always proved important in American thinking. John Adams reasoned that if Cuba or Puerto Rico became independent, black men would dominate their governments and might try to turn the islands into havens for runaway American slaves, a move that threatened to upset the South's economy by encouraging revolts. The problems that could result were too grave for the young nation to risk. Therefore Adams and others decided that while Latin American countries might be encouraged to gain their independence, a different course would be followed in the Caribbean. Americans wanted instead to concentrate on eliminating objectionable Spanish regulations that cramped the growth of their commerce.

Rhetoric and Spanish fears blurred the fine discrimination made by the American government between its political and economic policies toward the Caribbean. Washington planned and implemented pro-

---

1. Pedro Voltes Bou, "Repercusiones de la independencia de Estados Unidos en el comercio español de Indias," *Revista de Indias*, no. 76 (1959): 213–221.

grams to encourage American trade but not at the cost of major political or military involvement. Since Spain always combined political and economic policies into a single vision of its relations with the New World, considering Latin America and the Caribbean as one, it never fully accepted the distinctions Washington made.

A nation's policy is identifiable more by actions than by words, and, as misleading as those often might be, it helped define the characteristics of Caribbean politics. In 1810 a Cuban revolt erupted, reflecting many of the same concerns and following a similar pattern as those in South America except that Spain suppressed this one with the large number of troops on the island. But before it ended, Cubans had asked Washington for help, which the government refused. Yet at the same time officials in the United States wished the rebels in South America well. The president also kept silent about the harsh administration imposed on the island as a result of the revolution but deplored colonial policies in South America. Washington realized that the colony could be defended against Madrid's enemies. Spain's determination to hold onto Cuba became obvious during the Napoleonic invasion of the Iberian peninsula because, despite all the difficulties faced in governing the New World, Spaniards exerted the necessary effort to retain Cuba.

The problem of commercial relations with the United States never ceased to worry both governments during the years following the revolt of 1810. In 1818 Madrid instituted a series of new commercial regulations designed to reinforce its authority in the colonies. These proved so restrictive to American trade that the only way to sell goods to Cuba was by first sending them to Spain. This increased their cost so much that Spanish merchandise sold cheaper in Cuba. These regulations also seriously crippled the sugar trade with North America, irritating both Cubans and Americans. Spanish authorities believed that paying the price of reduced economic activity prevented further American penetration into the island. Thus, more for political than economic reasons, Madrid maintained its policies in the face of numerous criticisms from Cubans and Americans.[2]

---

2. Charles C. Griffin, *The United States and the Disruption of the Spanish Empire, 1810–1822* (New York, 1937), 278–288.

Europe's attitude toward Cuba continued to worry Spain and the United States after the Congress of Vienna. They especially watched France and Britain since both had expressed great interest in the Caribbean. Washington early took the initiative in warning Europe to stay out of the Caribbean. In 1808 the United States announced that it could not tolerate the transfer of any Spanish possession to some other European government, aiming these remarks at Britain and France. While not prepared to advocate Cuban independence, Washington explained that the United States would block any attempt by Europeans to seize Caribbean territory. American policy makers feared that British economic influence might grow and employed Spain's logic that this would represent the first step toward political hegemony in the Caribbean. Therefore until 1848 American officials supported Spanish rule in Cuba and Puerto Rico even though Spain did not believe Washington's avowed policy represented the true feelings of the United States.

Unquestionably the British wanted to expand their commercial and political influence in the Caribbean in order to protect existing trade in Florida and Honduras, apply pressure on Washington not to attack Canada, and affect French policies in Europe while wielding a similar club over the Spanish—a continuation of the policy it had followed in the New World over the past three centuries. British diplomats reasoned if they could not gain control over Cuba and Puerto Rico, then it would be best for Spain to continue governing them. If Paris obtained the colonies, then its influence would jeopardize Britain's much like the United States had since Paris might become interested in the Bahamas or threaten London's European policies with colonial blackmail. Moreover Britain believed that Madrid could be influenced more readily than either Paris or Washington. These factors led London to adopt the same policy as Washington. As a minor power in the Caribbean, France could do little to alter this. International rivalries thus preserved for Spain the remainder of its empire, even in the face of increased tensions there after 1815.[3]

---

3. Kenneth Bourne, *Britain and the Balance of Power in North America, 1815–1908* (Berkeley, 1967), 63–69, 71.

The difficulties Spain and the United States experienced in Latin America after 1821 became evident in their relations regarding Cuba and other Caribbean territories. Madrid accused the Americans of encouraging Cuban rebels. London pressured Spain to allow British commerce with Spanish colonies and even urged Madrid to curtail slave trading in the Caribbean, although to no avail. Since Canning believed that Americans threatened Britain's economic interests in the New World, he worried about any attempt by Washington to seize Cuba. An important reason for developing a policy that maintained the status quo in the Americas grew out of his concern for Cuba's situation. He continued his nation's policy of protecting Spanish rule in Cuba and Puerto Rico. Between 1822 and early 1823, when Canning's views drew President Monroe toward the development of his famous doctrine, diplomatic activity shifted to Cuba (Santo Domingo had been absorbed by Haiti and was no longer Spanish).[4]

During the 1820s, the United States defined for Spain the policies generated by the Monroe Doctrine, pointing out their applicability to Cuba and Puerto Rico. The country also guarded against a Spanish diplomatic offensive aimed at gaining a multinational guarantee of European intervention into the Caribbean. Relations became complicated at the same time by British insistence that slavery be reduced in the Christian world. Slave diplomacy also took on domestic political ramifications affecting Cuba's economic and international life. The issue of slavery made it difficult for Spanish diplomats to accept the American argument that it served the best interests of Washington for Cuba to remain in Spain's possession.

The status quo received the open blessings of most governments. Statesmen sometimes defied their citizens by publicly supporting it. Secretary of State Adams in 1823 called it vital to his country's interests.[5] Canning offered to sign a multilateral treaty in 1825 to protect the balance of power with Washington, Paris, and Madrid. Spain, always seeking such a treaty, approved, but Paris expressed only mild interest. The United States, following its policy of not

---

4. C. J. Bartlett, *Great Britain and Sea Power, 1815–1853* (Oxford, 1963), 69–70.

5. Lester D. Langley, *The Cuban Policy of the United States* (New York, 1968), 11.

signing entangling alliances, refused to commit itself. Unofficially American diplomats expressed concern that the treaty would never win the Senate's approval because it prevented the United States from moving into Cuba.

Spain viewed with mistrust Washington's rejection of Canning's proposal, fully aware of the implications. Washington's stance further indicated to Spaniards that the United States really wanted Cuba. When the Americans tactlessly requested Spain to allow commercial agents to live in Cuba to help merchants trading with North America, the Spanish rejected this, viewing such agents as a fifth column. However, Spain used this request to test American intentions while gaining concessions for commercial privileges. Madrid asked the United States to promise publicly to uphold Spanish rule in Cuba in return for permission to send more diplomatic personnel to the colony. Washington recoiled from such a commitment.[6]

In the same decade Spain and the United States faced another source of problems. Aware that Cuban dissidents might need some outside help to topple Spanish rule, Mexico and Colombia stood by with their armies. Madrid and Washington separately told the two Latin governments to stay out of Cuban politics; otherwise Europe and the United States would turn on them. The crisis subsided quickly because of the firm Spanish, American, and British pressures. Also the two South American governments sufficiently mistrusted each other to make cooperation impossible. Once again, the contending parties had rushed to the rescue of the status quo. But to ensure its interests, Spain sent a few more troops to Cuba and Puerto Rico.

The 1820s ended on a quiet note in the Caribbean. In the next decade the United States concentrated on expanding their commercial interests in Cuba, Puerto Rico, Santo Domingo, Haiti, and Central America. The only exception came from the United States where filibustering groups, sponsored by Cuban revolutionaries and private American citizens, attacked Cuba on a sporadic basis, often with the blessings of some Washington officials. Because the expeditions were small, the island's security never suffered, but they irritated Madrid enough to overshadow the economic rivalry that in the long

6. Jerónimo Becker, *Historia de las relaciones exteriores de España durante el siglo XIX* (Madrid, 1924), 1:549–556.

run would exercise a greater influence over the island's destiny.

The real question facing both nations in the 1830s involved the degree of economic influence that the Americans should have in Cuba. Spain wanted to keep it low; hence colonial authorities received instructions to enforce the complex system of regulations governing non-Spanish trade, even if this meant weakening Cuba's economy. Nevertheless traders still kept coming into Cuban ports, leading to many complaints about arbitrary colonial officials cramping international commerce or creating nasty incidents. Spain found itself in an uncomfortable position; on the one hand, it wanted to reduce this trade, but on the other, it could not exclude it completely without risking the loss of Cuba to an irate United States. By the mid-1850s, Cuba sold over 85 percent of its sugar to the Americans. The vast majority of Puerto Rico's import-export trade also involved North America, surpassing even Cuba in dependency on the United States. This is not to say that American businessmen toppled high Spanish tariff walls, because their trade conceivably might have been greater without such laws. Yet the enormous effort made by such merchants and investors created friction between both countries.

The United States reasoned that Cuba's proximity and the nature of the island's trade made their economic relations complementary and inevitably drew the two together in so natural a fashion that Spain could not stop it. Washington wanted to encourage this by having Spain modify its commercial regulations while reducing the harsh penalties inflicted on Americans who violated minor rules. Tariffs were the key issue since they averaged over 60 percent of a cargo's value and could run higher than 110 percent. The number of claims against Spain increased sharply after 1808. By the 1830s, these represented a complicated array of detailed counterclaims, charges, and protests. In the early 1830s, Spain and the United States agreed on a comprehensive settlement. Signed on February 17, 1834, Spain agreed to pay many American claims over the rest of the century. Madrid's willingness to accept such a treaty indicated its desire to reduce the tensions that threatened Cuba's security. In fact, this gesture proved of little use because Spain's commercial regulations—the cause of many claims—remained unchanged.[7]

American merchants continued penetrating Cuban and Puerto

---

7. Ibid., 630.

Rican markets. Still Spain refused to encourage such trade. John Forsyth, American secretary of state in 1840, noted that these laws harmed his nation's interests at the same time that the United States encouraged Spanish trade with its citizens by maintaining much lower tariffs. He warned Spain that Cuba's affairs always attracted his government's interest, commenting that it would never "look with indifference upon any occurrence connected with the fate of that island."[8] He repeated this to the British since they too continued competing for influence in the colonies.

In the 1840s British interest showed signs of increasing, especially in Central America. A change of some importance developed in the Caribbean in 1844 when Santo Domingo broke away from Haiti's control, causing European and American governments to compete for influence there. Finding their independence difficult to maintain in the face of Haitian hostility, the Dominicans seriously considered asking some power to accept them as a protectorate. By 1843 such speculations centered on possible Spanish domination. Both Britain and the United States worried about this possibility while the French stood by to protect Haitian interests. All knew that if the Dominicans came under the protection of some European power, the balance so delicately maintained in the Caribbean would be altered. But Spain questioned the wisdom of acquiring the island republic, which was riddled with problems. The United States cautioned the concerned governments not to show disrespect for the Monroe Doctrine, while the Spanish warned Washington they would find an American protectorate over Santo Domingo intolerable.[9]

The Dominican factor in the 1840s was only one of several issues. Another was Britain's increased efforts at eradicating the slave trade by pressuring Madrid to eliminate the peculiar institution in the colonies or at least stop the trafficking from Africa. The main problem existed in Cuba, which brought slaves from Africa in violation of international conventions and even imported them from Puerto Rico where the early signs of an abolition movement were discernible by

---

8. William R. Manning, ed., *Diplomatic Correspondence of the United States: Inter-American Affairs, 1831–1860*, vol. 11: *Spain* (Washington, D.C., 1939), 23.

9. Rayford W. Logan, *Haiti and the Dominican Republic* (New York, 1968), 33–35.

the end of the decade. Most governments ignored Puerto Rico when thinking of slaves, finding the Cuban situation more important. Even the southern half of the United States concentrated on the question of Cuban slavery, which in turn made Madrid nervous about the island's future. The Spanish always feared that the South would urge for the acquisition of the colony as another slave state to redress the increasing political imbalance developing in the Congress between those states that were free and others with slavery.

Between 1846 and 1848 the United States and Mexico were at war against each other. Because most European powers, including Spain, blamed the United States for coveting Mexican territory, they mistrusted Washington's statements about the Caribbean. The war seriously threatened to disturb peace in the New World, and when the United States acquired vast Mexican properties in North America, Europeans were convinced that the Americans would now expand southward into the Caribbean. During this war, each government felt its own interests might suffer. Washington thought Britain would expand its commercial and political influence, as it had done during the War of 1812. Americans were aware that Spain sent reinforcements to its colonies and wanted to help Mexico by opening ports to Mexican warships. Some even feared a Spanish invasion of the North American mainland. Washington expressed some concern that France might move into Santo Domingo, thereby further reducing its influence in the Caribbean.

Spaniards took an obvious interest in the Mexican war. Since they anticipated further American expansion into the Caribbean, they augmented Cuba's defenses while fostering closer relations with France, Britain, and Mexico. Yet Spain dared not risk aiding Mexico too overtly, fearing the Americans might seize Havana. Queen Isabel's government declared itself neutral despite the public's support for Mexico. Spain also faced a few problems caused by some Mexican privateers and rumors of Madrid's aiding other privateers, which generated an exchange of some strongly worded notes with worried American officials.[10]

When the United States won the war against Mexico, Europe

---

10. Manning, *Spain*, 43, 359, 400; Javier Malagón Barceló et al., eds., *Relaciones diplomaticas hispano-mexicanas (1839–1898)*, series I: *Despachos generales*, vol. 4: *1846–1848* (Mexico, 1968), passim.

faced a series of new political realities in the New World. Europeans saw the United States confident and rejuvenated by its quick war and vast profits. Most diplomats could not rule out the immediate possibility of the Americans flexing their military muscles in the Caribbean by seizing Cuba or possibly Santo Domingo and Puerto Rico. London and Paris saw the necessity of extending more diplomatic support to the Spanish, although reluctantly since Madrid might use such support to irritate the United States by some "irresponsible" act, possibly involving a naval incident or new restrictive economic measures. Both urged Spain to reinforce Cuba while recognizing that potential political competition in Santo Domingo would increase among all three European governments. In fact, Samaná Bay in Santo Domingo had long interested Washington, so the competitive effort now also centered on preventing the Dominicans from leasing this port to the United States.

The Americans saw an opportunity to press Spain into reforming Cuban and Puerto Rican commercial regulations. Britain and France stood to profit by this move since they assumed Madrid would never open its ports solely to the one nation that most threatened it without making at least an equal offer to European allies. Most diplomats did not believe that Spain would acquiesce in such a reversal of policy because of its poor relations with Washington. Yet if changes came, they also wanted benefits. Instead of waiting for commercial windfalls, they turned their attention to the political problems that existed in the New World after the Mexican war.

During the 1830s, Madrid and Washington competed for influence in South America, not just in the Caribbean. Washington encouraged trade with the southern hemisphere, breaking all previous trade records, at a cost to Spain's, which failed to match pre-1808 levels. The United States acted as Latin America's protector from European aggression as symbolized by the Monroe Doctrine. At the same time, Spain attempted to rebuild its economic and cultural influence in the New World in the face of growing North American objections. Each time Spain faced a diplomatic crisis with a Latin country, the United States invariably supported their fellow Americans. Spain called this a part of Washington's plan to acquire the remaining Spanish lands.[11]

---
11. Manning, *Spain*, 300–313.

After the Mexican war, President James K. Polk reassessed his Cuban policy; the result was a major change in official thinking that dramatically altered Spanish-American relations for the next fifty years. The U.S. government dropped its policy of not trying to acquire Cuba, deciding instead to gain control of it. This change in attitude did not include Puerto Rico, which lacked the strategic importance of Cuba. The American public had long believed Cuba would inevitably fall into their hands so the administration knew its new policy matched the nation's views. Backed by arguments grounded in economics and geopolitics, Americans considered the acquisition so natural that many could hardly understand why Spain would contest the new policy. Although Polk agreed with this logic, more specific reasons dictated his change. By this time, Havana had become a major port of call for American maritime traffic between the United States and newly acquired California and Oregon (Britain had recently acknowledged the latter as American). Officials, like their president, believed that if Havana were closed to Americans or if Spain went to war against the United States, then communications with the western part of the nation would be seriously threatened. In order to prevent such a catastrophe, Washington had to secure the port; that meant acquiring Cuba.

A second reason, also growing out of the Mexican war, concerned domestic politics. Mexico ceded territory to the United States that was hardly practical for plantations. Thus the southern portion of the United States, which advocated the extension of slavery, gained little new territory in which to expand. Southern politicians who envisioned the newly acquired lands' someday becoming free states felt that the balance of power in both houses of Congress would tip against them. The issue of slavery had grown in importance during the 1840s when cotton production rose as a result of technological developments in processing the fiber. In order to calm southerners, Polk wanted to acquire Cuba so slavery could flourish at no cost to the growth of new free states. Polk believed that slave economics could integrate the Cuban economy into the American since northern merchants would sell in Cuba the same sort of products now sold to the South but without restrictive Spanish laws, while southerners would impose their culture and business life on the Cubans.

The third reason, closely related to slavery, stemmed from economics. Since for years many of the problems faced by Washington and Madrid involved American complaints about Spanish commercial policies, this bone of contention would be eliminated. Friendlier relations could develop, and economic growth, which the United States wanted in the Caribbean, could progress with only the British and French to contend with. All three factors governing Polk's changes in policy were national in scope and grew out of earlier experiences. They threatened to alter radically the political and economic balance of power in the Caribbean while offering the possibility of heading off a major domestic political controversy.

In reaching his decision, Polk determined to seize the island if Spain refused to sell it. Some precedent for a sale existed, however, since Spain had sold Florida to the United States. Moreover Polk knew Americans generally approved of the force used against Mexico and might again for Cuba. He felt confident that negotiation would work and certainly that the nation could muster sufficient military power to seize the colony if need be. His secretary of state, James Buchanan, long an advocate of acquiring Cuba, proved instrumental in developing the revised Cuban policy. He wasted no time in implementing it because he thought it imperative to settle the issue quickly before Spain found support in Europe to resist Polk. He also believed that British threats to the island could easily be eliminated. Buchanan did not hide his wish to anglicize the island, which infuriated Spaniards. Yet when the secretary approached Spain in 1848 and 1849, he received a stern rebuke, rejecting all offers to surrender the colony.[12]

Spain's position was understandable, though not to the insensitive secretary of state. Buchanan was naive in thinking that Spain would sell the island. (Polk should be blamed for this attitude as well, but since his secretary authored the policy changes, he bears the responsibility for not fully appreciating or sympathizing about Spain's position.) Madrid did not consider the island's cost to the nation sufficient reason to sell it. The colony represented Spain's empire, the most

---

12. Langley, *Cuban Policy*, 24–25.

beautiful jewel in an ancient crown. If for no other reason than national pride, Cuba would be kept. Spanish officials felt so strongly about this that they considered Buchanan's offer an insult. They also knew the British and French could never tolerate the sale since it would radically compromise their power in the Caribbean, not to mention the influence they wielded in Madrid. The sale proved to be so politically explosive that any official daring to suggest that the island be surrendered would have been cast out of political life. No cabinet could have withstood the outcry of the public, Queen Isabel II, or other authorities in the government. Thus Spain took its only viable option when it rejected Buchanan's offer. For the time being, the United States could only contemplate future moves.

During this decade, increased filibustering from North America contributed to poor relations. Indeed Spanish diplomats spent years cataloging Washington's sins against Spain in the Caribbean and in South America. Anglo-Franco concern for the New World and slave politics in the United States further complicated the situation. It is little wonder that Washington reversed its old Cuban policy or that Madrid found in Buchanan's statements confirmation of what the Spanish had always believed: that the United States was a threat to Cuba. If anything, Spaniards thought the United States had finally decided to reveal its real Cuban policy, one that they believed had always existed.[13]

Filibustering greatly influenced Spanish-American relations. The most notorious case in the late 1840s illustrates the problem. Narcisco López, a Venezuelan working for Cuban independence, launched a series of expeditions from the southern United States between 1849 and 1851. His men were financed by Cuban revolutionary groups and private American citizens. Because his units always had hundreds of men, Spanish officials found it difficult to believe that Washington could not stop López. They blamed the United States for his activities while Cuban authorities braced themselves for his repeated assaults. Buchanan denied giving López any official or unofficial sup-

---

13. Becker, *Historio de las relaciones exteriores*, 2:55–80.

port at the same time that citizens in New York and New Orleans applauded the Venezuelan's work. The American press gave López wide coverage in often laudatory language, and Spanish newspapers exaggerated his strength. Colonial officials finally crushed his expedition, killing or imprisoning most of its members. Many Spaniards outside the government believed that colonial authorities had defeated a direct attempt by the United States to seize Cuba, rejecting the possibility that López had operated on his own. In all probability, however, Spanish officials in Madrid viewed López's activities more as a nuisance than as a threat to Cuba, although their fear for the island remained. Because many of the prisoners taken were American citizens, Washington felt morally obligated to ask for their release.

The United States realized that Spain had the capability of defending its possessions. Although negotiations for Cuba's sale failed in 1848–1849, the State Department knew now that force could not be used. Consequently Polk and Buchanan rejected the thought of military clashes for the time being, relying instead on diplomacy. The lesson Washington learned carried a heavy price because the Spanish executed a number of filibusters and won much sympathy in Europe.

The Foreign Office in Madrid took advantage of the moment to meet the American threat with more than just guns. The regime exploited these events to win public support between 1849 and 1852. During the winter months of 1851 and 1852, the ultraconservative Spanish prime minister, Antonio Bravo Murillo, asked his diplomats to determine if Britain and France would guarantee Cuba's security with a treaty, arguing that if the United States seized the island, British and French properties would be attacked next. He failed because the British disagreed with him. They wanted to curb Washington's perceived imperialist tendencies, but not by force. At the moment both London and Paris were more concerned with Central America, where they were learning how little they could do to block the expansion of North American economic and political influence. The situation could be worse in the Caribbean. Their inability to act stemmed mainly, however, from their determination to keep troops uncommitted in case relations with Russia deteriorated into war. In fact, within two years Paris and London went to war with Moscow in the Crimea. For them, Cuba was too far away at a time when greater problems lay closer to home.

The United States assured Bravo Murillo that a pact was unnecessary; it believed that Cuba should remain under Spanish control until freely given up. Realizing that the López expeditions had triggered Spain's flurry of diplomatic activity, American diplomats worked to prevent intervention in the Caribbean by warning Europe to keep out. They also told Spain that they still wanted Cuba, but only by negotiation. Meanwhile Paris and London searched for a formula to quiet the Caribbean while they faced European problems, finally suggesting that Washington become a party to Spain's multinational agreement. The United States, however, gave the suggestion little attention, convincing Spaniards that another American offensive against Cuba might be in the offing. Spanish fears were translated into numerous instructions to Cuba's captain generals in the 1850s, admonishing them to be watchful for new attacks.

By the end of 1852, another phase in Spanish-American relations had ended. The previous thirty years had witnessed difficult problems for both. North American influence continued to grow in the Caribbean at a faster rate than in South America. Yet it expanded more by accident than design, while Spain's receded in much the same way. For example, Spain's domestic history reflected continued political instability, which directly influenced relations with the United States. Spain's civil wars of 1833 to 1840 and again in the late 1840s between liberal and conservative elements ostensibly over dynastic questions seriously drained the nation's economic and military resources, making it difficult for the insecure monarchy to initiate a strong and purposeful foreign policy. Moreover, this instability worried Britain and France, which felt Spain could do little to preserve the balance of power in the Americas alone. Besides military weakness, domestic politics cramped Spain. In the 1840s, cabinets changed frequently, preventing politicians from planning and initiating any long-range foreign policy designed to counteract growing North American power. Spaniards realized that Cuba's best defense lay in short-term diplomatic efforts since few soldiers could be spared for colonial duty so long as civil war plagued the homeland. Fortunately for Spain, Britain and the United States believed Cuba should remain under Spanish control. Madrid thus did not have to rely on its armed services, which the Latin revolutions indicated might not be able to protect the remaining colonies—despite the success in suppressing López.

Similarly diverse events and social forces governed politics in the New World. The growing turmoil in the United States, developing by the late 1840s over the question of expanding or destroying slavery, led the government to seek a territorial balance between slave and free states. Acquiring Cuba became a viable solution to a pressing problem. The war with Mexico, supposedly only distantly connected to relations with Spain, proved more significant than historians have previously acknowledged since it gave the United States military confidence at the same time that the nation demanded further expansion. Slavery and the aftermath of Mexico burst the seams of the Cuban policy, which no longer served the interests of the United States.

Spaniards faced a cultural war with the United States as well, something North Americans hardly recognized. One Spanish diplomat, Andrés Borrego, wrote in the 1850s that Washington wanted to dominate the entire New World with its "ideas, sentiments, and customs." In a detailed analysis of the American situation for the Foreign Office, he stated that a struggle existed between the two in which the Hispanic people battled Anglo-Saxon culture.[14] For Spain, therefore, the survival of its culture in the New World hung in the balance, adding ideological complications to its foreign policy. Americans began to realize by the 1850s that cultural hegemony was a factor in their attitudes, but such a small one in the minds of policy makers that it can be discounted even though southern newpapers referred to it often. Unlike diplomats in Madrid, Washington's rarely discussed sociological implications for international relations.

Although both nations realized in the early 1850s that their relations with the other were important, neither fully anticipated the increased tensions coming in the next few years when the balance of power in the Caribbean slowly tipped in favor of the United States. Their rivalry increased throughout the area, as well as in Central and South America, while simultaneously Spain overcame the weaknesses it had endured during its civil wars. Unmatched in intensity

---

14. Manuscript No. 20228, Biblioteca Nacional, Madrid.

in the two previous generations, the confluence of European and American problems in the 1850s and 1860s was nothing less than profound.

5
RELATIONS AT MID-CENTURY

Caribbean problems continued dominating relations between Spain and the United States in the 1850s. In 1853 Franklin Pierce became president and, like his predecessor, wanted to acquire Cuba. In 1854 General Baldomero Espartero, a liberal politician with nationalist ideas on foreign policy, began a two-year term as Spain's prime minister and, like those before him, vowed never to surrender the island. Both men faced serious crises in Cuba, Santo Domingo, and Mexico. Because rivalry intensified, a new era in Spanish-American relations began around 1853 and continued to late 1868 when revolutions in Spain and Cuba bracketed the fifteen-year period. The American Civil War, Spain's annexation of Santo Domingo, intervention in Mexico, and war with Chile and Peru made the 1830s and 1840s seem quieter in comparison. Yet the later years clearly reflected problems that had germinated in earlier decades. Moreover the end of the 1860s provided a chronological frontier because by then Washington's power in the Caribbean proved greater than ever before. Spain's declined sharply along with French influence. Such social forces as slavery, which ended in the United States by 1865, seriously weakened Spain's grip on its remaining colonies, at the same time affecting the politics and economics of the Caribbean.

Spain and the United States stood on the verge of war with each other by late 1854. The main cause of this crisis was Pierre Soulé, U.S. minister to Madrid. Long an advocate of Cuban annexation, the flamboyant envoy went to great lengths to win the island. He thought that by disturbing relations at a time when Britain and France were increasingly absorbed by international problems involving Russia and therefore could not help Spain, Madrid would have no choice but to sell Cuba. Going beyond the pale of his instructions, he risked plunging both nations into war to give the United States an excuse for occupying Cuba. His major attempt in this direction came in 1854 when Cuban officials seized an American vessel, the *Black Warrior*, for minor infractions of port regulations in Havana. Neither Washington nor Madrid wanted the incident to explode, except perhaps Soulé. He wrote harsh notes to the Foreign Office demanding reparations and apologies. The envoy plotted with political enemies of the government as another means of winning the island. Meanwhile he received instructions to ask if Spain would sell Cuba. The Spanish, furious at his manner regarding the *Black Warrior* and for cavorting with the regime's foes, refused to discuss any sale with him. The entire affair gained for Spain much official and public sympathy in Europe and at home. In short, Soulé's efforts backfired, forcing Washington to consider other tactics.

The American government, in attempting to formulate new Cuban plans, ordered Soulé, James Buchanan (then minister to London), and James Y. Mason (stationed in Paris) in 1854 to meet and write down their suggestions. They met in October and wrote what became known as the Ostend manifesto. In it, the three pro-annexationists suggested Cuba be purchased. Failing this, the United States should seize the colony in order to ensure the Union's territorial security and economic future. News of the document quickly leaked to the press, infuriating Europeans more by its brashness than its content. Believing it to be proclaimed American policy, they criticized Washington to such an extent that Pierce decided to recall Soulé in an attempt to calm Europe, especially Spain. Washington's bellicose policy threatened peace, but Madrid wanted no war with the United States and exerted every effort to avoid it. Spain knew Britain and France would not help; therefore Madrid exploited world opinion, eliminated pretexts for the United States to act, and reinforced its army and navy in Cuba. Yet Spanish officials believed Washington would have little difficulty in seizing Havana. This possibility made it imperative that they maintain peaceful relations with Pierce.

During 1855 the Cuban captain general uncovered a revolutionary plot linked to exiled groups in the United States. The number of filibustering expeditions, such as those recently mounted by López, appeared to be on the rise; therefore authorities established a naval blockade around Cuba to keep subversives out, and the police and army arrested those on the island. Pierce feared this blockade would cripple American commerce with Cuba. Although this situation could have served as an excuse for him to occupy the colony, officials in Havana maintained the blockade until the military danger to Cuba ended. It forced the president to withhold any encouragement from other filibusters, one of the main reasons for the blockade.[1] Whether Pierce continued ignoring pleas from filibustering groups after Spain raised the blockade is not certain. But by the end of 1855, they were again organizing and, Madrid believed, with government support. Pierce feared that if filibustering posed too great a threat to Cuba, France and Britain might be drawn into a military confrontation with the United States since their interests appeared threatened.

Within this climate of suspicion another incident occurred. In the spring of 1855, a Spanish warship stopped an American vessel, *El Dorado*, possibly outside of Cuban waters, to check its papers. In quieter times, the case might have been handled as a minor incident; instead it grew into a major event, and newspapers in both countries gave it considerable coverage. Rash editorial writers on both sides of the Atlantic called for war while American agitation for Cuba's seizure once again captured much attention. Yet officials in both Madrid and Washington refused to take seriously the suggestion of war. Spain knew Cuba could not stand against an American invasion. Businessmen in Spain, Cuba, and the United States objected to war, fearing damage to their interests. Therefore each regime exploited the case for domestic political purposes over a period of several months before dropping it. (In fact, Spain never tendered apologies for the incident or paid reparations.)

Pierce knew that such incidents would occur again unless Cuba's economic relations with the United States were put on a sounder, more defined footing, as many members of Congress had urged. In short, he wanted a commercial treaty with Spain if he could not buy Cuba. Spaniards refused because it might have jeopardized their interests in Cuba as the Americans penetrated even deeper into Cuban

---

1. Herminio Portel Vilá, *Historia de Cuba en sus relaciones con los Estados Unidos y España* (Havana, 1938–1941), 2:98–106.

affairs. Yet at the same time Madrid did not want to irritate American warhawks, who advocated seizing Cuba. Thus while avoiding trade negotiations, Spain quietly instructed Cuban authorities to treat Americans with greater deference and publicly announced a reduction of some tariffs, mainly for wheat products, which the Spanish could not provide in sufficient quantities anyway. When a new minister, Augustus C. Dodge, arrived in Madrid in 1856, the Spanish saw no need to discuss Cuba's sale or a commercial treaty.[2]

Spain took greater interest in filibustering activities than on sale or commercial diplomacy in 1855 and 1856. The actions of William Walker especially drew Spanish attention. Walker initially filibustered in Central America with Washington's approval. Many Cuban revolutionaries helped him in order to gain his future aid in attacking Cuba. After he overthrew Nicaragua's legitimate government, Spaniards believed he would move on Cuba. Since Pierce was identified with Walker's achievements, Spain expected the revolutionary would receive considerable aid from the United States.[3] Spanish diplomats turned to Paris and London for help. Both said they could do little other than offer diplomatic backing since their armed forces were committed to the Crimean war. The British also worried that if they should become involved, Washington might retaliate by seizing the Bahamas or, worse, Canada. Failing in Europe, the Spanish turned to Latin America in 1856 in an attempt to form an anti–United States alliance to protect all Hispanic nations from Washington's imperialism. This, too, failed, mainly because of intra–South American rivalries and mistrust of Spanish intentions.[4]

During the closing days of the Pierce administration, Spain decided to send a new minister to Washington who had not criticized the United States publicly and who would follow orders strictly. The Foreign Office selected Gabriel García Tassara, more poet than

---

2. William R. Manning, ed., *Diplomatic Correspondence of the United States: Inter-American Affairs, 1830–1860*, vol. 11: *Spain* (Washington, D.C., 1939), 210–214.

3. James D. Richardson, ed., *Messages and Papers of the Presidents, 1789–1892* (Washington, D.C., 1896–1902), 5:371–373.

4. Luis M. Perez, "Project of Latin-American Confederation, 1856," *American Historical Review* 12 (October 1906): 97–99.

politician, to defend Spain's rights. His initial orders, which reflected the current state of Spanish thinking, stated that Cuban problems dominated relations between Spain and the United States. Anticipating the election of James Buchanan as president, the Spanish foreign office ordered all Spanish diplomats in the United States to watch his Cuban policy carefully in expectation of further trouble. Madrid regarded any proposal for a commercial treaty "prejudicial to our interests." Spain refused to apologize for *El Dorado* because, by the terms of Pierce's objections, Madrid would have to acknowledge that it controlled only a juridical band around Cuba of about three miles rather than the twelve then claimed. In short, his instructions dealt only with Cuba, indicating how important colonial matters were in Spanish-American relations.[5]

Although Pierce showed little enthusiasm for acquiring Cuba at the end of his term, his replacement did not. Fully aware of his past performance, Spanish diplomats expected Buchanan would work for acquisition after becoming president in March 1857. García Tassara realized that the men working with the new executive also wanted the colony. In fact, as his administration aged, Buchanan concluded that the only way to resolve the serious crisis over slavery would be to acquire Cuba, from which new slave states might be formed. Since Buchanan's critics condemned his domestic policies, the acquisition would distract the nation from its other problems. He asked Spain to sell the colony but Madrid said no. He next took the advice of some friends by asking Spain's creditors to pressure Madrid into selling Cuba, but this too failed. All his efforts made the Foreign Office, Queen Isabel, and the cabinet more determined not to surrender Cuba, especially if it appeared to have been done under duress.

Each year that he remained in office, Buchanan asked Congress to provide him with sufficient funds with which to purchase Cuba. In every instance, Congress rejected his request, either because of domestic political considerations or out of some fear that granting his wish would give him more power than permitted by the Constitution.

---

5. Minister of State to Tassara, December 7, 1856, Spanish Foreign Office, Correspondencia, Estados Unidos, legajo 1468, Foreign Office Archives, Madrid (hereafter cited as Sp/abbreviated file group for correspondencia and política/country).

The Spanish could not help but view any threat to Cuba's security as emanating from the White House, including all filibustering activities. In 1858, General Leopoldo O'Donnell, a liberal politician, began a five-year term as prime minister of Spain. His foreign minister, Saturnino Calderon Collantes, like his superior, vowed never to surrender Cuba and displayed stubbornness and ingenuity in working for Spain's interests.

Both governments struggled over Cuba to the end of Buchanan's administration in March 1861. In fact, the acquisition of Cuba became an obsession with the president as he slowly saw his country slip into civil war over slavery. But the Spanish refused to allow him to use Cuba as a cure-all for his troubles. O'Donnell exploited Buchanan's efforts as a means of drawing domestic support to his regime while winning sympathy in Europe. As a result, both O'Donnell and Buchanan stimulated more public discussion about their respective Cuban policies than anyone before them.

At the same time, they competed for political hegemony in Santo Domingo as their countries had in previous decades. Because interest in Cuban affairs increased in the 1850s, concern for Santo Domingo heightened. After Pierce became president in 1853, Spain reasoned that Cuba's security had to be protected. Santo Domingo's strategic importance to Cuba indicated that both nations would increase their efforts toward dominating the island republic. Madrid drew closer to the Dominicans by treaty. Ratified in 1855, it established closer economic and diplomatic ties between them. Meanwhile the United States attempted to negotiate a treaty with the Dominicans. Washington managed to develop a draft with them by 1855, which ceded Samaná Bay to the Americans. France, Britain, and Haiti objected to this, and Spanish officials in Santo Domingo pressured the local government not to ratify it.

In late 1855 Antonio María Segovia arrived in Santo Domingo as a special agent in charge of the campaign to destroy all North American influence while increasing Spain's. He wasted no time in executing his orders. He began building a pro-Spanish political party, brought in emigrants from Spain, negotiated a commercial and emigration treaty within a year, and had the Dominican president replaced by someone more disposed toward Madrid. He also prevented

Santo Domingo from ratifying its treaty with Washington by distributing foreign aid and threats of military coercion.

The speed and manner with which Segovia completed his projects irritated Washington, worried the British, French, and Haitians, and scared other Spanish diplomats in Latin America who feared the United States might go to war with Spain over Santo Domingo and Cuba. Therefore in 1857, Madrid recalled Segovia, replacing him with another energetic Spaniard who continued his work. In September 1858 the politician whom Segovia engineered out of the Dominican presidency, Pedro Santana, came back to power. By now old age, experience, and local political and economic unrest convinced him that a Spanish protectorate might solve his nation's problems. He asked Spain for this, but O'Donnell hesitated, concerned that Washington, London, and Paris would not approve. Yet he encouraged closer relations with Santo Domingo as protection for Cuba.[6]

American authorities thought Santo Domingo wanted to draw closer to the United States; they thus fought back against growing Spanish influence there. In April 1859 William L. Cazneau went to Santo Domingo with orders to negotiate a new base agreement. He failed because when Spain ended its victorious war against Morocco in 1860, it devoted more attention to Santo Domingo. President Santana also contributed to his failure because he hesitated to draw closer to the North Americans, believing their Anglo-Saxon culture too alien for his country. Santana consequently welcomed renewed Spanish interest in his nation. By the end of 1860 Spanish citizens and soldiers began arriving in Santo Domingo, ostensibly to become Dominican citizens. Santana did not prohibit Spanish diplomats from forming political groups to agitate for annexation to Spain. Local Spanish officials proved more enthusiastic about annexation than General O'Donnell who preferred merely closer ties, not a protectorate. He realized that direct annexation might cause the United States to occupy Havana, make the British and French increase their participation in Caribbean politics, and deny his government the diplomatic support he wanted in Europe and America. In fact, he ordered

---

6. Sumner Welles, *Naboth's Vineyard: The Dominican Republic, 1844–1924* (New York, 1928), 1:192–193.

the colonial government in Cuba, which had the major responsibility for Dominican activities, not to annex the island without his specific orders.[7]

At the end of 1860 and certainly by the start of 1861, O'Donnell reassessed his Caribbean policies. By this point, Europe expected the United States to collapse into civil war, thus leaving it prostrate in Caribbean affairs. The general worried about Cuba since some Americans wanted the island now as a means of preventing civil war. Although his nation felt confident and even bold after winning its quick victory over Morocco, growing French interest in Haiti, Mexico, and Central America also concerned O'Donnell, since Paris might encroach on Spanish property or restrict Spain's influence in the New World. Along with the queen, he thought that since Spain maintained virtually a protectorate over Santo Domingo, annexation hardly altered present conditions. He believed other Latin Americans might be inspired to return to Spanish rule as a solution to their own political instability if the island republic could be governed in an attractive fashion.

During 1861, while O'Donnell rethought his Dominican policy, Santana insisted on diplomatic negotiations with the Spanish. Running parallel with O'Donnell's contemplations, diplomats worked out the details of a transfer in order to give the appearance of a spontaneous return to Spain's authority. They considered it imperative that such an illusion be created in order to blunt American, French, and British criticisms. By early 1861, the Spanish knew France could not object since Paris was heavily involved in Mexican affairs. Madrid told London that slavery would not be reintroduced into the island (if it should come under Spain's control) or threaten the Bahamas. Spaniards knew by now that the Americans were too involved in their own domestic crisis to prevent annexation.

Yet O'Donnell hesitated to take the bold step of announcing it. Fearing the Spaniard might finally decide not to reincorporate Santo Domingo, Santana declared the annexation a fact on March 18, 1861, without informing Madrid beforehand. Cuban officials quickly

---

7. Jerónimo Becker, *Historia de las relaciones exteriores de España durante el siglo XIX* (Madrid, 1924), 2:570–574.

checked to see if the Dominican population objected. In the meanwhile, Santana's police silenced what little opposition had developed, leading authorities in Cuba to conclude that the country accepted Santana's proclamation. They recommended to O'Donnell that he approve Santana's move. The Spanish cabinet and O'Donnell were shocked. The Foreign Office communicated with European governments and the American legation for their views. Europeans did not protest, probably because they could not do anything to change the situation, but the Americans objected. Feeling that no major criticisms would be leveled against the government and pressured into it by the public, which approved of what they considered to be an accomplished fact, the queen officially accepted Santo Domingo back into the empire. Spain succumbed to the temptation, which French and British diplomats in Madrid believed would eventually cause more problems than O'Donnell thought.

The United States became highly agitated by the news. Washington warned Madrid about violating the Monroe Doctrine, but Spain ignored it, aware that the Americans could not stop them. The Liberal Union under O'Donnell's control could not retire to a different position. If they retreated before American objections, the regime would lose political power. Washington wanted Britain and France to join in protesting, but London and Paris avoided involvement. Yet some members of the Washington government wanted to do more.

During the spring, while Spain and Santo Domingo drew together, Abraham Lincoln became president and appointed William H. Seward as his secretary of state. The new cabinet official addressed a note to the president on April 1, analyzing the diplomatic posture of the United States, and made recommendations. In regard to Santo Domingo, he suggested that Spain be asked to explain its actions and, if necessary, call Congress to declare war on Madrid in order to expel the Spaniards from the republic, a move that would also take the American nation's mind off domestic problems. Lincoln rejected this proposal because he faced a civil war at home. Although Spanish diplomats were unaware of this memorandum, they understood that Seward advocated taking strong measures against Madrid. Yet García Tassara felt secure since words alone could not force Spain off the island.

The American public hardly took interest in the annexation. What little newspaper comment appeared criticized Spain. They questioned its spontaneity while fearing Spanish encroachment on American rights. Spanish citizens thought the event a great one, reconfirming Spain's growing importance in international affairs. The majority believed this would help protect Cuba at the same time that it suggested the possibility of other Latin states returning to the fold. Hardly any editorial writers raised the possibility of difficulties growing out of the annexation. A virulent, anti-American writer who often reflected the feelings of high ranking Spanish officials, José Ferrer de Couto, summarized popular opinion by calling the annexation a barrier "against the absorbing tendencies of the *yankees* in Central America and for Cuba."[8]

Official protests by the American legation failed to influence the Foreign Office. The Spanish argued that Santo Domingo had come back to Spain of its own accord. How willingly became clear by early 1863 when rumors circulated in Madrid and Washington that the Dominicans were revolting against the Spanish. Spain blamed the Haitians and Americans for fomenting this revolt, but in truth, Madrid had caused it by mismanaging the island and failing to carry out the obligations as stipulated in the transfer agreement. Spanish rule lowered the Dominican standard of living and crippled its legal and economic institutions. In the spring of 1865, it became painfully obvious to the Spaniards that they could not reassert their authority in Santo Domingo. By then Spain had lost about ten thousand soldiers to disease and fighting at a cost of millions of *reales* and with no end in sight. Throughout this Spanish tragedy, the United States remained quiet. The government declared its neutrality and refused to aid the rebels for fear that Spain might retaliate by recognizing the Confederacy. Seward and others believed the Dominicans could sap Spain's strength without their help. This in turn dispelled any worries about Madrid's threatening Washington's interests in the New World. Spain always believed that Seward had helped the rebels but could never prove it.

Spain's fear about the impact of the Dominican revolt on its inter-

---

8. José Ferrer de Couto, *Reincorporación de Santo Domingo á España* (Madrid, 1861), 7.

national position became evident when the cortés debated the crisis in the spring of 1865. In fact, the episode cost Spain whatever respect and sympathy it had had before 1861 in Latin America. Since Madrid wanted to have influence in the New World, the loss of this prestige and friendship proved a heavy price for annexing Santo Domingo. The revolt brought a storm of criticism down on O'Donnell and his Liberal Union even though he was not in power at the moment. Within European diplomatic circles, Spain's stock declined. Spaniards could not resist the temptation of regaining the island so easily in 1861 even in the face of possible negative consequences. South Americans now considered Spain rather than Washington the primary aggressor. Seward realized that after the Civil War, the United States would have to find more bases in the Caribbean in order to avoid future annexations by European governments. Spain's evacuation also weakened Cuba's security—a factor not lost to concerned nations.

Concurrent with problems in Santo Domingo were others in Mexico. Americans suffered property losses because of Mexican political instability, forcing Washington to take great interest in its neighbor's affairs. The Spanish always feared the United States might overrun that country and objected because of Cuba's security and because claims registered by U.S. citizens against the Mexicans and debts owed might never be paid. Prior to the Mexican civil war, which began in 1857, Spain and the United States carefully monitored each other's activities in Mexico. Americans, for example, worried that Madrid might aid conservative elements to gain power under Antonío López de Santa Anna who, having led his country's armies in its war against the United States in the 1840s, hated his northern neighbor. Washington also expressed concern over Spanish-Mexican relations, which deteriorated in the late 1850s when Spaniards were killed and their property destroyed. Spain worried that American claims would provide Washington with a good excuse to intervene and form a protectorate.[9]

In February 1857 the liberal political faction in Mexico announced a new constitution, which borrowed heavily from the U.S. Constitu-

---

9. James Morton Callahan, *Evolution of Seward's Mexican Policy* (Morgantown, 1909), 3–4.

tion. Spain saw this as a clear example of North America's penetration into Hispanic society. Liberal Mexican units led by Bénito Juarez received American public support, which also disturbed Madrid. Then Spain learned that Washington had signed a draft treaty with Mexico, which placed northern Mexican territory in collateral status for payment of debts. Although it was never acted upon by the Senate, the Spanish Foreign Office worried about the convention's implications.

Aside from the general prescriptions of Caribbean politics, Spanish-Mexican diplomacy reflected other concerns. During the late 1850s, their relations deteriorated as debts went unpaid and Spaniards were killed by various Mexican factions. When the Spanish public demanded that their government act forcefully, Madrid threatened to send troops to Mexico to compel payments and reparations and punish those responsible for killing Spaniards. Although Washington and London knew Spain had the right to these actions, neither wanted Spain to occupy Mexico. They thus tried to mediate Spanish-Mexican differences but failed because Mexico could hardly control its own domestic situation, let alone pay debts out of its empty treasury. Spain did not want to invade the country or establish a new government, yet it demanded basic justice, which the Mexicans could not provide. By the mid-1860s, Calderon Collantes decided that some action had to be taken or face rising criticism at home from outraged Spaniards. And like O'Donnell, he also wanted to head off an American attempt to establish a protectorate in northern Mexico.

London and Paris, similarly facing problems and worries over Mexico, proposed a multinational intervention treaty to Madrid. France, nurturing its own designs on Mexico, wanted to participate in order to prevent any other power from dominating the Latin country. London wished to preserve the status quo while eliminating the various sources of friction with Mexico. In October 1861 the three signed the treaty, stipulating they would only collect debts and protect lives. To calm Washington, they announced that none would impose a new government on the Mexicans.[10] Lincoln could do little

---

10. Carl H. Bock, *Prelude to Tragedy: Negotiation and Breakdown of the Tripartite Convention of London, October 31, 1861* (Philadelphia, 1966), 517–520.

to block the intervention. Seward merely warned them about violating the Monroe Doctrine and, when asked to be a party to the convention, declined.

By June the Spanish and British had left Mexico after they had discovered that France wanted to conquer the nation. The Spanish commander, Juan Prim, accused the French of violating the October convention and objected to their wanting to impose a king on Mexico. He withdrew his troops on his own initiative without prior permission from Madrid. Once O'Donnell received this news, he again faced a situation similar to Santo Domingo's annexation since he had to accept or repudiate an accomplished act. A long series of debates took place within the government, leading O'Donnell to confirm reluctantly Prim's evacuation in order to save face. He argued that Spain could never violate a treaty and then started mending his diplomatic fences with Paris.

The United States watched the intervention with suspicion. Washington approved of Prim's withdrawal and during the debates over Mexico in the cortés, kept quiet, commenting only when Seward felt he could help the anti-interventionists with assurances that the United States would not march into Mexico. By the end of 1862, Madrid and Washington no longer clashed over Mexico; they both knew that the real problem was between the United States and France. Officials in Madrid expressed less concern about American infiltration into Mexico because of the continuing North American Civil War; he also believed that Washington's concerns were directed more toward the Caribbean than Central America. Rather their fears centered on Cuba. The United States in 1865 might have been expected to expel the French from Mexico and then turn its large, experienced military machine on Cuba, easily seizing it from Spain. Some Spaniards even believed Washington might sweep the entire Caribbean clean of all Europeans.[11]

Some misconceptions about the Dominican and Mexican episodes should be cleared away. Spain's involvement in these areas did not materialize when Washington became involved in civil war; that event only speeded up the process. Spain's reasons for intervening

---

11. Tassara to Minister of State, No. 126, July 7, 1865, Sp/pol/USA/2409.

came as a result of a long process of confronting North American competition and in response to local conditions in each region. The two events developed simultaneously with the American Civil War, not as a consequence of it. Spain's retirement from these areas was also due to conditions there and less to the Civil War. In Mexico's case, evacuation came in response to Franco-Spanish problems and at a time when everyone knew the Civil War would continue. Spain left Santo Domingo after nearly two years of fruitless fighting. This is not to say that the Civil War failed to influence these events; rather, it was only one of several factors.

Two major problems directly related to the Civil War. The first involved the question of neutrality and recognition of the Confederacy, and the second concerned maritime incidents resulting from the conflict. In April 1861, when the fighting erupted, the United States declared it to be a domestic event of no concern to any other government. Washington also warned the rest of the world not to aid the South and then established a blockade around the southern coastline. Lincoln's envoys received orders to block any effort at recognizing the South or granting it belligerent status, and they were to prevent aid from being sent to the Confederacy. Spain, like France and Britain, declared its neutrality even though the majority of the upper classes and most officials sympathized with the South. Spain sincerely attempted to maintain a correct neutrality throughout the war out of fear that Washington might decide to retaliate by seizing Havana or all of Cuba.

One problem made Spain's stance difficult to maintain and led to dozens of complaints from Seward: Cuba's role in the American Civil War. Cuban ports proved convenient for southern merchants to acquire supplies while blockade runners invariably used them for refueling and obtaining the latest news about the war. Confederate raiders sometimes resupplied in them before attacking northern merchant ships, while southern diplomats passed through the colony on their way to and from Europe. Each time a Confederate ship or blockade runner used Cuban facilities, the United States protested, accusing Spain of voliating its own neutrality. These troubles, often resulting from the improper actions of colonial officials in Havana who either were incompetent or sympathized with the South, came without Madrid's blessings. However, some in Cuba and Spain argued that southern merchant ships should not be denied port facilities since they were vessels of the United States, not those of an unrecognized state. Denying them would be the same as acknowledging the existence of the Confederacy—which Washington did not want—leaving the United States trapped by its own semantics.

Neither government could resolve the problem during the war. The number of cases ran into the hundreds. Seward tried to negotiate a maritime jurisdictional treaty with Spain to define the territorial boundaries of Cuba so that the American navy could patrol without creating unnecessary problems for both. Spain refused because the United States wanted to recognize only a three-mile-wide water belt around Cuba; Madrid claimed twelve. Yet Seward felt obligated to persist because each time a maritime indicent occurred, he believed it symbolized Spain's forthcoming recognition of the Confederacy, an event that never took place. Madrid repeatedly denied that it would recognize or aid the South, but Seward continued to mistrust Spain. Finally this bantering came to an end with the death of the Confederacy in 1865.

These problems were augmented by other less important ones that nonetheless irritated both, since, like the maritime incidents, they were viewed as possible hints of the other's future policy. For example, when the Union Army occupied New Orleans, the local federal commander, Benjamin F. Butler, violated Spanish rights, as did other Union and Confederate commanders in Virginia, South Carolina, and Florida. Trade between the two and with Cuba suffered as a consequence of the war. Spain, the world's fourth largest consumer of cotton fiber, found its supplies virtually cut off, creating serious economic and political unrest in Catalonia, the area long recognized as an instrumental factor in causing the nation's major revolution in the fall of 1868.

The Civil War also affected the triangular relations among Spain, the United States, and Cuba for the rest of the blockade. The decline in trade with the North proved how great American penetration into Cuba's economy had been prior to 1861. This realization led local citizens to restudy the relationship of their economy to Washington in order to prevent future depressions. These problems inspired revolutionaries to continue organizing and fomenting unrest in the belief that once the Civil War ended, the United States would not hesitate to expel Spain from Cuba. And of course, Spanish and American officials believed that if the Confederacy won its independence, the South would seize the colony.

Immediately after the war ended, Spain's concern for Cuban security increased, reflecting the same urgency of the 1850s. Spanish dispatches duplicated those composed years earlier. Madrid's worries also mirrored past experiences. For instance, in 1867, a new envoy, Fecundo Goñi, arrived in Washington as García Tassara's replacement. Goñi's instructions were almost the same as those sent to Spanish envoys in the 1840s and 1850s.[12] Madrid decided to open partially Cuban ports to American trade in hopes this would again ease the pressure to acquire the colony. Spain's economic appeasement also indicated that it recognized the power wielded in the New World by the United States—an acknowledgment that the political balance of power in the Caribbean was tipping in Washington's favor.

If American influence grew, it came about for more than just military or political reasons because slavery provided a great catalyst for the growth of its power in the 1860s. The Civil War, fought over the question of slavery, affected Cuba's own slave society. Americans, Spaniards, and Cubans recognized that if Washington won the Civil War, then slavery had to end in the colonies since the Union would insist upon it. If the South won, then slavery could survive longer, although it would eventually face extinction because of growing pressure from abolition groups in the Americas, Spain, and Europe.

Abolition movements in Spain, Cuba, and Puerto Rico grew in strength in the 1860s, encouraged by the Civil War and, after 1865, by the end of slavery in North America. That in Cuba proved the most militant. Linked closely to revolutionary groups advocating Cuban independence, it threatened Spain's authority. Spanish authorities suspected the United States of using the abolition movement as a means of expelling Spain from the Caribbean. Most Spaniards and Cubans did not want to repeat the experience of the United States, rejecting civil wars, revolutions, and quick emancipation for achieving abolition. They generally concluded that gradual abolition, marked by

---

12. Joaquin Oltra, *La influencia norteamericana en la constitución española de 1869* (Madrid, 1972), 32.

compensation and implemented over many years, would serve their interests best.[13]

They recognized the inevitability of converting the colonies to an all-free-labor economy. Therefore, each captain general sent to Cuba and Puerto Rico from the late 1850s on carried instructions to reduce or stop the flow of new slaves into their districts and encourage the growth of a pool of free labor. After the Civil War, American pressures to accelerate this process led to renewed orders along this line. But at the same time, the captain generals faced the serious threats posed by abolition politics. Working out of clubs in New York and Cuba, various elements sought American aid for their movement, often shrouding their activities with an abolitionist mantle. Although they never received as much aid as earlier groups had in the 1850s, they continued hoping for such assistance. Americans publicly advocated freedom for Cuba, and most believed the island would inevitably become their own. In the fall of 1868, unrelated revolutions in Spain and Cuba kept revolutionaries hopeful of American intervention.

During the 1860s, Spain's war with Chile and Peru also disturbed Spanish-American relations. Between 1864 and 1871 Madrid was at war with these two Latin countries and broke diplomatic relations with nine others. Unsettled claims, hispanophobic incidents in Peru, and Peruvian attempts to form an anti-Spanish block in Latin America after Madrid occupied Santo Domingo and invaded Mexico led to serious difficulties between Spain and the two Latin nations. In order to gain compensation for injuries to Spaniards, which the Peruvians refused to pay, Spanish warships occupied Peru's Chincha Islands. National pride prevented either government from giving in to the demands of the other; both refused to compromise, preferring to leave the crisis in suspended yet dangerous animation to 1865. Then the Chileans, sympathetic to Peru and worried that Spain might decide to launch a campaign to regain control of its old colonies at a time that the Chileans were trying to expand their influence in Latin American politics, became involved by aligning with Lima.

British, French, and American diplomats, with the cooperation of

---

13. Arthur F. Corwin, *Spain and the Abolition of Slavery in Cuba, 1817–1886* (Austin, 1967), 129–151.

other European envoys, attempted to mediate the differences between the three, but to no avail. Meanwhile Spanish warships established a blockade on Chile's coast as a means of forcing the Latins to satisfy Spain.[14] Soon after, small naval clashes took place, and in 1866 the Spanish bombarded Valparaiso, Chile, and Callao, Peru, escalating the crisis into major proportions. More meetings between the Latin governments revealed their determination to continue the conflict. The British, French, and Americans worried about the damage to their business interests, the balance of power in the New World, and the possibility of one European gaining an advantage over the others as a result of this war.

Spain welcomed European and North American offers to mediate in order to end this futile conflict, providing the Latins would alleviate the genuine sense of injury Spain felt. Since Chile and Peru felt equally strong about their claims, Washington faced a frustrating situation, which appeared impossible to resolve. Seward worried that the Monroe Doctrine would be violated. Moreover both the Spanish and Latin Americans accused the United States of favoring their opponents. Spain based its opinion on previous experiences with Washington, while Chile and Peru reached their conclusion by Seward's correct neutrality, which meant denying them any aid. Finally in 1868 Seward managed to negotiate a cease-fire and brought representatives of the various governments to Washington for negotiations. On April 11, 1871, they signed an armistice. Then without much help from the United States, the various parties negotiated peace treaties, signing the final one in 1885.

The continuing problem of the New World from 1868 to the start of the last major Cuban revolution against Spain in 1895 bore many of the characteristics evident in earlier decades, although increasingly Spain lacked the ability to pose a serious threat to U.S. interests. Yet because both still had to ensure their possessions and advantages, their relations continued along a difficult course in the decades to come.

---

14. William C. Davis, *The Last Conquistadores: The Spanish Intervention in Peru and Chile, 1863–1866* (Athens, 1950), 206.

6
TOWARD THE CUBAN VORTEX

Relations between Spain and the United States from the fall of 1868 to late spring 1895 reflected the same problems faced by earlier generations. Cuba provided the major source of controversy because of its economic relations with the United States, insensitive colonial administration, and Spanish inability to reconcile Cuban nationalism with the economic aspirations and realities of the Caribbean world. In secondary roles, Puerto Rico, the Philippines, and Latin America irritated relations between Spain and the United States. Each saw a threat to their position from the other, while Spain endured the slow spread of American power into the Pacific and deep into the economic, cultural, and political life of its ex-colonies. The forces that in earlier years had begun tipping the balance of power in favor of the United States against Spanish interests continued operating at a faster rate in the late nineteenth century. Ultimately this progression subjugated Spanish authority in the Caribbean to unparalleled tests of endurance while, as before, the United States often benefited from situations it hardly controlled.

The period in question conveniently falls into two phases. The first, covering 1868 to 1873, witnessed heavy fighting in the Cuban Ten Years' War, a major revolution by colonists seeking independence from Spain. During this phase, a serious naval incident, much like those of the 1850s, involving the *Virginius* caused a small war scare. A second era took in the years between 1874 and 1895. While less hectic than the first, it signaled a continued decline in Spanish influence in the New World. The relative quiet proved deceptive since the Cuban revolution, which began in 1895, more than indicated that no nation could place major problems in suspended animation and thereby hope to solve them. Each strived to settle outstanding debts and claims, talked of more amicable relations, and expanded commercial relations. To a greater extent than in the 1860s, Cuban affairs virtually dominated Spanish-American relations for the rest of the century.

In the fall of 1868, Cuban nationalists revolted, fighting for over ten years. In announcing their grievances, they listed Spanish political and economic tyranny against them. Spain's denial of political and religious freedoms along with a burdensome taxation program irritated many Cubans who resented the power Spanish elements (*peninsularos*) enjoyed in their island. These issues were further confused by abolitionism and Cuban nationalism. Complicated questions concerning Cuba's destiny in the affairs of the New World and its economic relations with the United States added to an already difficult situation. The United States could not escape the consequences of this revolt either; its commerce with Cuba suffered, Americans were wounded and killed, and investments shrank. The seriousness of this fighting became apparent to all by April 1869 when the Cuban rebels felt strong enough to establish a republic at Gúaimaro where they named Manuel de Céspedes their president.

The rebels, still loosely organized and hardly in control of enough territory to warrant the establishment of a new Cuban government, demanded complete independence. More moderate elements considered the possibility of autonomy modeled on Canada's. But Spain refused to grant any concessions, let alone discuss future relations with Cuba, until the rebels first laid down their arms. Spanish officials believed that without such a preliminary requirement, Spain might face national disgrace, the public would force the current regime out of office, and the nation would appear weak before the rest of Europe. Therefore, even the liberals, in power after the fall of 1868 and who previously had been the most vocal element in Spain calling for Cuban reforms, refused to compromise. At the same time the Cuban revolutionaries would not lay down their arms.[1]

The domestic situation in Spain in the late 1860s and early 1870s influenced Madrid's position. Between 1868 and 1875, intense politi-

---

1. Lester D. Langley, *The Cuban Policy of the United States* (New York, 1968), 55–59.

cal instability plagued the Iberian nation. The era of the Liberal Union (1858–63) and even the period shortly after gave the appearance of greater stability in Spain to observers in other countries than during the first half of the Ten Years' War. In the years following 1868, whichever group held power always seized upon the idea of totally crushing the Cuban revolt as a means of rallying support to the government at home and signaling to the world Spain's ability to govern its own affairs. The rapid turnover of cabinets made the attractiveness of such a quick solution to an otherwise complicated domestic political situation understandable.

Ministerial instability also made the prosecution of the war more difficult. A provisional government came to power on October 8, 1868, after the expulsion of Isabel II from Spain, and until January 4, 1871, when Amadeo I became king, it had two regents. During the reign of the new king (January 1871–November 1873), Spain had no less than six ministries. The combination of the reign's failure to satisfy Spain's various political factions and the king's disgust with Spanish affairs led to the establishment of the first republic in February 1873. Before it fell to military rule in January 1874, four presidents governed, some staying in office hardly more than a month.

When it appeared that the Bourbons might regain power in 1873–74, the Carlists, who had claimed the Spanish throne since 1833, also confused matters by starting another civil war. Although eventually defeating the Carlists, Madrid had to fight them at the same time that troops battled with Cuban revolutionaries. Foreign powers occasionally intervened in Spain to protect lives and properties of their nationals, which discredited any minister who spoke of Madrid's winning in Cuba. Moreover Europe proved reluctant to extend recognition and aid to any political faction in Spain for fear it might soon fall. The potential threat of a major European intervention marked by some outside power's imposing a new government on Madrid, although unlikely, nonetheless worried some Spanish politicians, especially those who wanted a republic or a Carlist regime. The Spanish also feared that Britain, France, or the United States might seize Cuba and Puerto Rico. Thus domestic problems hampered efforts to end the Cuban revolution while intensifying Spanish concern over possible American and European intervention in the Caribbean.

Political conditions in the United States proved more stable. Ulysses S. Grant came to power in March 1869, remaining in office for the next eight years. Domestic and Cuban activities made his analysis of Spain's colonial war difficult because the revolutionaries looked to the United States for material support. They aroused public concern for their plight by a vigorous propaganda campaign, which eventually led some congressmen to advocate assistance. Cuban agitators in the United States were further aided by Spain's commercial policies, which irritated American businessmen. Other Americans believed the Cubans incapable of ruling themselves, which raised the question of leaving Cuba in Spanish hands or bringing it under the control of the United States. Many in Congress, as much disturbed by stories of Cuban and Spanish atrocities and fighting as by public pressure to aid the rebels, advocated giving the revolutionaries belligerency status while attempting to mediate between them and Spain. Washington felt other pressures from within as well. Daniel E. Sickles, the minister to Madrid, advocated Cuban independence. He also wanted the Grant administration to help gain Cuban freedom. The president sympathized but his strong-willed secretary of state, Hamilton Fish, did not. In the long run, the secretary's opinions dominated the government's foreign policy.

Fish concluded that enlightened Spanish rule would best serve the interests of his country. He never believed the rebels controlled sufficient territory to warrant the kind of support implied by belligerency, which carried with it the added risk of war with Spain at a time when the national debt of the United States remained large, the vast majority of her navy lay in disrepair, and the army was drastically reduced in numbers. The threat of war might also delay the conclusion of important yet delicate claims negotiations with Britain stemming from Civil War maritime problems.[2] Therefore in mid-1869, Fish proposed to Spain that Cuba be granted independence or some sort of autonomy and that the Spanish abolish slavery there and in Puerto Rico and allow the United States to mediate between them and Cuba. The secretary even was willing to negotiate with the Cubans to try to persuade them to pay a sum for independence, an amount to be

---

2. Allan Nevins, *Hamilton Fish: The Inner History of the Grant Administration* (New York, 1957), 1:180–181.

guaranteed by the United States. In this way, Fish hoped to end the struggle, which was damaging American commercial interests. To add force to his arguments, he threatened to recognize Cuba's belligerency if Spain rejected his proposals.

Madrid agreed to them provided the Cuban rebels laid down their arms prior to the start of negotiations. Spain wanted to end the war, but only in a way not prejudicial to its own national honor. Any hint of coercion by the United States would only add to the government's growing list of domestic problems. The Cubans, mistrustful of Spain's promise to grant concessions, refused to abide by Madrid's condition. The British, French, and Russians, concerned about the balance of power in the Caribbean as always, interfered by suggesting to Spain that it not fully agree to the secretary's proposals since the United States might somehow gain possession of Cuba. The Spanish agreed with this logic; therefore they seized on the refusal of the Cubans to negotiate without arms as the excuse to back away from Washington's proposals.[3]

In an attempt to placate the Americans after rejecting Fish's proposals, Spain drew up abolition plans and partially implemented them, although both Madrid and Washington knew this was merely window dressing. Spain expressed concern that its weakened condition might encourage France and Britain to join the United States in granting Cuba belligerency. This would mean that Spain could no longer purchase military supplies to suppress the revolt. Spanish diplomats also believed that the revolution tempted Paris and London to become further involved in North African affairs out of a belief that Spain could not divert her attention from Cuba to protect its interests in the Mediterranean. The Spanish therefore repeatedly stated that the rebels were virtually defeated and encouraged Americans to think that the Cuban revolt might be concluded by negotiation. The bunting was the abolition program implemented by the government. The entire project, Spaniards hoped, would prevent Grant from issuing a belligerency declaration and would silence critics in Europe.[4]

---

3. Jerónimo Becker, *Historia de las relaciones exteriores de España durante el siglo XIX* (Madrid, 1924), 3:38.

4. Franklin W. Knight, *Slave Society in Cuba during the Nineteenth Century* (Madison, 1970), 170–171.

The issue of belligerency died when Grant sent a special message to Congress in June 1870 on the revolution and his policy. The product of his secretary's thinking, it chastised Spain and Cuba for fighting. He rejected claims for belligerency, arguing that the rebels still had not earned such recognition. He criticized both parties for wounding and killing Americans, destroying their property, and damaging trade with the colony.[5] Immediately following Grant's message, Fish increased his efforts at mediating between Spain and Cuba. Neither welcomed this. The Spanish, recognizing that the United States might not intervene in Cuba as a result of the message, wanted to reduce friction by flaunting abolition plans. Yet the colonial administration failed to implement them properly despite enabling legislation from the cortés. Both Americans and Cubans, therefore, continued criticizing Spain for its antiquated colonial policies.

Sickles's views complicated matters for both governments. Spaniards found repugnant his suggestion that North American society would improve upon Spain's in the Caribbean. Meanwhile the envoy in Washington, Mauricio López Roberts, and the Foreign Office believed mediation would result in the loss of political face in Spain, leading to the overthrow of Spanish authority in the Caribbean colonies and ultimately in the Philippines as well. On a more individual level, Spanish officials wanted to continue in office, leaving them no option but to keep the United States from interfering in Cuban affairs on the one hand, while crushing the revolution quickly on the other. If successful, such a policy would encourage political stability at home, preserve the empire, and add prestige to the nation in Europe and American circles. Thus, Madrid again refused American mediation. Yet its plans nearly failed in 1873 when a maritime incident pushed Spain and the United States to the brink of war.

In November 1873, Spanish authorities seized the *Virginius*, a ship being used by the New York Cuban junta to send supplies into Cuba for the rebels. The next week, most of the crew, including some Americans, were executed. News of the episode soon surfaced on

---

5. James D. Richardson, ed., *Messages and Papers of the Presidents, 1789–1892* (Washington, D.C., 1896–1902), 9:4018–4023.

the front pages of newspapers in the United States, and there were loud protests. Fish complained to the Spanish, demanded that the ship be returned along with any remaining live Americans, wanted the flag of the United States saluted, and asked that those guilty of arbitrary actions be punished. He also warned that if Spain did not control its officers and avoid such incidents in the future, the United States would view this as indicative of Madrid's inability to rule Cuba any longer.[6]

The Spanish recognized the gravity of the incident but also did not appreciate Washington's intimidating them. Initially the Foreign Office insisted that Spain had a right to seize the *Virginius*, which had carried arms to Cuba on several occasions. Although Madrid believed in the justice of its actions, it decided to defuse the crisis by announcing that the episode would be investigated. At the time Spain believed European governments would condemn the executions as the British already had done and might not extend diplomatic recognition and support to the new Spanish regime. Therefore, the combination of fear of war with the United States and possible negative repercussions in Europe led Spain to offer Washington a compromise: an investigation of the affair, punishment for those who violated the rights of foreigners, indemnity to be paid families whose members were executed in violation of their rights, and if warranted, an official admittance of guilt and liability. In order to satisfy American impatience, Madrid would automatically admit responsibility if, by the end of the year, the investigation had not been completed and the issue was already settled. This, in effect, proved to be a complete retreat on Spain's part, but without loss of face, and was done to reduce the danger of war. Fish recognized Spain's motives and immediately accepted the proposals.[7]

Friction over Cuba declined momentarily. Spain soon paid $80,000 in indemnities to the families of executed Americans, a cheap price

---

6. French Ensor Chadwick, *The Relations of the United States and Spain* (New York, 1909–11), 1:323–357.

7. Julio Salom Costa, *España en la europa de Bismark: La política exterior de Cánovas (1871–1881)* (Madrid, 1967), 168–178; Vega de Armijo to Minister of State, no. 446, December 13, 1874, Sp/pol/USA/2410, Foreign Office Archives, Madrid.

for peace. Fish brought Sickles home as a further means of improving relations and sent Caleb Cushing to Madrid as his replacement. Cushing, more inclined toward peaceful diplomacy, harbored no serious ill feelings toward Spain, and Madrid respected the abilities of this experienced diplomat.

The temptation to compare the case of the *Virginius* to that of the *Black Warrior* is great; in both instances Madrid and Washington stood on the verge of war with each other, the American envoys favored Spain's loss of Cuba, and yet the two nations found ways to preserve peace. But the differences between the 1850s and the 1870s proved significant. In the later period, Spain's political instability and the seriousness of the revolt in Cuba complicated the situation. Moreover Spain's envoy in the 1870s was less obnoxious to the American government than the one serving in the 1850s. Most important, the *Virginius* affair, because of its similarity to earlier incidents, indicated that nothing had really changed in Cuba's colonial situation.

After the *Virginius* case, both nations turned their attention back to the fighting in Cuba, which dragged on, with neither side appearing to gain the upper hand. Casualties mounted along with damage to American interests. Secretary Fish asked France, Britain, Austria, and Russia to persuade Madrid to settle its differences with Cuba and offered his services. On November 5, 1875, he criticized Spain's policies and warned that if the war did not end within six months, then other governments might be forced into the conflict. Although the warning was issued to assuage Americans who were pressuring the administration to grant the rebels belligerency (which, in effect, would mean recognition of their existence as a legal entity), the Spanish worried even though they suspected, as a result of the *Virginius* case, that Fish and Grant did not want to fight over Cuba. Yet Madrid knew that American policy could always be altered radically if public pressure on Grant grew sufficient, and it was concerned about Washington's approach to the Europeans on Cuba.

Fish had suggested to the major powers that they help settle the crisis. Unknown fully to Madrid, however, Europe generally ignored Fish's suggestion because his proposal threatened to involve them in an imbroglio in Cuba at the very moment when a serious war scare threatened peace between the new French republic and Bismarck's powerful Germany. Britain wanted no part of American politics as long as there were more serious problems in Europe. The other European states offered Fish a collection of excuses for not wishing to discuss Cuba with Spain. The Spanish told Europe that the revolution was a purely domestic concern, using much the same logic employed by the United States during the Civil War. Spain's policy suited Europe for the moment; thus Fish failed to involve others in Cuban affairs.

Madrid still faced the question of future American policy. Dispatches from the legation in Washington spoke of the United States' possibly extending belligerency to the rebels. Meanwhile other reports concerning filibustering out of New Orleans and New York reflected Spanish worries. Madrid knew that Grant might be persuaded to carry out policies not favored by Fish and that he sympathized with those advocating assistance to the rebels. Spain feared Grant would act if Paris refused to support Madrid. In 1875, Spaniards still worried that the French might encourage Carlist rebels to overthrow the new Bourbon king in Madrid (Alfonso XII) by opening the border at the Pyrenees to them. Spain wanted this stopped so that it could concentrate full military strength on squashing the Cuban revolt. Any attempt by France to weaken the Spanish government would be viewed by Washington as a sign that Spain could not decisively end the revolt and might encourage Grant to aid the Cubans out of a need to bring peace to an area deemed of interest to Americans.[8]

Madrid's main concern, therefore, centered on the relationship of Cuban politics to domestic affairs in Spain. Usually in an international crisis, politicians measured an event or policy option against its potential impact on domestic affairs. In a war with the United States, not only Cuba but the restored monarchy might have been lost as well. King Alfonso could have been replaced by a Carlist pretender, another republic, or a military dictator. The king's gifted prime minister, Antonio Cánovas del Castillo, considered preserva-

---

8. On the war scare there are numerous dispatches, telegrams, and memoranda in Sp/pol/USA/2411 and in Sp/corr/USA/1474; on filibustering, numerous correspondence, reports, and so forth in Sp/corr/USA/1474.

tion of the throne his primary objective. Consequently he urged his representatives in Cuba to press the war to its successful conclusion quickly. Along with his cabinet, the prime minister also thought that the suppression of the "mulatto" revolution (which many Spaniards viewed as a struggle between the white Spanish and the racially mixed lower classes) would be a major victory for "European civilization," providing an early example of Europe's preoccupation with its "white man's burden."[9]

By 1876 informed officials in Madrid and Washington recognized that the Cuban rebels could no longer fight with any serious hope of gaining independence. They could not defeat Spain and were running out of supplies. Spain hinted to the United States that it might be willing to start some negotiations with the Cubans to effect an end to the useless fighting, provided, of course, that the rebels laid down their arms prior to any talks. Cánovas believed this tactic would discourage any American aid to the Cubans. The cabinet worried at the moment about the United States's ordering ships into the Caribbean; Washington had already sent vessels to the area in case some intervention might be necessary to save American lives. The Spanish took no chances; they sent five more ships into the area.[10]

Amid continuing reports of filibustering, Spanish representatives began negotiating quietly with Cuban rebels.[11] These talks were suspended for a while in 1876 while the Americans held their presidential election. The Hayes-Tilden campaign was important since it reflected American attitudes and hinted of possible future policy, so Spain observed it carefully. At one point the legation in Washington reported that "the triumph of Mr. Hayes over Tilden is without a doubt preferable for Spain" because the former would compromise on Cuba, encourage peace there, and allow Spain to continue governing her.

---

9. Salom Costa, *España en la europa de Bismark*, 178–182.

10. Mantilla to Minister of State, no. 6, January 15, 1876, Sp/corr/USA/1475; Minister of State to Mantilla, February 10, 1876, Sp/corr/USA/1475; Minister of State to Francisco Merry y Colom (envoy to Berlin), January 21, 1876, Sp/pol/USA/2411; Mantilla to Minister of State, no. 179, December 27, 1875, and no. 3, January 4, 1876, Sp/pol/USA/2411.

11. Mantilla to Minister of State, no. 129, November 15, 1877, Sp/corr/USA/1475.

In fact, the Spanish believed Hayes to be a far more prudent politician than Tilden, who, by drawing on much support from the South, took a more hostile attitude toward Spain.[12] Once a friendlier administration than Grant's came into power, Madrid believed peace could be reestablished in Cuba without American interruptions.

In preparation for a final settlement, Madrid and Washington signed a protocol in January 1877, stipulating that American citizens charged with crimes in Spanish territories would have their rights protected. Necessary details were spelled out in subsequent clauses in order to avoid future complications. At the same time General Arsenio Martínez Campos arrived in Cuba to command Spanish operations. A popular man, respected by Cubans and Spaniards alike, he came with orders to end the Ten Years' War, mainly by diplomacy. Important Cuban rebel leaders began surrendering, and although sporadic fighting continued into the next decade, he managed to negotiate the Treaty of Zanjón. Signed in February 1878, it ended the war for all intents and purposes. It called for colonial reforms (which never came) and amnesty from Spain in exchange for a cessation of hostilities and allegiance to Spanish authority.[13]

Although the war ended, 1878 was not a significant date in Spanish-American relations; many historians have called it that, however. It did not signify that Washington's relations with Cuba or Spain changed or that Spanish authority had been restored on a permanent basis. If anything, the termination of this struggle represented merely a cease-fire, which lasted hardly seventeen years. It indicated to the United States that Cuban problems might decline in importance for a while but certainly would not end all friction in the Caribbean.

The war's end, however, was a major event in Spanish domestic history. Its conclusion graced the monarchy with the laurels of victory and thereby contributed greatly to the nation's relative political stability for the next two decades. This is not to say that peace reigned in Spain because many economic problems and Carlist agitation continued to frustrate Spanish authorities at a time when the nation was experiencing significant demographic and sociopolitical changes as a

---

12. Ibid., no. 26, March 18, 1877.
13. Herminio Portell Vilá, *Historio de Cuba en sus relaciones con los Estados Unidos y España* (Havana, 1938–41), 2:247–248.

result of industrialization and continued stagnation in the agricultural south. Nonetheless Zanjón helped usher in a period of some peace and prosperity to an extent not seen in Spain during that century. This in turn encouraged Cánovas and others to involve Spain in Mediterranean politics with a greater sense of direction and authority than could be done earlier. At the same time, officials had the opportunity to restudy colonial authority in Cuba while shoring up deteriorating relations with Latin America.

Officials in Washington and Madrid knew that they still faced conflicts over Cuba. The United States again raised the question of American claims, which had grown in number as a result of the Ten Years' War. In fact, there were so many of them that both nations devoted the rest of the nineteenth century to resolving them.[14] Reports of filibustering continued to crowd the desks at the Foreign Office throughout the 1880s and 1890s, duplicating the worries that had existed prior to 1861. The Cubans also repeated their previous activities.[15]

Although the Spanish in the 1880s and 1890s did not seriously believe that the United States would conquer Cuba by force of arms, they did realize that the economic realities that had previously embittered relations with Washington continued unchanged. Both governments, therefore, paid a great deal of attention to Cuban economics. Each wanted to improve its position in Cuba while reducing tensions with the other. Yet neither was willing to compromise to gain the tranquility they sought. Spain knew that any compromise ultimately meant American dominance of the Cuban economy. The same idea occurred to the Americans. But both went through the motions of finding solutions to their problems. For example, John W. Foster went to Spain in 1883 as an American envoy carrying with him instructions to negotiate a reciprocal commercial treaty involving Cuba, Puerto Rico, the Philippines, and Spain. Washington wanted tariffs

---

14. Many documents regarding reclamations during the 1870s through 1895 are in Sp/pol/USA/2410 and 2413.

15. Hundreds of reports, memoranda, and telegrams on filibustering are in Sp/corr/USA/1476–1481 and in Sp/pol/USA/2412–2414.

reduced on American goods going into Spanish territories. The Spanish foreign minister, Servando Ruiz Gómez, welcomed the opportunity to negotiate a downward revision of tariffs. An advocate of free trade, he realized that without a change, friction over Cuba would continue at great peril to Spain's political stability. Yet no treaty came about.

The economic situation that Ruiz Gómez and other officials faced in both countries did not lend itself to easy resolution. Spain maintained a "discriminating flag" policy whereby Spanish goods came into Cuba with a lower tax than items from other nations. The United States retaliated by imposing higher tariffs on Spanish goods entering North America. At the same time, American investments in Cuba in both trade and capital-producing businesses (such as sugar plantations) steadily increased. In fact, sales to Cuba by the United States amounted to one-fourth of all the latter's trade with Latin America.[16] Therefore Washington's insistence that Spain change its policy remained intense over the years. A critical point came after 1890 when the McKinley tariff went into effect, calling for higher duties on incoming foreign goods, which could be altered by commercial treaties on a bilateral basis. Thus, if Spain wanted American tariffs reduced on its merchandise, such as on olive oil, wines, cork, and cigars, it would have to sign a commercial pact with the United States. This meant opening the Cuban market even further to American business.

The Spaniards found themselves in a more difficult position in 1891 when the United States began negotiating a series of commercial treaties with European governments. Spain had just abandoned its free trade policies to appease Catalan and Basque industrial interests and Castilian wheat growers. Each of these domestic groups wanted to maintain their favorable position in the colonial market, which they saw threatened immensely by the treaties of the United States. Sixty percent of Catalonia's trade, for instance, went to the colonies. Since this area was at the time demanding some form of political autonomy within Spain while labor agitation threatened the political

---

16. John W. Foster, *Diplomatic Memoirs* (New York, 1909), 1:247; Leland Jenks, *Our Cuban Colony: A Study in Sugar* (New York, 1928), 31–32, 39.

stability in the nation, Madrid could ill afford to irritate the Catalans any further by acquiescing to American demands for tariff revision. Yet Madrid considered Cuba's security of such great importance that it negotiated a draft of such a treaty with Foster. When the final decision had to be made by the government on the treaty, domestic considerations prevailed, compelling the cabinet to reject it. A similar situation existed in Washington where pressure mounted not to ratify the treaty since it did not really open up the Cuban economy.

Historians writing about Spanish-American relations usually forget that during the 1880s and 1890s the Philippines—still a Spanish colony—played a role in diplomatic affairs. Indeed, when economic problems were discussed or maritime incidents analyzed, the Philippines drew the attention of both regimes. Each expressed concern for its relations with this colony. During the 1880s and 1890s, the United States had expanded deeply into the Pacific by way of Hawaii. At first this interest proved only economic, but later it became political as well. Spanish authorities quietly monitored this growing American interest in the area, fearing that someday the Philippines might have the same influence on Spanish-American relations as Cuba did now. In fact, by the 1880s, both faced the same sort of problems with the Philippines as in the Caribbean, only to a lesser extent. American trade with this colony grew, and naval strategists in Washington became interested in the territory's position in the Pacific. As with Cuba, various incidents brought the colony to the attention of Washington and Madrid. For example during the 1880s, colonial authorities seized an American ship, the *Masonic*, for violating regulations regarding cargo manifests. The vessel's owners took the case to a Spanish court, which agreed that the seizure was illegal, but complicated negotiations between the two governments proved necessary to obtain an indemnity.[17]

Both nations viewed problems emerging from the Philippines, Cuba, and Puerto Rico as part of the broader issue of each country's influence in the New World. Although the Philippines lay in the Pacific, this colony was nevertheless linked to Caribbean and South American politics since Spain, on the one hand, considered its active

---

17. Foster, *Diplomatic Memoirs*, 1:305–306.

involvement in these areas vital to the preservation of its remaining colonies. On the other hand, the United States participated in American and Pacific affairs in order to expand its economic interests and to protect its territory from potential military threats. Both saw the entire area of the New World, and by implication, the Pacific as well, as a field of political, economic, and cultural rivalry. After the Ten Years' War ended, they expressed renewed interest in the whole region. Washington expanded its influence southward while Madrid rebuilt friendlier relations there, which had faltered badly during the 1860s and1870s.

Neither hesitated to take the initiative in implementing policies designed to further their influence in the Americas. Spain encouraged Spanish immigrants to move by the thousands into Latin America to provide employment for those who could not find it in the Iberian peninsula. These immigrants then became tools for building closer relations with Latin America by fostering cultural ties (*hispanismo*) between the two. Madrid negotiated a series of commercial, scientific, postal, diplomatic, criminal, and communication treaties with the South Americans. Recognizing that the long-cherished hope of old colonies returning to Spain's flag survived only as a dream, Spanish authorities assumed that the Latin Americans would remain independent. Consequently their attitude changed; for example, they established the Ibero-American Union to encourage more intimate relations among equals.

A pattern quickly became discernible. Whenever Spain signed a new treaty, the United States paid only mild attention since its officials considered Spanish influence in the Americas nominal. However, each time Washington involved itself in a Latin American project, Spain worried about its implications for Cuba and the effects on its position on the New World's politics. The cases where Spanish-American concerns appear abound. For instance, between 1875 and 1885, troops from the United States crossed into Mexico to suppress bandits who raided American territory. Yet Madrid never felt sure that Washington's intentions would remain so limited since Spanish diplomats remembered how just a decade before, Americans had talked of acquiring land from Mexico.

Another case considered more serious by the Spaniards, since it was closer to the Caribbean, came during 1880–81 when James G.

Blaine, secretary of state, became involved in a dispute among Guatemala, Mexico, and Costa Rica and earned their enmity. Spaniards followed the course of events there and were delighted when the Latin Americans told Blaine to leave them alone.

Spain took more seriously Blaine's attempt at the same time to organize a conference in Washington for all the governments of the New World to discuss commerce, the prevention of war, and other hemispheric problems. Blaine resigned his office in 1881 for domestic reasons, too soon to complete his plans, and his successor cancelled the conference. Yet interest in such a meeting never died at the State Department, where plans were developed throughout the 1880s for a conference. During this decade, Spain viewed the convention as a direct threat to its interests since it could evolve into an alliance aimed against all European involvement in the Americas. While Blaine was formulating his plans, Madrid instructed its envoys in Latin America to discourage participation because this would "endanger the natural influence of Europe in the nations of the Latin race."[18]

Besides the more specific question of an inter-American conference, Spaniards monitored the general problem of southward economic and political penetration by the United States in the 1880s. One foreign minister in the mid-1880s said that Spain had a responsibility to reduce such American influence if it could.[19] When Madrid learned in 1886 that the Latin Americans might form a customs union similar to the *Zollverein* (established in Germany prior to 1848), Spain worried. Europeans recognized that this type of union had been one of the major causes of Germany's unification into a powerful nation. Madrid did not rule out the possibility of the same occurring in Latin America and consequently wanted Europe to block such a union. Spain protested to the Latin American governments that an American *Zollverein* would harm European trade with them.[20] But a

---

18. Minister of State to all Spanish ministers in Latin America, n.d. [1882], Sp/pol/USA/2412.

19. Minister of State to Valera, "very reserved," March 15, 1886, Sp/corr/USA/1479.

20. Minister of State to all Spanish ministers in Latin America, May 31, 1886, Sp/pol/USA/2413.

real threat developed in 1889 when President Benjamin Harrison came into office, bringing with him Blaine as his secretary of state.

Blaine immediately revived the idea of a Latin American conference and this time had the president's approval. But even though they wanted to protect themselves from European interference, the Latin Americans mistrusted each other too much to accomplish anything important. They rejected the customs union and proved reluctant to negotiate any other formal bonds. Realizing that they were divided among themselves, Spain mounted a large counteroffensive against any such conference, warning Spanish-Americans that if Europe felt threatened, Paris, London, Madrid, Berlin, St. Petersburg, and others might feel compelled to intervene more actively in American affairs. Clearly viewing this conference as Blaine's attempt to expand North American influence still further within the Hispanic world and linking it to what they considered a renewal of American attempts to buy Cuba, Spain commented to the Latins about the danger to their society's culture. Madrid also recommended to the major European powers that they cripple Blaine's efforts since he might hurt their business interests. Europeans saw the dangers Spain spoke of and made some effort to thwart the Pan-American movement with some well-placed protest notes and mild threats.[21]

Other Latin American controversies before the start of the Cuban revolution in 1895 illustrated the continuing rivalry between Madrid and Washington in South America. In 1893 Venezuela had challenged the borders maintained by British Guiana. Earlier, in 1887, Venezuela had broken diplomatic relations with London over the question, but by 1893 public interest in the unresolved dispute in the United States forced President Grover Cleveland to become involved. He attempted to settle the issue, only to earn the enmity of several Latin American governments, British criticisms, and Spanish objections. Further problems with the British came in April 1895 when a dispute arose over claims with Nicaragua. In July Washington told the British that any European intervention into the New World would be

---

21. Minister of State to Sagasta, April 16, 1888, Sp/pol/USA/2413; Maruaga to Minister of State, no. 117, November 21, 1888, Sp/pol/USA/2414.

interpreted as an unfriendly act toward the United States. Eventually the problems between Latin America and Britain were settled but not before Cánovas and other Spanish officials worried about the further exertion of North American authority southward. The British difficulties with the United States led Spain into thinking that if a serious crisis developed between Madrid and Washington over Cuba, London might support the Spanish in order to curtail the growth of North American power. In fact, this never came about because Anglo-American relations improved during the late 1890s.

When the 1890s began, Spain and the United States did not realize how quickly their attention would revert back to Cuba. In 1892 the Spanish celebrated the four hundredth anniversary of the discovery of the New World by Christopher Columbus. They spared no expense or effort in using the occasion to foster closer ties with the Hispanic Americans, and the celebration became a major social and political event for them and the ex-colonies. With some success Spain reminded Europe and America of its contribution to the spread of European civilization throughout the world. Spanish diplomats took advantage of the friendly mood of the ex-colonies to negotiate more commercial agreements and other related conventions.[22] Even the United States participated in the celebration, and on both sides of the Atlantic, politicians and writers expounded on the friendly relations existing between Madrid and Washington. It seemed as if Cuban problems had been eliminated. But in truth, serious problems remained, which could not be glossed over with rhetoric and celebrations.

Cuban revolutionaries, such as José Martí in New York, continued working for independence even though Spain had thoroughly reimposed its authority on the island after the Ten Years' War. The government in Madrid in 1893, headed by Práxedes Mateo Sagasta, chief of the moderate constitutionalist party, took a fresh look at Cuban problems. Antonio Maura, his minister of the colonies, suggested giving Cuba a unicameral legislature, an advisory council made up of local citizens to advise the Spanish captain general in Havana, and

---

22. Juan Ortega y Rubio, *Historia de la regencia de Maria Cristina Habsbourg-Lorena* (Madrid, 1905), 2:101.

real autonomist rights at the municipal level. However, once Maura laid his proposals on the prime minister's desk, Sagasta rejected them for fear the public would not accept them. Already his political opposition had begun to criticize him for endangering Spain's control over Cuba. Maura was forced out of office, and the status quo in regard to colonial policy returned. Yet the fact that such proposals were developed indicated that the Cuban problem could not be ignored. Washington pressured Madrid to initiate the sort of reforms that Maura had suggested, which in turn further convinced Spaniards that such proposals would be detrimental to Spain's interests by bolstering those of the United States.[23]

The pattern of diplomatic and political behavior of the two nations, although repetitive, suggests the course of events in the late 1890s. Throughout the nineteenth century, American political and economic power in the New World steadily grew. Cuba's proximity to the United States and the complementary nature of its economy drew the island closer to North America, irritating Spain and threatening to sully its honor should the colony be lost. Europe paid little attention to Spanish *dignidad* and worried more about the military and political balance of power in the Caribbean and the effects of Washington's policies on their commercial dealings with the entire New World.

These factors became more apparent as the century grew older. Continued North American interference in Central American and Caribbean affairs and the growing militancy of the American press, as reflected in the newspapers of William Randolph Hearst after 1895, reminded Europeans of the growing power of the young republic. Yet neither Spain nor the United States could bring political stability to the Caribbean, and they could not live together in harmony. Their differences encouraged filibustering, economic imperialism, threats of wars, revolutions, and damage to each other's properties. Spain failed miserably to resolve the Cuban problems with any sense of feeling for the colonial subjects, and the United States never displayed sufficient confidence or domestic unity of purpose necessary to take the Caribbean colonies from the Spanish.

---

23. Ibid., 146–147.

The United States made resolution of the Cuban problem by Spain difficult. It led Spaniards into believing that if reforms were initiated, Cuba would fall into American hands. Yet the Americans could not exercise the option of seizing the island. Greater efforts at reform by Spain might have come if the Spanish could believe that the Americans would not seize the colony. This might have been accomplished by signing a treaty to that effect, but many Americans opposed such a proposal. American support for the rebels, which met more often than not only with Washington's official disapproval, complicated matters.

The complexity of the Cuban problem for both nations can be summarized as serious conflicts of interests, which deep-seated mistrust and stubbornness on both sides prevented from being resolved. Each considered its goals in the Caribbean of primary national importance. This made dispatches from the 1870s and 1880s read like those of the 1840s and 1850s. The issues and both nations' reactions to them basically never changed.

Yet there were a few differences toward the end of the century. Spain enjoyed greater political stability from the 1870s through the 1890s than prior to 1858. In a relative sense, Cánovas and alternately Sagasta held on to power long enough to initiate and implement policies that their predecessors could not. Moreover stability gained for Spain greater European respect and a reputation (although inaccurate) for having a strong navy and army. If Spanish authorities failed to reform their colonies, the reason lay in the successful attempt of various business interests and rabid nationalists in Spain to preserve the status quo in Cuba and Puerto Rico. At the same time, the United States stood as a powerful nation in the New World in the second half of the nineteenth century—at least far more so than before the Civil War. U.S. industrial strength might have indicated to most that, at least in economic circles, American influence would continue growing in Latin America. Thus in both countries friction over Cuba was as much the result of economics as of politics.

The two nations experienced other similar conditions that prevented the resolution of Cuban problems. The publics in each proved more reluctant than their governments to compromise on Cuba. They also confused practical political considerations with national honor, patriotic rhetoric, and racial ideologies. The nature of political life in the two nations, therefore, prevented officials from deviating from long-established diplomatic and colonial policies. Europeans encouraged this inactivity since many believed that maintaining the status quo would best protect their economic interests. This stance often explained the reluctance of any Europeans to support either the United States or Spain. This is not to say that they avoided involvement in Latin America's affairs; on numerous occasions Europeans landed troops there, tried to acquire new land, or became involved in its diplomacy. Yet to maintain the status quo remained uppermost in European minds and thus contributed to the length of time in which Cuban-American-Spanish relations were brought to a head.

The factors no diplomat could control and that ultimately shattered the carefully maintained status quo were the developments in the domestic lives of every involved nation. No European could prevent the growth of American economic power, change those Spanish attitudes that prevented colonial reform, or discourage the insistence of Cuban revolutionaries for independence. No individual official or group in power fully realized that the only status quo in Latin America was change, be it in politics, economics, or nationalism. This reality ultimately sucked Spain and the United States into the Cuban vortex of war.

7
THE SPANISH-AMERICAN WAR

Spanish-American relations between 1895 and 1898, when the Cuban revolution and the war between Spain and the United States occurred, have attracted the attention of many historians. After 1898 people from all walks of academic, political, and journalistic life joined in analyzing the events of the 1890s. In the past twenty years rhetoric and interpretive studies have given way to more solid research conducted in European archives, American newspapers, private papers of Spanish and American participants, and records of various Spanish, American, and Cuban agencies. Therefore more information on Spanish-American relations between 1895 and 1899 exists than for any other period in their diplomatic history.

The start of another Cuban revolt in early 1895 triggered the process that culminated in the war of 1898. Initially guided by José Martí and other Cuban nationalists, the revolution soon acquired the guerrilla characteristics that scarred the Ten Years' War. It began for the same reasons as the first—and with similar goals. And like the Ten Years' War, the United States expressed great interest in Cuban affairs. The revolt became the main topic of discussion in Spain. Prior to it, the Spanish regime had acknowledged that reforms were needed in Cuba; however, once the fighting started, Madrid refused to consider any or to negotiate with dissident Cubans until it restored authority on the island.

This proved a difficult task. General Martínez Campos (who had negotiated the end of the Ten Years' War) commanded Spain's army in Cuba. He failed to suppress the revolution, which was broader based than before. Its leaders were also more stubborn in their demand for independence. At the same time (1895) he recommended compromising with the Cubans, a suggestion Cánovas would not consider. Rejecting the general's suggestions, he replaced him with another, Valeriano Weyler, known as a ruthless and efficient officer. Commanding an army of about 250,000 men, he herded Cubans into concentration camps (policy of *reconcentración*) to break down and destroy sources of support for the rebels, hunted down guerrilla fighters, and jailed political enemies. His efforts soon made him an internationally hated figure, especially in Cuba and the United States; even in Spain some questioned the need for his brutal tactics.[1]

In 1896 and 1897 the fighting increased sharply, primarily as a Cuban reaction to Weyler's policies. The number of dead and wounded multiplied, as did complaints from Spanish, Cuban, and American businessmen and property owners. Stories of barbarity on both sides, crippling blows to the Cuban economy, and public concern in the United States made the conflict an issue of diplomatic importance. Americans pictured Weyler as a villain and called on Spain to remove him. But the general still enjoyed wide support in Madrid since, in Spanish minds, he had dealt with traitors while drawing sympathy from those who understood under what trying conditions he worked. Therefore complaints against him were brushed aside in order to give him time to defeat the rebels before the United States decided to intervene.

By the spring of 1897, many Spanish saw that Weyler could not suppress the revolution, which seemed to grow. Some Spaniards suggested compromising with the rebels, agreeing with many Americans who advocated a negotiated settlement. Spanish liberals were especially vocal in this regard. A well-known leader of the Liberal party, Segismundo Moret, who served as Sagasta's minister of the colonies in the fall of 1897, suggested before he joined the cabinet that Cuba be granted autonomy much along Canadian lines. More conservative elements rejected this position, although they acknowledged that some reforms would soon have to be initiated. During the summer of 1897, for instance, a heated debate took place on Moret's proposal. At the time Cánovas and a conservative group held power. The prime

---

1. Ernest R. May, *Imperial Democracy: The Emergence of America as a Great Power* (New York, 1961), 94–111.

minister was willing to grant some concessions but only after the rebels stopped fighting. In August an anarchist assassinated him, and by October the liberal Sagasta once again found himself in charge of Spanish affairs.

Sagasta concluded that since Cánovas had failed to settle the Cuban revolt, he would have to change Spain's policy. He ordered Weyler back to Spain, replacing him with a less ruthless and more flexible individual. Next he established an autonomous government for the Cubans. Because these measures represented such a radical departure from previous policy and were executed with lightning speed, many moderates and conservatives criticized Sagasta for jeopardizing Spanish authority in the island. Tempers flared and anti-American riots threatened the consulate in Barcelona because many believed the United States had forced Sagasta to offer Cuba its autonomy. Yet his efforts failed to placate the Cuban rebels, who wanted nothing less than complete independence.

Between 1895 and early 1898, the United States and Spain engaged in discussions over Cuba. Europe participated since its interests were also in jeopardy. Washington could not avoid involvement since its citizens deplored the inhumanity of the fighting while some also complained about the damage done to their commercial interests. At the start of the revolution, Americans had nearly $50 million invested in the Cuban economy, which the fighting could destroy. The combined import-export trade with the colony before the revolt amounted to about $100 million annually. After the revolution began, it dropped sharply to less than $66 million in 1895, $47.5 million in 1896, and in the following year to $26.7 million.[2] Businessmen pressured the Cleveland administration to protect their investments and shore up declining commercial relations with Cuba.

Nationalists and military strategists also worried about the threat to American influence and security in the Caribbean. Newspapers reported the war in virulent anti-Spanish terms. It was over the Cuban issue that the famous newspapers of William Randolph Hearst (*New York Journal*) and Joseph Pulitzer (*New York World*) competed and

---

2. Lester D. Langley, *The Cuban Policy of the United States* (New York, 1968), 103.

grew by condemning Spanish policies on the island. General Weyler was labeled a "butcher" and a "human hyena." Spaniards were reported to have satisfied their lust at the expense of virtuous Cuban maidens while "inventing tortures and infamies of bloody debauchery."[3] Although sordid and inaccurate, this sort of yellow journalism went far to arouse anti-Spanish feeling and the belief that Spain had to be expelled from the Caribbean. The impact of such public feeling, as measured by circulations of the Hearst and Pulitzer papers, which each reached about 800,000, could not be resisted by Congress. Early in 1896, it passed a resolution recognizing Cuban belligerency; but the president ignored it since the Constitution delegated only to him the power to implement foreign policy.

Cleveland refused to be pressured into intervening in Cuba, which would mean war with Spain. He urged Spain to act more humanely and emphasized the need for colonial reforms. The president further asked that Spain respect American property and not waste the lives of his countrymen. Madrid and Washington were concerned when the American press began discussing intervention more emphatically by 1897, making military involvement politically less risky than ever before. Yet the president continued cautioning his nation. Despite this, Americans privately aided the Cubans, which in turn led to numerous Spanish complaints and made them suspicious of any mediatory offers coming from Washington. Maritime incidents and more American protests complicated relations in 1896 and 1897. Employing much the same reasoning as in previous decades, Spanish diplomats feared President Cleveland might abandon neutrality. Yet they felt unable to comply with his requests as long as the Cuban rebels refused to negotiate something less than complete independence.

In March 1897, William McKinley became president. Unlike Cleveland, he believed that if pressed hard enough, the American government should intervene. He found Spain's inability to end the fighting so expensive to Americans that he tried to convince Madrid to compromise with the rebels. He ordered his envoy in Madrid, Stewart Woodford, to ask for a rapid settlement of the war, reforms

---

3. *New York Journal*, October 10, 1897, p. 1.

in the legal status of the island, and protection for American property. He also offered to mediate between Spain and the rebels, saying that if Madrid rejected his suggestions, the United States might have to intervene. Despite Cuban obstinancy in negotiating with Spain, the president concentrated his efforts on convincing the Spanish to accept a compromise. Spain believed this unfair since it saw no evidence of McKinley's pressuring the Cubans.

Yet along with his cabinet, Cánovas believed the most prudent course to follow (summer 1897) would be to offer some suggestions for reforms, which might bring peace and could be discarded if the Cubans refused them. This would place the blame for further fighting on the Cubans. In July he offered a package of reforms, which the Cubans predictably rejected since these presupposed continued Spanish ownership of Cuba. The Spanish next turned to the United States with the argument that the Cubans, having refused to negotiate, could not be granted any unilateral concessions since this would embarrass Spain abroad and jeopardize peace at home. Thus during the summer and early fall, the Spanish determined to crush the revolution.

While these various negotiations proceeded between Madrid and Washington, naval strategists and businessmen increased their pressure on McKinley to end the war, suggesting even military intervention. The president renewed his diplomatic efforts at the end of 1897, but to no avail. Both the Cubans and the Spanish wanted to wait until the military situation in Cuba became clearer. While the fighting slowed in the fall, each knew it would continue on a sporadic basis until summer, and both wanted another round of fighting before considering any compromises. This situation proved unsatisfactory to the impatient Americans, who saw nothing but hardships ahead for them if conditions continued unchanged.

Also of concern to McKinley, Cánovas, Sagasta, and informed elements in both countries was Europe's increased interest in the Cuban problem. Spanish diplomats complained to European ministers that American aid and the promise of possible future support encouraged Cuban rebels to keep fighting. The United States informed the governments of France, Britain, Austria, and Russia that Spain's maladministration and inability to suppress the revolution had prevented the colony from returning to peace and hinted that Madrid no longer deserved to control it. Europeans, Spaniards, and Americans also monitored changes in the political balance of power in the Caribbean. The British and French recognized that Washington's star was rising in the New World and, for all intents and purposes, wrote off the Caribbean to the Americans by the late 1890s. Already the U.S. Navy was being rebuilt into a powerful force not to be lightly challenged in the Americas. Moreover with tensions increasing in post-Bismarckian Europe as alliances shifted in strength and character, Britain and France sought new friends, and the powerful United States appeared as an attractive candidate to each. Therefore they were reluctant to side too openly with Madrid against Washington.

American diplomats realized that as U.S. power grew, Europe would respect Washington's position more than in previous decades. President McKinley went to great lengths to justify his Spanish policy. His stiff notes to Spain invariably were followed by reports to European diplomats. At the same time, he indicated that his government would not tolerate any European interference in Cuban affairs. Because of his attitude, the president felt compelled to rationalize each action publicly. The last thing the United States wanted was to face a united concert of European powers backing Spain for some gross violation of Europe's sensibilities. The risk for Washington proved small, however. Divided opinions regarding what policy to follow on the war inhibited any European regime from joining others in a stand. No power wished to act alone, and thus Europe did not block American expansion into the Caribbean.

Two events in February 1898 finally pushed the McKinley administration closer to war. A private letter written by the Spanish envoy in Washington, Enrique Dupuy de Lôme, to a friend ended up on the front page of the *New York Journal* on February 9, calling the president a poor politician and an opportunist and suggesting that Spain had practiced deceit on the United States in regard to certain commercial matters.[4] Americans felt insulted and saw the letter as proof of Spain's chicanery in Cuba. While the Spanish quickly recalled their envoy, the incident turned public opinion further against Spain. A week later, on February 15, the U.S.S. *Maine*, recently sent to Havana in anticipation of anti-American riots, mysteriously blew

---

4. Langley, *Cuban Policy*, 181–219.

up, killing over 250 of its crew. The American press initially struck a note of caution while waiting for further facts. Soon, however, many Americans began to blame the Spanish for destroying the warship and called for revenge. Both the letter and this tragedy jolted relations between Spain and the United States to such an extent that both governments saw the conduct of diplomacy virtually moved out of their offices. On March 9 Congress authorized the president to spend $50 million in military preparations. By the end of March, many Americans and Spaniards believed Washington would have to intervene in Cuba to protect the economic and political interests of the United States.

Much of the reason for this lay in McKinley's demands on Spain made in mid-March. He asked that the concentration camps in Cuba be closed, that Cubans be granted autonomy, and that an armistice be declared. The Spanish, pressured at the same time by business interests with investments in Cuba to avoid war with the United States, agreed to some changes. On March 30, the colonial government began dismantling the camps and sent agricultural workers to their homes. Yet Spain refused to declare an armistice or change the status of the present Cuban administration because Spanish citizens generally rejected any leniency for the Cubans and the rebels still demanded nothing less than independence. On April 9 Sagasta agreed to permit his generals in Cuba to declare an armistice if they thought this would lead to a peaceful settlement of the war. Many Spanish policy makers now believed that if they were to retain Cuba, Spain would have to fight the Americans since Madrid could not make further concessions. Therefore Spanish diplomats tried again to obtain European support. Recognizing the seriousness of the crisis, France, Britain, Russia, and Austria feebly requested the Americans on April 6 to exercise restraint. The weakness of this gesture was obvious to all since the State Department, previous to April 6, had been asked to approve the collective European text by several of the powers. In fact, most Europeans at this point believed that the United States would intervene in Cuba regardless of what they did and in spite of the genuine attempt by Spain to avert war through its series of concessions to Washington and the Cubans. Proof came on April 19 when Congress authorized McKinley to invade Cuba.

McKinley's decision to end the Cuban war by military intervention is the subject of much controversy. Some historians have argued that he submitted to public pressure to fight Spain. Others believe humanitarian concern for the plight of the Cubans motivated him, and a small minority have suggested that key members of the administration persuaded him. The most plausible arguments have recently come from Walter LaFeber and Philip Foner, who demonstrated that he followed the traditional, unsentimental policy of doing what he thought best for the United States. They argued that McKinley grounded his decision solidly on economic and political considerations. LaFeber, for example, suggested that rapid American industrialization in the 1890s led to a search for new markets outside of the United States. Realistically placing his thesis within the context of contemporary thinking, he wrote that American businessmen saw Asia and the Caribbean as logical outlets for their products. LaFeber believed the president did not want to annex Cuba because of the problems posed in assimilating a society different from that of the United States. Moreover, both American and Spanish businessmen merely wanted to end, not expand, the war.[5]

LaFeber's ideas are further confirmed and advanced by Foner, who developed a tempting thesis that the war was completely imperialistic, and came because Americans wanted new markets. He argued his Marxian viewpoint convincingly with impressive evidence. Foner believed the origins of American involvement in Cuba were rooted in nineteenth-century economic philosophy and needs, and he suggested that the catalyst leading to the war came from the Cuban revolution, which lasted long enough to threaten significantly American commercial interests in the Caribbean. To protect these, the Americans had no other option but to expel Spain.[6] Unquestionably economics played a dominating role in causing this conflict. Throughout the nineteenth century, commercial issues often brought both na-

---

5. Walter LaFeber, "That 'Splendid Little War': An Historical Perspective," *The Texas Quarterly* 11, no. 4 (Winter 1968): 89–98.
6. Philip S. Foner, *The Spanish-Cuban-American War and the Birth of American Imperialism, 1895–1902* (New York, 1972), 1:310.

tions to the verge of war. Most centered around problems Americans faced in preserving or expanding their commercial ties with Cuba. The Cuban war simply accelerated this friction. From the American point of view, the logical solution to the problem was to eliminate Spain from the Caribbean—the decision the United States took in April 1898.

Spanish thinking in early 1898 proved equally important as a cause of this war. Authorities in the 1890s, like their predecessors throughout the century, believed any concession to Cubans and Americans threatened to sever the colony from the kingdom. Granting Cuba autonomy, negotiating a compromise peace, or implementing significant colonial reforms therefore disturbed them. Any of these measures would have proven less expensive and more attractive than fighting the Cubans, or worse, the Americans, but Spain was not prepared to risk losing Cuba. In the late 1890s, Spaniards did not want a war with the United States for military reasons. They had a weak navy while the Americans had a new and strong one. Moreover the large number of troops on the island could quickly be matched with American forces. The island's proximity to the United States further suggested that the Americans would have less difficulty than Spain in supplying their troops. Domestic Spanish considerations influenced Madrid's foreign policy as well, and although historians have not conducted sufficient research into this aspect of the war's origins, a few obvious conditions suggested the climate of opinion in Madrid.

Many historians believed Sagasta's government accepted war as a question of national honor and a challenge to the nation's dignity. Undeniably some chivalrous idealism existed in the characters of Spanish policy makers and influenced their thinking when it came to the United States. Their common belief in the superiority of Spanish over Anglo-Saxon society made it difficult to ignore any insult to Spain's interests from the Americans. The public always rallied to the government's support whenever the United States threatened Spain and in the spring of 1898, Spaniards did it again. But if national honor were the only reason for war, then Spain had a group of incompetent leaders. Previous experiences provided a better guide to Spanish behavior than Quixotic borrowings. It is a tragedy of the war's historiography that many writers assumed that the Spanish were usually ignorant, stubborn, and even stupid, when in fact the events of these years proved otherwise.

If the Americans felt their economic system could only be preserved by fighting Spain, the Spanish monarchy believed its survival lay in not avoiding this war. The regime, controlled by Sagasta in those crucial months before the conflict, reasoned that the rebellion could end only in Spain's favor if the rebels were convinced the United States would not help them. Sagasta tried to delay a final resolution of the crisis in order to give his troops time to defeat the Cubans by hinting to Washington that he might allow the Americans to mediate Spanish-Cuban differences. He saw no other realistic solution to the problem, which would protect the monarchy from collapsing and Spain from experiencing national disgrace. By January 1898, Sagasta concluded that the United States would not help end the rebellion by discouraging the colonists. He now faced a more serious problem because his plan had failed.

To sell the island or grant it independence risked provoking the Spanish army or at least Weyler's allies who might overthrow the regime and possibly the monarchy. Such concessions spelled defeat in the minds of many Spaniards. Moreover a retreat would leave Spaniards living in Cuba at the mercy of the Cuban rebels, an unthinkable breach of Sagasta's responsibility. Sagasta and other members of the cabinet considered giving up the island by war with the United States as a semihonorable way out of their predicament. They also thought of prevailing again on Europe to prevent Washington from seizing it. Yet they rejected these two alternatives as impractical. Sagasta decided by January that the best course to follow would be, first, to continue fighting as long as possible or at least into the fall when the weather might curtail further campaigning by either side and, second, to obtain whatever support possible from Europe against the Americans. In short he opted for the traditional Spanish reaction to Cuban crises involving the United States.

Spain never capitulated to the United States. Each concession to the Americans—and there were many—came after a careful consideration of options open to Madrid. For example, the decision to close the Cuban concentration camps probably was more of a response to Spanish complaints than to American demands. Spain's declaration of an armistice on April 10 grew from a combination of

European and American pressures, the stalemated military situation in Cuba, and the need to make a dramatic gesture to quiet critics in Spain. Spanish diplomats hoped the armistice would encourage Europe to help them, silence the opposition then plaguing the cabinet, encourage the rebels to negotiate, and appease the United States. Rarely did the Spanish initiate a policy solely because of American pressures. Like officials in Washington, action emerged after a consideration of multiple factors even though American pressures were important.

The Spanish believed their gestures could delay the crisis, which they felt inevitably would involve Spain and the United States in war. Even though both Americans and Spaniards had had a century to prepare mentally and militarily for such a conflict, the Spanish wanted more time to ready the nation for the imminent possibility of war. Sagasta and others used various means to avoid war so that if it came, critics would not be able to accuse the regime of failing to do enough to prevent it. By the end of April, Spain realized that the only way to avoid war was to give Cuba its independence. This meant admitting defeat at the hands of the rebels and Washington. Since such a move spelled greater disaster for the regime and the monarchy than losing a war, the ministry placed the nation on alert, confident that all Spaniards would close ranks at such a moment. After McKinley's declaration of hostilities arrived in Madrid, the Spanish announced that the two countries were at war.[7]

In retrospect, the war itself seemed anticlimactic after a century of nervous rivalry over Cuba. Most Americans, Europeans, and well-informed Spaniards realized that the United States would win and take Cuba from Spain. The details of the short war are familiar enough. In May George Dewey's squadron destroyed Spain's in the Philippines. American troops quickly landed in Puerto Rico and occupied it with hardly a contest. Admiral Pascual Cervera's Spanish fleet went down at Santiago de Cuba on July 3 after a short naval engagement. American soldiers arrived in Cuba, where a limited ground war terminated at the end of the summer with the surrender of the remaining Spanish forces. Finally on August 13, 1898, Manila fell to the United States.

---

7. Raymond Carr, *Spain, 1808–1939* (Oxford, 1969), 386–387.

The fighting had hardly started before Spanish and American diplomats began negotiating a peace settlement. Acting for the Spanish, the French envoy in Washington signed a protocol ending the war and detailing a tentative set of peace clauses on August 12. Spain surrendered Cuba, Puerto Rico, and one island of the Marianas in the Pacific to the United States. Madrid also granted the Americans permission to occupy Manila while the United States determined whether to retain the whole of this colony. During these talks, Spain tried to have Washington acquire legal title to Cuba, which would include the colony's $500 million debt. The Americans rejected this offer, arguing that Madrid had to shoulder the debt as a consequence of its maladministration of the island. Moreover the American government had earlier, through Congress, announced that it would not retain permanent possession of Cuba, implying occupation only until the colonists could govern themselves.[8]

On October 1, 1898, the formal peace negotiations began in Paris. Cuban problems dominated the early stages of these talks. The Americans insisted that Cuba be made an independent nation; Spain suggested that it become American territory. Since Madrid's bargaining position was weak, the final settlement called for the United States to occupy the colony until it could govern itself peacefully but with the understanding that Washington would have considerable influence on the island's domestic life. Puerto Rico became American property.

The most controversial clause involved the Philippines. Historians have argued for years about why McKinley asked for it. The most widely accepted theory holds that the Philippines would serve as a base for the expansion of American commerce in the Pacific and Asia. Admittedly historians uncovered some pressure on the president from the business community to acquire the Philippines. Other Americans, mesmerized by an ideology of expansionism and a desire to carry the fruits of their society to more underdeveloped areas, also led many to advocate its acquisition. Imperialism, missionary zeal, an acquiescence in the public's desire for such a possession, and faith

---

8. U. S., Department of State, *Papers Relating to the Foreign Affairs of the United States, 1898* (Washington, D.C., 1901), 820.

in America's future role as a world power undoubtedly mixed with McKinley's concern for the expansion of American economic interests. Since the Spanish could do little but comply, both nations ratified the Treaty of Paris in early 1899, which officially ended the war. With the stroke of a pen, the most radical change in Spanish-American relations since the 1820s came about because the Cuban problem had finally been laid to rest.

The immediate costs of the war to both nations varied. Spain lost 50,000 men to disease and combat in Cuba and the Philippines; surrendered its Caribbean and Pacific colonies; suffered the destruction of the navy; inherited Cuba's financial debt and Spanish war expenses; and, worst of all, experienced national humiliation. The United States paid less, losing several thousand men by disease and fighting. In short, the conflict resulted in a lopsided victory for the Americans. Even the Germans profited by the war at Spain's expense. For years Berlin had bickered with Madrid over some small islands in the Pacific and at the end of the war had forced Spain to surrender them with a little gunboat diplomacy.

It would be difficult to overestimate the significance of this short war on the domestic histories of Spain and the United States and on the course of international relations in the early twentieth century. The conflict obviously affected the recent internal histories of Cuba, Puerto Rico, and the Philippines as well. At first glance, within the context of late nineteenth-century European history, it seems to be only another example of one nation adding by force to its possessions what it could not take by persuasion from a weaker country. During the last third of the century, virtually every major European power became involved in a hectic race for colonies that they considered prestigious, important for national security, and necessary for industrial and general economic development. Europe claimed or occupied almost all of Africa; established trading posts, colonies, bases, and protectorates over most of Asia; and explored the South Pacific and the Arctic regions. As the amount of available land for colonies declined, stronger powers took territory away from the smaller ones. Spain's experience reflected this pattern. In 1891 Portugal suffered humiliation when Britain forced it to recognize London's right to advance into African territory claimed by Lisbon. Five years later, the Ethiopians expelled Italy as a result of the battle of Adowa, blocking

Italian colonization there until the mid-1930s. France, Britain, and Germany also took advantage of each international crisis to acquire new lands in the Middle East. Germany's appropriation of Spanish islands at the end of the century typified the colonial policies of the age.

More important for the future conduct of international relations, the major governments now realized the unquestionable truth of earlier predictions about the United States's becoming a world power to be dealt with in the New World, Asia, and probably in Europe. Both its navy and army had proved their fighting abilities. Its industries competed with Britain's and Germany's on a worldwide basis. Yet the war did not make the United States a major power; it simply accelerated that achievement and the world's acceptance of the fact. The conflict added to its already vast resources. The acquisition of islands in the Caribbean made it the dominant power there, while the Philippines led to the construction of naval bases, which, with the newly acquired Hawaiian islands, made it easier for American naval and commercial forces to play a key role in the future of the Pacific. The greatest change came in the Caribbean where the Americans overwhelmingly dominated its political and economic life. Most Europeans had begun recognizing this fact by the late 1880s or early 1890s, but it took the war to confirm the reality. By accelerating the drive toward hegemony over the Americas, the Spanish-American War capped a century-long rivalry for control of the Caribbean and, indirectly, of Latin America between Europe and the United States.

American imperialism grew slowly as a mood in the early 1800s and eventually into a national policy by the 1840s. During the second half of the nineteenth century, it reflected much the same pattern as reflected by European states, although with less tangible results before the 1890s. Historians still differ about the origins of American imperialism and its characteristics, but the early signs of it unquestionably are found in the Mexican War in the 1840s and in Seward's desire to establish naval bases in Santo Domingo and in his acquisition of Alaska in the late 1860s. Ideologically many Americans believed the United States should accumulate new territories in the post–Civil War years. The acquisition of Hawaii in July 1898 reflected the increased interest in new lands. Penetration into the Pacific—which Hawaii symbolized—indicated that imperialism had become a fact of life for the United States prior to the Cuban conflict. The war with Spain was part of this process and, if anything, sped it up by rekindling the sense of manifest destiny that the nation had entertained as a philosophical tenet of its politics prior to 1861.

The war burdened the nation with the responsibility of being a world power. In openly acknowledging that isolationism no longer influenced American foreign policy, the war contributed a new factor. Until 1898 most Americans still subscribed to the notion that they were hardly involved in world affairs and would not become so—a mystique nurtured throughout the nineteenth century but no longer viable after 1898.

The consequences of the war of 1898 on the domestic life of the United States proved considerable as well. Businessmen who long had dreamed of vast markets and investment possibilities in the Caribbean and in the Pacific believed their hopes would come true and acted accordingly by expanding their commercial contacts outside the United States. The acquisition of new territories encouraged such an expansion of American world trade that it harmed Britain's and Germany's in the first several decades of the 1900s. The positivist sentiment the war generated in the United States and that was so lacking in Spanish society after 1898 sharply contrasted the two nations while hinting of their future destinies.

The war proved detrimental to Spain. The negative results of the conflict were so significant that diplomatic historians need to examine them more closely when analyzing Spanish diplomacy in the twentieth century. The defeat stung Spain, which had always viewed the United States not only as a threat but also as a society with an inferior culture, marked by vulgarity and a lack of refinements Spaniards saw in Hispanic society. Thus their defeat at the hands of the United States humiliated them by questioning the dynamism of their culture. Equally demoralizing was the destruction of their image of Spain as a world power, a delusion that events in the nineteenth century failed to dispel until 1898. As one historian has noted, Spaniards lost even further confidence in their government while turning "defeat into moral disaster."[9]

Diplomatically Spain's position changed after 1898. Throughout

---

9. Carr, *Spain*, 387.

the nineteenth century it had considered its primary goal protection of the homeland and preservation of the remaining colonies. Other European nations rarely threatened Spain, but the colonies could easily have been lost without a foreign policy designed to protect them. Concern for Cuba often dominated Spain's diplomacy in the New World and repeatedly became important in relations with Britain and France. With the loss of its Caribbean holdings, Spain had to establish new diplomatic goals and priorities. By the early years of the twentieth century, Spaniards fulfilled this conscious and even subconscious requirement by design and accident, leading them to concentrate on North African and Mediterranean politics. Spain's attempt at expanding into North Africa after 1900 reflected a return to a more traditional foreign policy that dated back many centuries.

Directing more attention to European and North African affairs did not signal a complete retreat from Latin America. In fact, Spain's relations with Hispanic Americans actually improved as a direct result of the war. As long as Spain remained a property owner in the New World, Latin Americans could not help but feel that Madrid posed a threat to their own security, despite their recognition by the 1880s that the United States endangered them more. During the Spanish-American War, Cuban revolutionaries won some sympathy from their neighbors (as they had in the 1870s and again in the early 1890s), who wanted to see the Spanish expelled from Cuba. Yet Hispanic American diplomats knew that if the United States won this war, they could expect further interference southward by Washington. Moreover Spain's energetic efforts in the previous two decades at cultivating closer economic and cultural bonds indicated that Madrid recognized the legitimacy of these American regimes and that friendly relations were possible with them and could be profitable after the war. If the United States won the conflict, Spain might also serve as Latin America's European agent in seeking support to block North American imperialism in the Americas. Therefore from the point of view of national self-interest, the Latin Americans could not take sides against Spain between 1895 and 1898. They avoided controversy by declaring their collective neutrality and remaining silent on Cuban issues.[10]

---

10. Foner, *Spanish-Cuban-American War*, 1:151–162.

The most important impact of the war on Spain lay not with European and Latin American relations but in its domestic life. Spaniards from all classes, trades, and opinions felt the consequences. Most questioned the nature of Spanish society, and many criticized their government for the defeat. While criticisms of the monarchy were not new and actually had been on the increase during the early 1890s, the fact that it presided over the loss of Cuba further encouraged recriminations. Radical elements of the extreme political right and left sought to change the government, and other commentators suggested remodeling Spanish society and culture. Regeneration became a topic of heated controversy. Some suggested Europeanizing Spain; others proposed returning to those qualities that made their society the force it was in the Middle Ages. For obvious political reasons, politicians identified with those who wanted to improve Spain. In a policy known as *regeneracionismo*, most Spaniards identified with this eclectic recognition of Spain's need to change. It cut across all social lines and spilled into economics, politics, philosophy, literature, the arts, and religion.

Spanish society rapidly changed in the late nineteenth century as industrialization expanded and internal migration led to increased urbanization. Regionalism in the Basque and Catalan regions to the north grew more pronounced as the century came to a close, and friction grew between the supporters of the Catholic church and its critics. These tensions generated much of the criticisms leveled against Spanish government and society. The war with the United States accelerated this sense of negativism much as it reinforced the confidence of the Americans. Spaniards believed that the war marked a turning point in their domestic history while, in fact, it merely reflected conditions already prevailing. It led people to criticize what the war accentuated as Spain's faults; it did not create new domestic conditions. Objections to the government's policies or to society's characteristics came after 1898 from the same elements that had benefitted the least from them before the war: poorly paid soldiers and officers, Catalan and Basque nationalists, businessmen, artists, literary figures, university professors, and journalists.

Such a large number of intellectuals and writers identified with the symbolic nature of 1898 that they soon became known as the "generation of '98." United only by their criticism of current affairs, they represented every shade of political and philosophical thought and came from various professions and social classes. Their representatives were a gallery of brilliant young writers and intellectuals born in the late 1860s and 1870s, who were most active after the turn of the century. They contributed some of the finest contemporary literature to European society and, like their predecessors of the golden age of Spanish literature in the 1600s, lived in a period of political and social unrest. Joaquín Costa, typifying the politically conscious element of the group, analyzed contemporary problems in historical and philosophical perspective, suggesting which elements had weakened Spanish culture and offering remedies borrowed mainly from European traditions alien to Spain. Other writers suggested either copying from Europe in wholesale quantities or retreating behind the Pyrenees to an older cultural heritage of Arabic origin. Novelists, poets, dramatists, and philosophers such as Unamuno, Valle Inclán, Pío Baroja, Machado, and later Maeztu and Ortega y Gasset joined in the debate. Even Spain's leading artist of the day, Zuloaga, identified with *regeneracionismo*.

The war encouraged political critics of the monarchy. The restoration's system of government, as developed by Cánovas in the mid-1870s into ministerial form, had to be justified by its supporters in the face of such policies as those that had led to the war. Catalan and Basque nationalists insisted even more on their special privileges, while republicans condemned the government and worked to expand their political support. Regaining its confidence in North African campaigns after 1900, the army now talked of reentering Spanish politics, something that had been kept to a minimum since 1875. These various elements were united by several factors. The defeat made them realize that Spain was not the world power that many Spaniards used to think. The majority recognized that Spain had lost Cuba because of an inept and corrupt administration and policies that had catered to the selfish interests of Spanish businessmen. Most Spaniards also saw the need to improve their society and faced their international embarrassments with determination. Such an honest evaluation of the nation's international position helped dictate the role it played in European diplomacy during the coming decades.

Relations between the United States and Spain underwent a radical change as a result of the war. Since Cuba had been the key source of friction between them for nearly a century, its transference to American control eliminated this factor in their relations, rapidly reducing friction between both governments. No longer would Madrid fear for Cuba's safety or Americans face Spain's restrictive economic policies. For the first time in the history of their relations, they were not competing for political and economic prizes that each considered essential to their national survival.

In the next thirty-seven years, relations proved to be far friendlier than in the nineteenth century. Concerns now grew out of general European and world conditions. In the 1900s competitive relations continued in different yet milder ways, such as economically and culturally in Latin America. Often Spain would identify with Europe and the Mediterranean world against the United States, but these were issues not characteristic of relations prior to the war.

Spain and the United States faced several immediate problems after 1898 that were direct legacies of the fighting. The question of claims and the complicated task of restructuring commercial relations with Cuba, Puerto Rico, and the Philippines, not to mention with each other, caught their attention. As symbolic of how things would change, Spain's future interest in the welfare of its old colonies bore the same features as its concern for South America. The cultural bond fused by centuries of shared experiences drew the Spanish to the Latin Americans in more peaceful and intimate ways than in the late nineteenth century. Cuba and Puerto Rico took part in this, much like any Central or South American nation.

The United States, aware of its growing stature in world affairs, no longer considered relations with Spain as very important and certainly felt no danger from that quarter. American and Spanish diplomats considered contacts between them their most important in 1897 and 1898 but certainly not afterward. For Washington, Berlin, London, Paris, and the Latin Americans, broader concerns in the Americas, Europe, and Africa took precedence over diplomacy with Spain. The Spanish also rated relations with the United States after those with Europe and the Mediterranean world. This situation went far to explain why both nations felt little bitterness toward each other after the war.

Also a consideration was their cultural relations. Each expressed an interest in the other's society, culture, history, and politics throughout the nineteenth century. It reflected a curiosity that had existed alongside their political and economic rivalry.

8
A CENTURY OF CULTURAL RELATIONS

Cultural relations among nations, complicated and diverse, hardly lend themselves to the often clearer definitions characteristic of diplomatic history. Yet contacts of a nondiplomatic or economic nature are contributing influences to the political associations of governments and countries. Those between Spain and the United States in the nineteenth century represented more than the clash of cultures. The prejudices that remained were more within the purview of politically and sociologically conscious individuals with strong racist attitudes and less of an influence on literary figures, historians, painters, or tourists. There were literary hostilities as well, yet in general, cultural relations between the United States and Spain were healthy, diverse, and plentiful, involving novelists, poets, historians, tourists, painters, and architects. Spain's cultural impact on American society proved far more pervasive and influential than that of the United States on Spain.

The dramatic Spanish effect on early North American society came mainly from literary relations. A contributing factor was the fascination Americans had with Spain's history, which many believed represented a romantic blending of the past with contemporary Iberian affairs. Despite the predominantly English base of North American society, the physical closeness to Hispanic America and the early Spanish control of territory near the United States also fired American interest in the Iberian culture. Such intimate ties encouraged Americans to express an early concern for the one country that had played such a major role in the discovery and development of the New World.

Interest in Spanish affairs came from many quarters. The political problems faced with Madrid accounted for some of this concern.

Americans displayed an intellectual curiosity about the country that had done so much to change European history since the sixteenth century. Thomas Jefferson and Benjamin Franklin claimed they could read and speak Spanish with some facility and encouraged others to study it. Most of the British colonists, however, knew little or nothing of the language and, in fact, mistrusted Spain. What little opinion crept into print reflected a deep-seated belief that Spain was a clerically dominated and decadent society generating bigotry that maintained harsh colonial policies. Beyond that, colonists knew little of the country that even Europeans found difficult to travel in, let alone study.

At this early stage, ignorance of the Spanish encouraged a romanticization of their society and history. On the positive side, the colonists thought of Spain as a place of fiestas. Spain's reputation for having beautiful women and bullfights already existed. But some colonists thought that all Spaniards were flamenco dancers, deceiving devils, or a lazy people. Early Americans added to this crude set of images by mythicizing Spain's history. They knew vaguely of Ferdinand and Isabel's efforts to Europeanize the Americas. Philip II's involvement in European religious and political conflicts also appeared in their history books and in classroom lectures, in highly uncomplimentary terms. Many educated Americans considered these Spaniards important figures in the history of the world. The apparent contradiction between American disrespect for Spanish political affairs and their virtual fascination with Spanish literature and history proved difficult to explain. Ignorance of the facts, acceptance of Spain as they thought it was, and a selection of what interested them might well have been the causes of this confusion of opinions. Yet such contradictions hardly disturbed eighteenth- and early nineteenth-century Americans who could praise Spain's literary accomplishments in one breath and in the next curse its officials for some new incident in the Mississippi Valley.

Educated Americans and virtually every student heard tales about Columbus and Cervantes much as schoolchildren today are introduced to the American mythology concerning George Washington and Abraham Lincoln. And even today, textbook histories of the United States from elementary through university levels virtually canonize Columbus as an American hero. Besides their fascination with Columbus, Americans knew about Miguel Cervantes, one of Spain's great classical writers. In the eighteenth century, people could read his novel, *Don Quixote*, in various English editions. A large number of informed Americans believed that Spanish society as portrayed in this volume existed in contemporary Spain. The novelist's view of seventeenth-century Iberia became their main source of information about Spanish society in the eighteenth and early nineteenth centuries. The practical wisdom of fat Sancho Panza and the ridiculous nature of Spain's nobility depicted by Don Quixote appealed to Americans as an accurate reflection of current class characteristics in Spain. Indeed it would not be difficult to assume that *Don Quixote* caused Americans to think they understood Spain's irritating policies in the New World as being the work of officials drawn from the nobility portrayed by Cervantes.

The overwhelming influence of this book was tempered in the 1800s as more diversified contacts with Spain developed through diplomats, merchants, travelers, magazine writers, historians, scholars, literary figures, and artists. Cultural relations were dominated by writers through whom Spain's influence on North Americans flowed.[1] Those who visited Spain in the first half of the century found the country difficult to travel in because of a lack of hotels, a poor system of roads, and a limited number of hotels and inns. Americans generally considered Spain's physical and psychological impenetrability an admirable quality, leaving for them an unspoiled and mysterious land to explore much in the same way that in the second half of the twentieth century parts of Latin America and Asia became. Scores of American travel books on Iberia and Europe discussed Spain's uniqueness. Prior to 1870, they emphasized the descriptive; afterward, they offered more analysis of Spanish society.

Important literary figures contributed to this body of ideas throughout the nineteenth century but especially between 1820 and 1850. Henry Wadsworth Longfellow and Washington Irving wrote about Spain in the 1830s. Later Caleb Cushing contributed his views long before he was appointed minister to Spain. Irving's *The Alhambra*, which served many Americans as their guide to Spain, be-

---

1. Stanley T. Williams, *The Spanish Background of American Literature* (New Haven, 1955).

came the most popular American book on Spain sold in the United States during the 1830s and 1840s, and it still commanded respect in the twentieth century. Along with the works of other Americans, such as William Prescott, it glorified Spanish history and found that the fusion of the past with the present gave Spaniards a sense of tradition that Americans lacked.

These books superficially glossed over contemporary Spanish conditions; after the American Civil War, writers produced more analytical works. They still reflected the fascination of earlier generations but tempered this with more accurate descriptions of current situations in Spain. The change became apparent with the publication of John Hay's *Castilian Days* in 1871. He found Spain a priest-ridden, violent, and bigoted society that other Americans had known, yet he avoided passing moral judgments on Spaniards to the extent that earlier writers had. Besides the usual travelogue descriptions, he commented on the social and political forces at work in mid-century Spain. Throughout the 1870s and 1880s, romantic notions declined in importance. By the 1890s, commentary became more critical as the crisis complicating relations between Washington and Madrid affected both publics.[2]

Periodicals reached more Americans in the nineteenth century than books did. Because articles were shorter, discussed more diversified subjects, and enjoyed wider circulation, a larger number of people read them. Thousands appeared on Spain in virtually every type of magazine. They were short stories, poems, features on history, culture, politics, economics, religion, and literature. Prior to the American Civil War, these reflected many of the characteristics found in travel books, including romantic accounts, inaccurate reflections, and sentimentalized pieces devoid of sophisticated analyses. Most authors disguised their inability to understand the nation by arguing about the impenetrability of the Spanish mentality, thereby preserving the mystique of a romantic and mysterious Spain. In some cases, writers with a degree of knowledge about the country wrote useful and accurate accounts of Spanish culture, contemporary politics, and economics. In most instances, however, authors reflected their wonderment at how Spain's past lived in the present. This

---

2. Ibid., 1:51–75.

blending of history with the contemporary that so fascinated Irving, Longfellow, George Tichnor, and the popular historian William H. Prescott was also found in magazines.[3]

American magazine writers generally commented on Spanish politics in critical language, although there were some exceptions. In 1869, when Spain adopted a new constitution, which included civil liberties and democratic clauses, many Americans expressed the hope that a more enlightened government would now guide the nation. They welcomed the development of democratic institutions and hoped the political instability of the past would not reappear. One writer, expressing widely held views on Spanish subjects, argued that Spain could not "return to the prison-house from which it has emerged."[4] Such optimism died after the restoration of the Bourbon monarchy in the mid-1870s, which was followed by economic and political friction with the Americans. Consequently political commentary reverted back to its highly critical attitude. By 1898 favorable remarks on Spain's government rarely appeared in American publications.

While political discussions proved critical of Spain in the second half of the nineteenth century, the romantic notions of previous years survived in thousands of articles, which still talked of pretty señoritas, fiestas, love, and wine. The celebration of Columbus's anniversary in the 1890s generated a spate of articles on him. For most Americans Spanish history still continued to be dominated by the discovery and harsh conquest of Latin America, the inquisition and armada, and, of course, Cuba.

American historians were responsible in large part for the romantic approach to Spanish history, more because of the topics they selected to write about than for their research and interpretations. More than any other group, historians generated interest in Spain. They used the medium of colorful history to romanticize Spanish culture even more than novelists and magazine writers did. The works of Irving and Prescott, for example, remained best-sellers throughout the century. (In fact, they are still reprinted and read today as both moving

---

3. Ibid., 113.
4. Lyman Abbot. "The Spanish Revolution," *Harper's New Monthly Magazine* 40 (January 1870): 273.

history and beautiful literature.) Yet the original fascination of these men for Spain reflected the attitudes of their contemporaries. The color, age, and violence of Spain's past excited Americans. Punctuated by monarchs, wars, chivalry, cruelty, religious crusades, feuds, and vastness, Spanish history offered an intellectual adventure. Moreover Spain's colonization of North America's neighbors to the south made such history relevant, especially when it concerned the discovery and conquest of the New World.

A group of scholars emerged in the 1830s who produced major classics in Spanish historiography. George Bancroft, John L. Motley, and Prescott were part of this generation. Prescott's *Ferdinand and Isabella* (1837), *The Conquest of Mexico* (1843), *The Conquest of Peru* (1847), and *The Reign of Philip II* (1855–58 but never finished) were histories of majestic proportions sweeping across continents, centuries, and exciting events. They were written in a grand style as historical and literary gems, matching the public's taste for history. Prescott's and Motley's books sold well for decades. In each case, the author conducted extensive research, often into European archives. They also attempted to be accurate and perhaps appealed to the democratic prejudices of their readers by often being critical of Spanish religious intolerance and political monarchism, suggesting that Spain's culture needed more civilizing. Perhaps the best example of the era for this viewpoint was Motley's three-volume *The Rise of the Dutch Republic* (1856), which made in effect a similar statement throughout the study.

Standards for research improved in the second half of the nineteenth century while the writing styles and public interest in historical studies declined. Undoubtedly the increasing emphasis on scientific history—on research and documentation as opposed to good literature and the expression of excitement through historical events—resulted in more accurate accounts. Henry Charles Lee, for example, went one step beyond Prescott and Motley with his detailed and objective investigations of religious affairs of the Middle Ages. His books on the inquisition became standard works on the subject and remain important today.[5]

5. *History of the Inquisition in Spain* (1906–07), along with his earlier *History of the Inquisition of the Middle Ages* (1887), totaling six volumes, were basic works in the field.

The main problem Americans faced in trying to study Spanish institutions was that except for a few merchants who traded with the colonies and in Latin America, only a handful could speak Spanish; thus it was difficult to find anyone to teach it. As the nineteenth century grew older, the number of Americans who knew Spanish increased. Schools and colleges began offering the language. Merchants found it more useful as American foreign trade expanded, and tourists acquired some facility. When old Spanish lands in the Mississippi Valley and in the Southwest came under American control, new residents often learned Spanish out of necessity. In this century, Texas, California, New Mexico, and parts of Arizona, Nevada, and Colorado sported a bicultural background. Unquestionably by mid-twentieth century, Spanish had become a second American language, with native speakers also coming from Puerto Rico, Cuba, and states bordering on Mexico.

In the 1800s the study of Spanish and its literature grew slowly, mainly at major universities. Classes drew their greatest impetus from the efforts of George Ticknor, Henry Wadsworth Longfellow, and James Russell Lowell who taught in succession at Harvard. Ticknor's classes and his books on Spanish literature early established the language as a subject worth studying in universities. His *History of Spanish Literature* became a classroom classic. Longfellow also trained teachers, published on the general subject of Spanish literature, and edited Hispanic works.[6] Lowell contributed publications and prepared language instructors for years before being sent to Spain as minister in 1877. These three men did more to encourage the study of Spanish literature than any other Americans in the last century. Their articles coupled with lectures led to a growing respect for Spanish letters. Their translations and edited works made Spain's literature more readily available to Americans, and they considerably augmented the holdings of Harvard University's library.

Several American envoys in Spain were specialists in Spanish literature. As part of their duties, they encouraged closer cultural relations between both nations. After their return to the United States, they described Spain and its society. While on duty, they often com-

---

6. Iris Lilian Whitman, *Longfellow and Spain* (New York, 1927), 235.

mented to the secretary of state on domestic Spanish events, providing historians with a valuable source of material on nineteenth-century Spain. Washington Irving arrived in Madrid as envoy long after he had made his first trip to Spain. He was already recognized as a leading American expert on Iberia by 1842 when he became minister, and Spaniards welcomed him as the agent of friendlier relations. Caleb Cushing, who served from May 1874 through March 1877, enjoyed a similar reputation. His successor was James Russell Lowell, who stayed until March 1880. Each wrote of his experiences and lectured on Spain in the United States and on Americans while in Europe. John W. Foster, stationed at Madrid from June 1883 through August 1885, also described his experiences, combining history, travelogue, and analysis of contemporary Spain into a readable account. Stewart L. Woodford, the last envoy before the Spanish-American War, kept a diary in which he concentrated on diplomatic matters but also attempted to discuss domestic conditions.

Lowell's comments reflected much the same type of materials collected by other envoys. He analyzed Spanish society in fairly objective terms and, like others, declared his love for its culture and history. Lowell commented often on its politics, noting, for instance, that Spain had adopted a parliamentary government "but has never acquired the habit of constitutional procedure when shorter methods seem for the moment more effective or convenient."[7] Lowell observed that while "the instincts of absolutism are still predominant, yet the last forty years have made a great change in the Spanish people."[8] Such optimism, expressed in a dispatch not for public consumption, reflected a theme running through the published and unpublished writings of American envoys to Spain. The sense of affection found in the writings of American literary figures also appeared in numerous dispatches from Madrid.

Foster proved more sympathetic toward Spain than even Lowell. His comments, prepared in the late 1890s, exemplified how even on the eve of the Spanish-American War, national resentment against Spain rarely spilled over into cultural relations. In his memoirs,

---

7. James Russell Lowell, *Impressions of Spain* (New York, 1900), 31.
8. Ibid., 34.

Foster commented that "of all the countries of my foreign residence, I found Spain the most interesting from almost every point of view."[9] He discussed its history in the same romantic terms as most other Americans before him had done. On contemporary matters, his notes were superficial and trite. (He wrote, for example, that "the most distinctive national features of Spanish life is the bull-fight."[10]) Yet he balanced such shallow commentary with useful and accurate descriptions of contemporary government officials and Spanish politics. Books by Foster, Lowell, and others generally provided much accurate information on contemporary Spain not readily found in other American publications.

Some of Spain's envoys were also literary figures. None became as intimately acquainted with the North American culture as some of Washington's envoys were with theirs nor did they publish on the United States as often. Yet when in Washington, they described Spanish society to Americans. Of the several men of letters sent to Washington, the first important figure was Calderon de la Barca. At home Spaniards respected his views on political and literary subjects, which he continued to explain while serving between 1835 and 1839. Gabriel García Tassara, in the United States from 1857 to 1867, belonged to this literary circle. Known in Spain as a poet and conservative politician, in Washington he reported voluminously on American politics (often critically), economics, and society. In public he talked about Spain and, although irritated with the Americans for desiring Cuba, the diplomat encouraged cultural relations by facilitating the exchange of books between the Library of Congress, the Smithsonian Institute, and various Spanish government agencies. The most significant literary figure sent to Washington was Juan Valera y Alcalá, envoy between 1884 and 1886. At the time many Spaniards called him their most popular novelist.[11]

During the nineteenth century, Americans in general continued to believe that Spanish culture, particularly as exemplified by *Don Quixote*, slowed the process of modernization in Spain, which they

---

9. John W. Foster, *Diplomatic Memoirs* (New York, 1909), 1:276.
10. Ibid., 279.
11. Williams, *Spanish Background*, 1:275.

believed resulted in economic friction with the United States.[12] Most writers chose to view Spain through some romanticized prism, often avoiding realities that they either found ugly or incomprehensible. Their reaction to Spain was often poetically worded:

Bells of the Past, whose long-forgotten music
Still fills the wide expanse,
Tingeing the sober twilight of the Present
With color of Romance!![13]

Yet by the late nineteenth century, some Americans were breaking away from this tradition by viewing contemporary Spain more realistically, discussing Spanish politics, economics, religion, and sociology in accurate and unbiased terms.

Spaniards also expressed interest in the new nation's culture, although not as intensely as Americans did on Spain. They wrote less about the United States, making it difficult to assess American impact on Spain. Most commentary on the United States appeared in the highly publicized and polemical newspapers. The reasons for diminished Spainish interest in Americans were several. Many believed that the Anglo-Saxon culture was inferior to Spain's and therefore was not worth studying or even respecting. Others were simply bound up in the crowded affairs of their own lives and had no time to read about the United States. Illiteracy among all Spanish classes restricted the flow of information. The poor system of roads and postal service made communication of any sort difficult. Despite the influx of American tourists into Spain, their general inability to speak Spanish further discouraged Spaniards from acquiring a better understanding.

Despite these enormous handicaps, some Spaniards were interested in the United States. A few traveled in the United States, and others wrote and lectured about it. Some literary figures borrowed from American fiction; others recognized the bond that existed in the his-

---

12. Frederick S. Stimson, *Origenes del hispanismo norteamericano* (Mexico, 1961), 115–116.
13. Quoted in Williams, *Spanish Background*, 1:282.

tories of both. During the late Napoleonic era and again most notably in 1869, liberal politicians expropriated certain American political traditions for their own use. Curiously enough, many of these were French in origin and came back into Spain by way of French publications on the United States. Concerned Spaniards welcomed each American literary figure visiting Spain and questioned diplomats. Many citizens considered political freedoms and economic opportunities, stories about which spread all over Europe in the nineteenth century, to be more than interesting. Liberals, especially in northeastern Spain, thought Spaniards might learn from them. Consequently a body of literature, descriptions, and translations on American society appeared in Spain, especially after the Napoleonic wars. While less of a movement existed in Spain to expand the nation's understanding of such a political foe, concern existed throughout the century, oblivious to Spain's political restrictions, censorship, or distance from the New World. If for no other reason, Spaniards found Americans interesting because of the newness and heterogeneous characteristics of the United States, which encouraged a love-hate respect for these Americans.

During the first three decades of the nineteenth century, Spaniards knew little about the United States other than what small pieces of information came from other parts of Europe or by way of colonial officials assigned to sectors near the Americans. A few comments, most of them inaccurate and hostile diatribes critical of Washington's Latin American policies, appeared in the small number of newspapers. By around 1830, however, some translated American works appeared along with commentaries on the United States, mostly by Frenchmen. At the same time, writers such as Irving were visiting Spain, bringing with them the cultural baggage of the new nation. With the end of the repressive and reactionary regime of Fernando VII in 1833, which even prohibited the publication of *Rip Van Winkle* (considered politically subversive), press censorship lightened, and both moderate and liberal Spaniards began reading books once proscribed. They studied American political institutions, drawing from them such inspiration as needed. Numerous laudatory articles appeared on Benjamin Franklin and George Washington. Later admiring Spaniards would write about Abraham Lincoln and Woodrow Wilson. The American Constitution and its Bill of Rights also became a popular subject for newspapers and magazines.[14]

In the first half of the 1800s, Spaniards expressed a greater interest in American literature than in its history or politics. They were already fascinated with Indian stories. Many early American publications came into Spain by way of France, reflecting French literary tastes. Charles Baudelaire translated Edgar Allan Poe's works into French, which appeared in Spanish by the late 1850s.[15] Books by Walt Whitman and Nathaniel Hawthorne also came to Spain by way of France in the 1840s and 1850s. Other books were translated directly from English into Spanish; of these, the works of Washington Irving and William H. Prescott, who both wrote on Spanish topics, drew the most attention. New editions of their books were published throughout the 1800s and are still reprinted today. By the end of the nineteenth century, the works of most leading American fictional writers had appeared in Spanish—James Fenimore Cooper, Ralph Waldo Emerson, and Mark Twain, among others.[16]

Despite the publication of American fiction in Spain, their impact on nineteenth-century Spanish literature proved small, never matching Spain's influence on American works. Since books from the United States usually appeared in Spain only if they were popular in France, many Spaniards were under the sway of French literary tastes, hardly a significant basis for influencing Spanish literature by way of American productions. Spanish interest in American political commentaries sometimes diverged from French tastes, however.

For a nation so devoted to politics as Spain, studying American political institutions seemed a natural activity. When Spanish liberals debated between 1810 and 1812 on the nature of their political institutions, they drew some inspiration from the American example, but not to the exclusion of British and French traditions. Often they paid homage to those American ideals that originally came from the French. Therefore it is difficult to isolate a particular facet of American political thought that interested Spaniards without suspecting

---

14. John DeLancey Ferguson, *American Literature in Spain* (New York, 1916), 3.

15. John Eugene Englekirk, *Edgar Allan Poe in Hispanic Literature* (New York, 1934), 23–24.

16. For a bibliography of translations, see Ferguson, *American Literature in Spain*, 203–260.

British or French origins. As the century grew older, more specific interest in the United States could be discerned. Republicans in Spain studied the political institutions of the United States on an informal basis, searching for possible remedies to their nation's ills.

By the time of the American Civil War, and certainly afterward when the Union had proved it could survive such a powerful shock, liberal Spaniards expressed greater interest in the U.S. system, and conservatives found they had more to fear from the strong republic than ever before. The growth of Lincoln's saintlike stature following his assassination in 1865 encouraged many liberal politicians to identify with his political beliefs. They borrowed from him what they needed when arguing for more democratic institutions or abolition of Spanish slavery. Consequently during the 1860s, a flurry of publications appeared in Spain on the United States. Some translations of American publications came off the presses and others were issued in translation from various other European languages. Most of these mid-century works emphasized historical and political conditions in the young republic. Spaniards wrote articles and books specifically tailored to Spanish audiences in which they generally praised American political institutions. A counterattack by such conservative writers as José Ferrer de Couto in the 1850s and 1860s failed to offset the liberal views of the United States, which were still in the minority at the time.[17]

The zenith of nineteenth-century American influence on Spanish politics—with the exception of the Spanish-American War—came in 1869 when Spain adopted a new constitution. Spanish historian Joaquin Oltra found that much of the text and political philosophy underlying it came from the Constitution of the United States. He

---

17. For examples, *Causa célebre. Asesinato del Presidente Lincoln, atentados contra Mr. Seward y otros* (La Habana, 1865); Antonio Angulo Heredia, *Estudios sobre los Estados Unidos de América. La democracía y el self-government* (Madrid, 1865); Juan Bigelow, *Los Estados Unidos de América en 1865*, trans. Narciso Blanch e Illa (Madrid, 1866); J. A. Spencer, *Historia de los Estados Unidos desde su primer período hasta la administración de Jacobo Buchanan por . . . continuada hasta nuestros días por Horacio Greeley* (Barcelona, 1868); José Comas, *El mundo pintoresco: historia y descripción de los Estados Unidos* (Barcelona, 1868); and E. Laboulaye, *Estudios sobre la constitución de los Estados Unidos* (Seville, 1869).

discovered even that certain passages in the Spanish document were lifted almost verbatim from the American one. This Spanish constitution did not last long, however, and in 1875 a new one, reflecting more closely the realities of Spanish politics, symbolized the decline of American political influence on domestic affairs in Spain and the lack of general interest in internal American conditions.[18]

Yet American publications, literary translations along with some histories, continued to appear in Spain. No longer did literature and political history monopolize Spain's information about the United States. New articles and books discussed industrialization, the American economy, the growth of cities, and immigration. Authors made comparisons with conditions in Spain, especially in regard to economic policies. In many instances, Spaniards wrote with some admiration about American economic strength and searched for models to apply to their own agricultural and industrial problems. They aired American tariff debates, which particularly interested Catalan industrialists who were just beginning to experience industrialization in their region. Agricultural affairs in the United States also drew interest since Spain, still a predominantly rural society, faced serious difficulties in production, labor relations, and consumer demands. Urban boss politics in the United States were often paralleled to its rural version in Spain (*caciquismo*), with little effect on the institution. Although comparisons with American situations failed to inspire the application of new solutions to Spain's problems, attempts were at least made to understand available options.[19]

Spanish institutions were virtually unchanged by the impact of

---

18. Joaquin Oltra, *La influencia norteamericana en la constitución española de 1869* (Madrid, 1972), passim.

19. Emilio Jonveaux, *Los Estados Unidos de América del Norte. Estudios histórico actual* (Madrid, 1871); Rafael M. de Labra, *De la representación e influencia de los Estados Unidos de América en el derecho internacional* (Madrid, 1877); José Jordana y Morera, *La agricultura y los montes de los Estados Unidos* (Madrid, 1880); Cornelio de Witt, *Historia de Washington y de la fundación de la república en los Estados Unidos de América*, trans. Luis de Terán (Madrid, n.d.); Enrique Leopoldo de Verneuill, *Historia biográfica de los presidentes de los Estados Unidos, con presencia de las obras de Irving, Spencer, etc.* (Barcelona, 1885); Pablo de Rousiers, *La vida en la América del Norte* (Barcelona, 1899).

American experiences. Since many still believed that North American culture was inferior to their own, they were reluctant to adopt its social values, literary techniques, and economic or political institutions. The small impact of American society on Spain's could also be explained by the fact that less than 30 percent of all Spaniards could read. In the United States, the literacy rate in the nineteenth century was double Spain's. It would be difficult, if not impossible, to detail what the Spanish masses thought of the United States, but it can be assumed that they shared much the same feelings of other West Europeans.

Most of the lower classes of Western Europe found much to admire in the United States. Hardly had the new nation been born before it earned a reputation for being a land of opportunity. As the century passed, its economic prowess became obvious to all. The collective experiences of European immigrants, including some from Spain and Portugal, planted this image in Spanish minds. Obviously urban labor leaders lamented the growth of big business in the United States with its inherent evils, yet they could identify with workers in America. Those of republican political leanings, although still in a minority, could be expected to be sympathetic to American institutions.

Spanish upper classes—which might include the bourgeois, high-ranking army, church, and government officials, and the nobility—were generally hostile to the United States, more for practical reasons growing out of international political and economic problems. Ideological and religious considerations also contributed to this hostility. Army officers counted among their number many liberals, but they objected to the threat Washington posed to Spain's national interests in the Caribbean. The nobility proved reactionary and highly critical of any democratic society. The Catholic church found Protestantism in North America offensive, believing the United States might act against a Catholic power much as Spain had against Protestant nations in the past. With the major exception of Barcelona, Spaniards living in cities and rural areas knew little about the United States and might have been counted to have few opinions regarding Americans.

Barcelona, long a center of liberal and republican activity, had close ties to America. The city maintained extensive commercial bonds with the United States (mainly for cotton and manufactured consumer goods) and reflected those predominantly French attitudes toward world affairs and economics that the more conservative Castilians still suspected. Barcelona had always been considered a more modern, progressive, or decadent city—depending from what part of Spain one came—than other areas of the nation; therefore some differences of opinion existed among concerned Spaniards regarding the United States. Generalizations about Barcelona were difficult to make, because even here contradictions developed. For instance, the city traded heavily with Cuba, and its merchants faced potential hard times if the United States seized the colony. On the other hand, some recognized that American economic growth provided a model for their own development. Labor leaders learned from their American counterparts, and some local politicians admired Washington's institutions. Catalan nobles who still had not become involved in industrial projects were as conservative as members of the Castilian upper classes and thus often criticized the United States.

Despite the various currents of opinion in Spain on the Americans, reactions after 1898 were understandable. The high rate of illiteracy and widespread disaffection with the Spanish political system contributed to the lack of significant resentment against the United States. Unquestionably no nation suffering such a defeat as Spain's could be expected to forgive the victor entirely. However, since Spaniards realized that their problems were mainly Spanish in origin, they wasted little energy on recriminations. Small pockets of resentful Spaniards existed much like elements in the United States mocking Spain, but both were in the minority and hardly interrupted cultural relations between the two nations after 1898. These contacts actually grew and diversified in the twentieth century. Yet in the early days of the 1900s, formal economic and diplomatic relations dominated contacts between the two nations.

9
DIPLOMACY IN A NEW CENTURY

From the end of the Spanish-American War through 1918, relations between Spain and the United States improved.

These years, marked by few serious diplomatic controversies and emotional issues, stood in sharp contrast to earlier ones. Yet problems growing out of the war continued to concern both countries. Their necessary readjustments in the diplomatic and economic positions called for considerable thinking by policy makers. Moreover some of the irritations of the past had carried over into the new century. This became evident as Spain and the United States renewed commercial and diplomatic ties, battled for ideological and cultural influence in the New World, quibbled over claims, and grappled with boundary problems in the Philippines. Yet none of these problems weighed them down with the importance they would have had in earlier times. In fact many new issues were settled rapidly by negotiation.

Since neither nation significantly threatened the other anymore, an atmosphere of genuine reconciliation developed quickly. Both hoped for better times. For instance, when reporting back to Madrid after his first day of work on June 3, 1899, the Spanish envoy in Washington, José Brunetti y Gayoso, noted that Americans no longer resented Spain and predicted that remaining issues could be settled amicably.[1]

Each nation wanted to eliminate outstanding points of friction, some of which had emerged from the peace agreement regarding

---

1. Brunetti y Gayoso to Minister of State, no. 4, June 3, 1899, Sp/pol/USA/2427, Foreign Office Archives, Madrid.

boundaries. An American naval unit sailing around the Philippines noticed that the settlement had failed to include two islands that had been part of the Spanish colony as property of the United States. The treaty included detailed border descriptions precisely to avoid problems of this sort. The two islands, Cagayan and Sibutú, lay in the southwestern corner of the Philippine archipelago below Mindanao and east of north Borneo but outside the boundaries set for American-held territories in the Pacific. Washington immediately claimed sovereignty over them since the treaty was supposed to give it authority over the entire area, despite the precise delineation of the boundary line.

Brunetti quickly announced that these islands were Spanish because the United States had insisted on an exact border description at Paris and at that time failed to include these two islands among its demands. The Spanish noted that article III of the peace treaty omitted any mention of these two pieces of land, obviously an accident, but one that Spain took advantage of in order to gain concessions from the United States. Officially Madrid argued that Washington could not have accidently left these islands out of the treaty. Thus with the war hardly over, Madrid boxed Washington into an awkward legal position caused by American carelessness.

The Americans realized an error had been made by their negotiators in Paris but believed the spirit of the treaty called for these islands to come under their control. Recognizing that their position was legally weak and Spain's almost impossible to contest, Washington offered to buy the islands in March 1900. Spain had never intended to keep them if it could dispose of them honorably since administering two small islands halfway around the world made little sense, given the cost and administrative nuisance involved. Spanish diplomats (probably with hidden smiles of amusement) appreciated the uncomfortable position of the United States and decided to dispose of the islands—at a profit. The usual haggling over price took place with Spain careful not to accept too low a figure for face-saving purposes while the United States urged a rapid yet inexpensive settlement. They finally agreed on $100,000, and by January 1901 the islands were under American jurisdiction.

The ownership problem posed by these two islands never became serious to either government. Both viewed their policies toward them by assessing their possible impact on domestic politics and in the end each received what it wanted. The Spanish disposed of a nuisance at a small profit and honorably while the United States acquired the missing pieces necessary to ensure the security of the Philippine archipelago. Washington particularly wanted these territories to forestall some other power, such as Germany, from acquiring them. To all the participating diplomats, the easy settlement suggested that relations between Spain and the United States had indeed improved in the new century.

Before the problem of the Philippine islands was solved, a more persistent and nagging one drew the attention of both governments and occupied them for the better part of a decade. During the Cuban revolution of the mid-1890s and later, Americans had filed claims against the Spanish that amounted to millions of dollars. Both governments discussed the issue at Paris and finally agreed that Spain would surrender Puerto Rico and some small Caribbean islands; in return Washington accepted responsibility for paying off American claims in any way deemed proper. The burden for solving the difficult problem of claims consequently lay with Washington as stipulated by article VII of the Treaty of Paris. It proved to be a far more complicated matter than either side anticipated. Prisoner exchanges, political detainees in Cuban jails, and the transfer of administrative control of the Spanish colonies to American authorities never posed any problem when compared to the question of claims.

The United States created the Spanish Claims Commission, which began sifting through the cases in March 1901. The commissioners faced a prodigious task since the claims amounted to almost $65 million. Those which it decided to consider could be settled only after gathering information in the United States, Cuba, and Spain to validate them. Much of the necessary data had to come from Spanish interviews and documentary collections, sources that Madrid husbanded. American investigators found that the Spaniards felt uncomfortable about their work since many cases concerned the excesses of Spanish soldiers involved in robbing or killing Cuban civilians and abusing women, which hurt their national pride. Moreover, allowing Americans to read archival material posed a security risk and violated the privacy of Spanish officials. The fact that Spain lost the war obviously increased its sensitivity to the issue even though it did not have any liability to worry about. The Spanish Foreign Office, however, did not want to cooperate too openly since it might want to file counter cases for Spanish citizens. This never occurred, but the possibility did not help the American commission in the early days of the 1900s. Therefore investigators turned to the State Department for help.[2]

American diplomats joined in urging Spain to cooperate. Finally in 1904, Madrid permitted an agent to gather necessary information with the help of a Spanish representative. The reasons for Spain's change of attitude could be attributed to several conditions. By then resentment over the war had declined. In 1902 a favored-nation commercial treaty between the United States and Spain went into effect and in the following year a copyright agreement was drawn up, both of which encouraged a more cooperative spirit. In short neither public overreacted to Spanish-American diplomacy in 1904, allowing diplomats greater freedom of action. Thus the commission worked on its cases, completing them in 1910.

More irritating to both nations than claims was the issue of the U.S.S. *Maine*. Nothing in Spanish-American relations in the early 1900s drew more public attention in each country than this emotionally charged event. Spaniards in all walks of life believed Spain had not blown up the ship and always argued that the United States used the incident to steal Cuba from them. Moreover they resented the charge since it insulted Spanish honor. The fact that American naval investigators never conclusively determined the cause of the explosion (although blaming a Spanish mine as the probable one) coupled with Washington's reluctance to study the case more thoroughly led to recriminations in the Spanish press during the early 1900s. Each time a piece of evidence circulated in the United States about the ship's being destroyed by Cuban revolutionaries, Americans, or by accident, Spanish newspapers gave it wide coverage while denouncing the American government for its mismanagement of the case.

Americans divided on the question of how the *Maine* blew up.

---

2. Spain's uncomfortable feelings were expressed in dozens of dispatches, Sp/pol/USA/2439-2441.

Some believed Spain responsible; more skeptical individuals suspected either a Cuban mine or an internal explosion in the ship's magazine or boiler compartment. These guesses were confused by investigations. An American naval board in 1898 blamed Spain for the explosion but found contradictory evidence—all without raising the ship for examination. An independent Spanish investigation concluded that the vessel exploded because of an internal blowup.[3] As the years went by, Americans demanded that the issue be settled, the ship raised, and the dead on board buried. Spaniards joined in such requests, believing these moves would clear their nation. When Washington hesitated, many Spaniards accused the American government of hiding its guilt. Following much discussion, however, the ship was raised in 1912. After studying it and removing the dead, the navy towed the ship to its final resting place off Cuba. The raising confirmed Spanish belief in their innocence. An American naval board found evidence of an internal explosion yet refused to turn over the conclusion of the earlier investigative body. By the 1970s sufficient evidence had appeared to prove that the ship had suffered an internal explosion of no fault to Spain.

During the early years of the 1900s, however, newspapers and magazines in both nations covered the *Maine* in great detail. This issue made it difficult for either government to improve relations substantially for fear of public reaction and mistrust growing out of national concern for the ship's fate. The *Maine* drew attention even after 1912; in 1914 some Americans planned special ceremonies to honor the ship's dead. The Spanish press and government protested.[4] When the Germans began sinking ships in the Atlantic during 1915, both nations recalled the *Maine*, to the discomfort of their governments, for in both instances innocent ships that were not at war and did not have any hostile intentions were attacked.

Like the Spanish press, American newspapers sometimes stirred their readers. Prior to World War I, periodicals in the United States carried stories insulting to Spain. For instance, rumors continually circulated about King Alfonso XIII's having mental problems or his

---

3. Shirley F. Jackson, "The United States and Spain, 1898–1918" (Ph.D. diss., Florida State University, 1967), 83.

4. Ibid., 106.

acting in an irresponsible or rude manner. The *New York American Journal* reported in 1902 that the king was dissipated and disagreeable. In such cases, the Spanish Foreign Office protested, especially since newspapers in Spain reported such stories.[5] Earlier in the same year another case developed when a Spanish consul protested that drunk American sailors had insulted Spain's flag in Santiago de Cuba. This too led the Foreign Office to object and demand punishment for the guilty.[6] These various cases of hostility were never long lasting when compared to more fundamental issues, such as commerce.

The Spanish-American War had disrupted trade between Spain and the United States and among the Cubans, Spanish, and Americans. All recognized that reestablishing commerce would be one of the early priorities for the postwar period. Moreover Spain and the United States sought to expand commercial contacts with the Latin Americans, especially the Spanish who wanted to make up for trade deficits, which they believed were being created by American expansion into the Cuban market after 1898. The Spanish also determined that closer trade relations with the South Americans would further their program of *hispanismo*. Thus because of the broad significance of commerce to both Spain and the United States, economic issues dominated their diplomatic relations from 1899 to 1917.

Despite the intentions of both the United States and Spain to foster closer commercial relations, difficulties remained throughout the early years of the century caused by economic considerations and sociopolitical rivalry in Latin America. Immediately upon renewing diplomatic relations, the two encouraged trade. By 1900 American imports from Spain amounted to about $6 million; exports to Spain reached nearly $13.4 million. The emphasis on commerce appeared enormous, considering that the annual trade figures were higher in 1900 than they had been in any year since 1883.[7] Yet American busi-

---

5. *New York American Journal*, August 10, 1902; Brunetti y Gayoso to Minister of State, no. 185, November 4, 1902, Sp/pol/USA/2440, in response to Minister of State to Brunetti y Gayoso, August 18, 1902, Sp/pol/USA/2440.

6. Joaquin de Pereyra to Minister of State, no. 93, May 7, 1902, Sp/pol/USA/2440.

7. Jackson, "The United States and Spain," 180–181.

nessmen mistrusted their Spanish counterparts and therefore hesitated to extend them credit, a necessity in international trade. Spain maintained unusually high tariffs on incoming American products as a result of legislation of the early 1890s. These problems continued to disturb economic relations despite the fact that in 1902 the two governments signed a commercial agreement granting each other status as favored nations.

Each also competed economically in Latin America, using its commercial power to undercut the other. For example, Washington threatened to restrict incoming Spanish goods if Spain did not reduce its tariffs on American products; at the same time, the United States negotiated special trade agreements in Latin America that were detrimental to Madrid. Americans pointed to Spain's economic policy toward the United States as an indication of what Latin Americans could expect from Madrid. The Spanish used virtually the same argument in reverse.

Another international influence that both faced was Europe's commercial ties with Spain. Prior to the Spanish-American War, German-manufactured products duplicating American goods began coming into Spain, where they were cheaper because of lower Spanish tariffs on European commodities. This traffic increased after 1898 to the consternation of the Americans. Despite negotiations with Spain for a more equitable tariff system, this imbalance continued. On the other hand, the Spanish competed poorly with France and Italy in exporting such items as wines, luxury foods, cork, and animal skins to the United States, often being undercut by European competitors who had already negotiated more favorable trade agreements with Washington.

Both recognized that the solution to many of their difficulties lay in a comprehensive commercial treaty. Despite the limited one signed in 1902, they waited until 1906 before negotiating a more encompassing one. The American minister to Madrid, William Collier, advocated mutual reduction of tariffs as tentatively agreed to in 1902 by proposing model rate scales. On August 1, 1906, the two governments signed such an agreement. By its terms, tariffs went down on most traded commodities.[8] As a result, commerce between the two

---

8. For provisions, see ibid., 189.

increased dramatically over the next few years. In effect, goods entered each country on a competitive basis with those of other nations although at a higher rate than offered by domestic producers. Since each sold to the other items not readily available in the domestic market, internal production hardly suffered. In 1910 they further reduced duties.

Trade from 1899 onward reflected much the same pattern as that of the previous century. Spain exported to the United States wines, cork, olives, and luxury items such as art and furniture, while the Americans generally shipped cotton, machinery, barrels, and a variety of manufactured consumer products. By the turn of the century coal exports to Spain had also increased. Yet cotton and coal caused difficulties for Washington because of the heavy transportation tax imposed by the Spanish, which was not covered by earlier agreements. This situation became especially acute after 1910 when American exporters again faced the challenge of European competition in Spain. In 1912, for instance, Spaniards purchased 2.32 million tons of coal in Europe but none from the United States, which was then the largest producer in the world and, without the Spanish tax, could have supplied Spain cheaper than Britain or Germany did.[9] Thus the State Department raised the issue of changing the transportation tax in 1913, meeting with little encouragement since the Spanish government needed that income to pay rising expenses at home and in North Africa. However, Spain agreed to revise this tax downward in exchange for commercial concessions by Washington. Before the details could be discussed, World War I broke out in the late summer of 1914.

Both the United States and Spain declared their neutrality and began to reassess their international positions. Each recognized it might face difficulties in obtaining products that the bellicose nations needed. Moreover they saw the opportunity to trade with both sides while increasing commerce with each other. Spain moved quickly to ensure adequate quantities of coal by reducing duties on imported supplies. In spring of 1915, Madrid also reduced the transportation tax. Because the Germans were sinking Spanish ships and the British continually protested about Spain's commercial relations with the

---

9. Ibid., 194.

Central Powers, Madrid hoped to increase commerce with the United States and thereby preserve neutrality.

Washington faced a similar situation: its ships were being sunk and its commercial relations with the warring factions were constantly threatened by one side or the other. Therefore the United States also worked to improve commercial contacts with neutral nations. Various tariffs were readjusted and import-export regulations revised accordingly, leading to a steady increase in Spanish-American business throughout the war. Between 1914 and 1916, trade grew to the point where 32 percent of Spain's exports went to the United States, and the United States sold a greater volume of goods to Spain than previously.[10]

Another factor contributing to increased trade came from reduced commercial relations of the United States and Spain with the rest of Europe. Germany exported less to Spain after August 1914 because it needed much of its own production for the war. Berlin still tried to buy war supplies from Spain, but found it more difficult since it was selling less to them and thus could not build up reserves of pesetas essential for its own needs. Eventually most warring nations obtained sufficient Spanish credits and made the necessary arrangements to increase their purchases in Spain. But in the early days of the war, this was not the case. At first goods once purchased from the Germans might now come from the United States. A similar pattern developed in regard to French exports to the United States, which were partially supplanted by Spain. The fighting worked to the advantage of Spanish and American commerce until the United States entered the war in the spring of 1917, complicating economic exchanges.

To understand more fully the post-April 1917 commerce between Spain and the United States, Latin America's prewar relations with both have to be taken into account. In the twentieth century Spain wanted to continue developing closer cultural and economic ties to the ex-colonies. In this it faced the United States as the prime rival. Madrid's attachment to Latin America grew after 1898 when it no longer posed a political threat to the South Americans. Spaniards

---

10. Ibid., 203.

continued viewing the powerful Anglo-Saxon nation in North America as a political, economic, and cultural threat to all Hispanic people. After 1898, they believed more than ever that Washington wanted to extend its imperialist tentacles into the Caribbean, down the spine of Central America, and deeply into South America, using economics to this end. Unquestionably Spaniards saw evidence of this reach all around them. Their own experiences in regard to Cuba, Puerto Rico, and the Philippines, coupled with the growing economic and military power of the United States, lent urgent relevance to their fears, concerns that many Latin Americans shared.

Spaniards generally believed that North Americans lacked the spirituality that gave meaning to the Hispanic culture. They also thought that North American society challenged all Hispanic people by its ruthlessness and insensitivity. Spaniards worried that the attractiveness of North American prosperity with its emphasis on materialism as the basic quality of life instead of on spiritual considerations might destroy both Hispanic society and any hope of Spain's wielding influence in the New World. They knew that because of the military successes of the United States in 1898, Latin Americans also had the same worries; thus Spaniards saw an opportunity to expand their influence in the Americas. Hardly a Spanish publication of the day rejected the challenge of leading all the Hispanic people away from the North American danger by uniting the ex-colonists with them in their *raza hispanica*.[11]

One of the first steps taken after 1898 was to discourage all Pan-Americanist movements since they implied separation from Spain and hinted of closer ties to Washington. Spain wanted to replace such a system with a Hispanic one. Diplomats, philosophers, and merchants told Latin Americans that with Europe respecting North American power as never before, the Hispanic people had to make common cause with Spain. They argued that Britain and France could no longer checkmate the United States when Washington used the Monroe Doctrine unreasonably because of their own problems in Western Europe. As it happened, Washington began to interfere

---

11. Frederick B. Pike, *Hispanismo, 1898-1936: Spanish Conservatives and Liberals and Their Relations with Spanish America* (Notre Dame, 1971), 142-145.

militarily in Latin American affairs more often than in the 1800s, making Spanish arguments inviting.

Spanish diplomats worried privately that their efforts might fail each time Washington sent troops into the Caribbean or Central America. They studied American policy toward Cuba with the same concern as they did Washington's attitude toward other Latin American countries.[12] They also watched the construction of the Panama Canal with apprehension, since many Spaniards knew the circumstances surrounding the birth of the Panamanian government and the implications of the canal's influence on North American policy in Central America. They thought that the interference there of Presidents Theodore Roosevelt, William H. Taft, and Woodrow Wilson threatened their Latin American policy.[13]

Combating the United States in the New World proved difficult, since the Spanish could not agree on the best approach. Liberal Spaniards suggested using propaganda. They believed that emphasizing how Spain continually advanced in science, commerce, education, and politics would offer an attractive alternative to North American institutions. Spanish conservatives suggested using Catholicism as the principal element in binding the Latin Americans to Spain. They correctly realized that the church continued to be the cultural glue bonding all Hispanic people, irrespective of political and economic differences among themselves. They stressed to the Latin Americans the grave danger posed to their religion by the Protestant United States.[14] This reasoning produced some favorable reactions in South America, although not to the degree Spain had wanted.

Spaniards also believed they could use commercial relations to their advantage. Solid economic experience encouraged them to advocate commercial competition with the United States in the southern hemisphere. They used Cuba as an example, where trade with Spain from 1891 through 1895 had amounted to 166 million pesetas at an

---

12. For dispatches on this, see Sp/pol/USA/2439–2443. When U.S. troops went into Nicaragua in 1909, the Spanish minister in Washington called it "deplorable." Villalobar to Minister of State, no. 179, December 3, 1909, Sp/corr/USA/1482.

13. For dispatches on this, see Sp/pol/USA/2442.

14. Pike, *Hispanismo*, 182–183.

exchange rate of between 7.5 to 5.5 pesetas to the dollar. Business with Puerto Rico averaged about 49.5 million pesetas. In 1900 Spain's commerce with Cuba totaled 62 million pesetas and 13 million pesetas with Puerto Rico. Consequently Spain had another reason to seek new markets in Latin America: to make up for lost business.[15]

Confident of their economic prowess, Spaniards launched a major campaign to increase trade with the Latin Americans. This would also serve to quiet the Catalan industrialists who constantly irritated officials in Madrid with their demands for expanded foreign trade and closer ties to the South Americans. Spain met with less than dramatic success. Commerce increased, but it never matched the rapid growth of Spanish business with the United States. Moreover Spain never made up the lost Cuban trade. Yet historians have at times confused Spanish economic policies for Cuba and Latin America. In regard to South America, expanded trade was desired not only for economic reasons but as a further means of fostering *hispanismo*.

The reasons for Spain's inability to increase trade to the desired extent were clearly linked to North America's role in the New World and to domestic Spanish economic conditions. The United States enjoyed unique trading advantages in the Caribbean, which were reflected in lower tariffs and transportation costs. The small and inefficient Spanish merchant marine could not transport goods to Latin America in sufficient quantities or as inexpensively, forcing Spaniards to charge more. Moreover the Latins preferred North American products. Deliveries from Spain decreased as did the size of the shipments, which never met Latin American demands. Spaniards probably could have made a greater profit simply by concentrating their New World efforts on selling more to the United States. But because Spain closely tied international economic policies to diplomacy in Latin America, concentrating on the North American market virtually to the exclusion of South America would have been counterproductive in terms of Madrid's program for the Americas.

The other weakness Spain endured was the inability of its economy to satisfy the gargantuan demands of Latin America. Both North

---

15. Ibid., 210–211.

American consumer and industrial manufactures went to South America in large quantities. Spain could not ship similar items since it had to purchase them from Germany and the United States. Cigars could be bought directly from Cuba without involving Spain. Spanish cotton products competed with those of the United States. Moreover such items as wines, olives, and corks had only a limited market anyway. When coupled with inefficient industrial management and a restless labor force, it became clear why the Spanish lacked even the fundamental economic base from which to invade the American markets massively.

Issues of economic and cultural competition particularly mixed with political concerns in Mexico in the years immediately before World War I. Until about 1911, Spain and the United States ranged across the whole of Latin America in their rivalry, only momentarily concentrating attention on a specific country. However, Mexico was an exception because of its continuous political and social unrest. Mexican problems illustrated the nature of Spanish-American competition in the New World on the eve of world war. Both expressed interest in its affairs. Many Americans had invested considerable sums of money and time in Mexico, interests that Washington was prepared to protect. This meant that domestic Mexican affairs would draw more than casual attention from the State Department. Spain also maintained close ties to Mexico by virtue of the thousands of Spaniards living and investing there and, of course, because of the country's Hispanic background.

Mexico's political unrest originally stemmed from the fact that President Porfirio Díaz had stayed in power too long. Becoming chief of state in 1877, he was still in office in 1910, when various critics were plotting his overthrow. Over the years Díaz had encouraged foreigners to live and invest in Mexico as a means of improving his nation's economy. To some degree this plan had worked, especially when American businessmen built railroads and worked oil fields. When various opponents of the Mexican president began scheming, both Spain and the United States could not ignore the plight in which this put their citizens; most of the Mexican government's critics charged, among other things, that foreigners exploited Mexico unfairly and should have their properties confiscated and the owners expelled or punished.

In 1911 Francisco I. Madero replaced Díaz as chief of state. But more conservative elements than Madero rose in rebellion before he was hardly ensconced in the presidential palace. In 1913 Victoriano Huerta successfully forced Madero out of office. Anti-Huerta elements led by Emiliano Zapata, Francisco "Pancho" Villa, and Venustiano Carranza worked to overthrow the new president, seeking support from the United States. Madrid and Washington watched apprehensively, filed claims, protested when their citizens suffered, and, in the case of the United States, stationed troops along the border for an emergency rescue of Americans.

Huerta managed to stay in office longer than some of his competitors, creating problems for Spain and the United States because his enemies despised Spaniards and Americans. Therefore in their struggles against him, they confiscated foreign properties to finance the revolts. Between 1913 and late 1915, some Spaniards were killed. But because Spain could do little more than protest, Spanish residents turned to Washington for protection. President Woodrow Wilson in 1913 hesitated to intervene on their behalf or even for Americans. He asked the rebels to leave all foreigners alone, but they ignored him, and more Spaniards and Americans suffered the consequences. Mexicans even raided across the border into the United States, and in 1914 hundreds of Spaniards streamed across the same frontier to save their lives. In the same year Huerta left office and Carranza replaced him.

In the early days of the fighting (1911–13) Spain tried to identify with the more conservative elements in Mexico, hoping in that way to protect Spaniards. But when even these conservatives turned on Spaniards, Madrid asked Washington to intervene more actively on behalf of its citizens. Wilson hesitated; he did not want to jeopardize American interests there or to send troops (which he finally had to do anyway). Because Wilson believed such intervention was immoral and irresponsible, he did not help the Spanish as much as they had wanted. His behavior led Madrid to conclude that Wilson was deeply involved in domestic Mexican politics and worked against Spanish interests. Spain's newspapers criticized him. More outspoken critics accused Wilson of everything from indifference to blatant imperialism. Public resentment grew as the number of Spanish casualties multiplied and were reported in detail by the press. Soon Spaniards blamed the United States rather than the Mexicans for this new bloodshed and loss of property.

Washington replied that a responsible nation could not intervene in another's domestic affairs without considerable provocation. Wilson faced a genuine dilemma: he believed such intervention was morally wrong and might jeopardize Washington's growing influence in the rest of Latin America. He thus refused to secure Spanish interests at the expense of his own nation's. He chose to use diplomatic channels to redress Spanish and American wrongs, later was forced to intrigue with various Mexican elements, and finally in 1916 sent a military force into Mexico to destroy Villa. Yet it was his reluctance to take action early in the crisis that led to much of the increase in tensions between Spain and the United States just prior to World War I.

Mistaken motives on both sides coupled with Wilson's misassessment of Mexican events stimulated fears about the other's encroaching in Latin America (especially since Wilson had sent troops into various parts of the Caribbean). Along with Spain, he failed to take advantage of a situation that offered an opportunity to improve relations between Madrid and Washington. He probably concluded that friendship with Spain could not be bought with American or Mexican interests.

World War I influenced Spanish-American diplomacy more dramatically than the events in Mexico. It brought forth a multitude of issues involving peace initiatives, neutrality, modified economic polcies, propaganda, *hispanismo*, and incidents typical of all hostilities. When war broke out in late summer 1914, both countries sought to define their positions in relation to the events in Europe. Spain maintained close commercial ties with Germany and France, which it shared a border with. Many members of the government along with conservatives in the country generally sympathized with the Germans; those on the periphery, especially in Catalonia and in the Basque country, favored the French. Officials in Madrid, finding their nation divided on which side to support, concluded by late fall to remain neutral. The United States also faced divided opinion at home, although a majority of Americans favored the French and British. Unlike Spain, the United States did not share borders with either side and its economic relations with the warring parties were not so important. Also a vast majority of Americans wanted to stay out of the war. Thus Washington declared its neutrality.

Spain and the United States during 1914 wanted to mediate for peace and to a certain extent considered cooperating with each other toward this end. Yet simultaneously they competed for the privilege of being the chief instrument of peace in Europe. In order to encourage such negotiations, they concluded a peace and arbitration treaty, originally proposed by the United States in fall 1914. Spain delayed a final settlement on it until the war made the treaty a potentially valuable instrument for peace; Madrid could serve it up as proof that even two nations recently at war with each other could maintain amicable relations and settle differences through diplomacy. However, this treaty did not suggest that Washington and Madrid would grow more intimate because they now rivaled each other in persuading Europe to stop fighting.

Europe had not experienced a lengthy war since the days of Napoleon. Most conflicts in the 1800s had lasted a few weeks or months. The Crimean war was fought outside of Europe proper. Consequently most Americans and Spanish diplomats believed, like many Europeans, that this new war might be short. Therefore they rushed to launch peace offensives before it ended. The Americans, generally sympathetic to the Entente, concentrated their efforts on London and Paris; the Spanish, with close ties to the Central Powers, began discussions with Berlin. The differences in sympathies in themselves caused suspicion between Madrid and Washington.[16] Yet at the same time neither wanted to do anything to disturb its neutrality, which meant more than their international rivalry. Each simply saw its peace initiatives as a way to preserve neutrality. The longer the fighting continued, the greater chance existed that one or both would be forced into taking sides.

By May 1916 Spanish diplomats were continually questioning neutral and warring governments about peace. King Alfonso XIII invited President Wilson to join him in this peace offensive, thinking that with two governments involved, the chances for success might improve. Wilson declined in the belief that the Entente would reject

---

16. *New York Times*, February 6, 1915, p. 7.

such overtures at the moment. Spanish diplomats, undeterred, next approached each regime with suggestions for peace, which were rejected. For months Madrid and Washington exchanged notes on the nature of a combined peace offensive, but with no serious intention of cooperating. Mutual suspicions prevented any coordinated effort.

Finally in January 1917 the Spanish refused to coordinate their own diplomatic efforts with Wilson anymore.[17] They believed he did not really want cooperation and had used gestures of friendship and interest in a joint effort to achieve the dominant role in bringing peace to Europe. Madrid also did not want to irritate either the Entente or the Central Powers by such efforts. Spanish diplomats believed that cooperation with Wilson, whom they could not control, was impossible, especially since they did not respect his skill as a diplomat. He might jeopardize their relations with France, which they could not risk for economic and political reasons.

In the spring of 1917 the United States joined the Entente to form the Allies in the war against Germany. King Alfonso could now steer a more independent course from Wilson. This stance in turn created the same type of friction between Washington and Madrid that had existed from 1914 to 1917 between Spain, the United States, and other neutrals on the one hand and against the warring nations on the other. Moreover the rivalry, which remained hidden from the public during the first two and one-half years of the war, now surfaced, brought about by the exigencies of war. For example in trade, Spain could purchase oil and other items from the United States only after American war needs had been satisfied and with the consent of the other Allies. Washington also applied economic pressure on the Spanish through the sale of such items as coal and oil to force Madrid into a more pro-Entente position. Washington failed (as it did during World War II) because Madrid believed it more important to maintain a neutral position than to benefit from greater commercial relations.

During the first several years of the war, trade between the two nations actually had increased. Both sold to the other and to the various warring factions. In 1914 Spain purchased from the United

---

17. Ibid., January 1, 1917, p. 5.

States products and materials valued at nearly $24.7 million; by the end of 1916, this reached $27.9 million. The Americans bought $30.4 million in goods during 1914 and $52.8 million in 1916.[18] Each believed the economy of the other complemented its own and wanted to expand commerce even more. But when the United States entered the war in 1917, the conditions influencing both changed. Economics now became a weapon. Also the Germans began sinking ships again, including Spanish vessels trading with the United States, Britain, and France. The Americans reduced sales of war-related items to Spain at the same time.

By March 1918 Madrid concluded that the Entente would win the war, yet it realized that the fighting was far from over. It thus agreed to sell supplies to American forces in France secure in the knowledge that Germany could do little to prevent this trade or jeopardize Spain's neutrality. Spain also began experiencing an economic slowdown at home, which threatened to increase unemployment at a time of rapid inflation. To ease this pressure, economic officials in Madrid urged increased trade with the Entente. Thus a combination of the two factors led Spain to sell the Allies copper, lead, pyrites, iron ore, food, and cotton products in exchange for such traditional items from the United States as fuels and industrial machinery. Yet to the end of the war, economic problems disturbed both countries. Embargos, blacklists, priorities, and dangerous transportation routes easily combined to restrict trade.

American propaganda in neutral Spain also complicated relations after 1917 when Washington launched a massive campaign to gain public support for the Entente. This made it difficult for Madrid to remain neutral since both Germany and the United States maintained large propaganda agencies in Spain. Each protested the other's activities to the Spanish and accused them of not being neutral. Yet propaganda did not sway Spanish public opinion to any significant degree. Rather a combination of propaganda, successful military efforts by the Entente, closer economic dependency on France and the United States than on the Central Powers, and the personal sympathies of Alfonso made Spain pro-Allies by mid-1918. But because

---

18. Jackson, "The United States and Spain," 202.

propaganda was visible, many people gave it more credit than it deserved when in fact it only irritated diplomats.[19]

As the war drew to a close, Spain and the United States again sounded out the involved European governments about peace. Once the armistice was signed on November 11, 1918, the Spanish increased their efforts to coordinate with Washington but failed. For instance, when Wilson's adviser, Colonel E. M. House, went to Europe in November to begin talks with the Germans, the Spanish asked him to visit Madrid and discuss peace.[20] All the warring powers, however, ignored Spain; the United States dominated the peace offensive through Wilson, who refused to share his position with Alfonso. Because Spain had been a neutral, the victors did not believe Madrid could dictate peace or influence its terms.

Historians who have mentioned Spanish-American relations during World War I have failed to analyze the influence of Latin America upon this diplomacy, yet it proved important since the South Americans continued affecting the two nations as they had done for decades before. The war intensified ideological and economic rivalry in the New World while offering both nations new occasions to expand their influence southward. Spaniards viewed their opportunity in two ways. First, officials and Hispanic nationalists believed that Spain could draw the Latin Americans and themselves into a closer political, cultural, and moral union while Europe weakened itself in war. Conservative Spaniards hoped they could use the war to erode North American influence in the area, and liberals believed Latin America might be drawn to Spain since many Spanish citizens and South Americans favored the French cause. Second, Spaniards of all political persuasions wanted to increase trade with their Hispanic cousins by filling gaps created by the war.

Spain failed to expand commerce with the Latin Americans, in spite of its increased talk about closer cultural bonds. Seven Latin governments declared their neutrality, another five severed relations with the Central Powers, and eight went to war with the Germans. These governments represented a mixture of political and ideological

---

19. Ibid., 226-235.
20. Minister of State to Spanish Embassy (Paris), November 30, 1918, Sp/pol/USA/2442.

currents rather than the unified block that many Spaniards thought them to be. In general, the Latin Americans advocated some limited involvement in the war either diplomatically or economically, often throwing their lot in with the Allies, especially after April 1917. This situation made it difficult for Spain to draw the Latins into a unified body. Each time they made an effort in this direction, the United States counteracted.

Commercial relations between Spain and the South Americans proved especially disappointing. Between 1913 and 1918, Spain supplied Latin America with about 3.5 to 4.5 percent of the latter's imports. The figures dropped in 1920 to even lower points. A similar pattern for exports also confirmed Spain's inability to compete economically with the United States and other nations. During the war years, about 15 percent of Spain's foreign commerce was with the Latin·Americans; 23 percent involved France, another 20.7 went to the United States, and 15.9 percent went to Britain.[21] After entering the war, the United States implemented similar policies toward Spain and Latin America. Propaganda coupled with economic pressures produced more results for Washington than for Madrid. The Spanish envoy to the United States in 1917, Juan Riaño y Gayangos, correctly predicted that with the United States in the war, Madrid could expect a "break in the neutrality of all the American republics." He believed the North Americans would also dominate Latin America's export trade, which they did, especially with foods, arms, and raw materials.[22]

In looking back at the years between 1899 and 1918, it was obvious that rivalries and mistrust in Europe and America played greater roles than in the 1920s but less than in the nineteenth century. While the bitterness of their war of 1898 rankled a declining number of individuals, the first two decades of the 1900s were understandably marked by problems left from 1898 but that were absent in the 1920s. After World War I, economic problems and new crises in Europe drew both nations into the mainstream of European affairs in broader dimensions than either could imagine in 1918 and to a lesser extent

---

21. Pike, *Hispanismo*, 222–223.
22. Riaño y Gayangos to Minister of State, no. 20, April 12, 1917, Sp/pol/USA/2443.

into Latin America's. Domestic unrest in Spain further interested Americans as well by the mid-1930s, creating a new volatile period in Spanish-American diplomacy.

10
A QUIET INTERLUDE

After World War I, Spain and the United States slipped into quieter relations, expressing greater interest in expanding trade than in nurturing diplomatic conflicts even though Latin America still stirred passions in both. Cultural exchanges increased as tourists poured into Spain, writers rediscovered Iberian charms, and Spaniards acquired a healthier respect for the American colossus. Amicable contacts lasted until the events of the mid-1930s rudely opened old wounds, inflicted new ones, and aroused ideological and national feelings in both. Before the Civil War, however, each country considered its diplomatic and economic associations with the other of declining importance. Such an attitude suggested why little rancor disturbed their diplomacy during the 1920s and early 1930s.

Both turned their energies to domestic or international problems. Spain attempted to expand its influence within the League of Nations while the United States, not being a member, could not. Madrid also continued waging an expensive and bloody colonial war in North Africa that did not involve the United States. The North Americans retreated into their own continent, shouting the return to "normalcy" and the pseudo-isolationism that such a vague misnomer implied. In truth, Americans involved themselves in many international affairs, especially in broadening their foreign commerce in Latin America, Europe, and Asia. Admittedly they preferred to avoid participating in European political affairs but even in this Americans could not totally avoid the demands made upon them as a world power. Consequently relations were not completely uneventful between Spain and the United States.

Domestic developments in Spain set the background for some of the problems both faced. A checkered pattern of peace and domestic violence, economic hopes, and recessionary cycles continually upset the Spanish. Between 1918 and 1923, Spain faced economic contraction, as did most other European nations. Mines closed, shipbuilding declined, steel production faltered, agricultural and industrial unemployment increased, prices fell, and strikes multiplied. Although the intense labor problems, which often burst into violence, subsided by 1923, and failed to cause a bolshevik-style revolution, conservative Spaniards were shaken. Many concluded that the central government could hardly control the situation, maintain law and order, or establish economic stability. In July 1921 the Spanish army in North Africa experienced a humiliating defeat at Anual inflicted by a few thousand natives, thereby effectively destroying ten years of Spain's hard work in expanding its control over the area.

The combined political, economic, and military troubles facing Spain encouraged conservative politicians and army officers to increase their participation in politics. In September 1923 General Primo de Rivera declared that he would seize power if he were not legally brought into the government. With no real choice open to him, Alfonso XIII felt compelled to appoint the general prime minister. In effect, Primo de Rivera ruled as a dictator under various titles until January 28, 1930. During the 1920s, Alfonso's personal power diminished while that of Primo de Rivera increased. The army officer provided Spain with a sense of stability and peace that conservative Spaniards longed for after the eventful five years since 1918. He initiated reforms, encouraged economic growth, and participated in international affairs. He terminated the Moroccan war, electing to spend the nation's resources on building roads, public offices, schools, and a reorganized government.

In the United States, the American economy underwent change after the war. A temporary decline, unlike the more massive one in Spain, characterized the economy's performance. Yet by the mid-1920s, Americans enjoyed an economic boom that was reflected in expanding world trade, increased consumer production, and a rise in the standard of living. Like Spain, the agricultural sector continued to face serious economic hardships, but American farmers never resorted to the desperate acts of protest and violence witnessed by

Spaniards. As with Spain, the United States avoided overcommitments in international affairs. Washington did not join the League of Nations and never faced a crippling colonial war. Each nation fostered trade relations with Latin America and worked to improve its quality of life.

The two nations sported interests common to most other countries in the 1920s. They talked of world disarmament—Spain in the League and the United States through a series of conferences in Washington. Both created trade barriers in the form of increased tariffs in order to encourage the development of domestic industries. In return, each was linked to the world's economy more than they realized. The consequence was that when the depression arrived at the end of the 1920s, the two felt its effects dramatically in continued inflation, then falling prices, rising unemployment, declining international trade, and faltering monetary systems.

Between 1918 and 1923, most Americans believed Spain supported a liberal monarchy. Although they imagined that Alfonso favored some democratic reforms, Americans felt he could not provide the nation with peaceful domestic life. The unrest of the immediate postwar years confirmed this. When Primo de Rivera came to power, Americans hoped Spain would enjoy more prosperous times. The increase in the number of dictatorships in Europe at the same time suggested to many in the United States that democratic institutions could not provide Europe with the stability Americans enjoyed. Therefore they generally concluded that benevolent dictatorships might help Europeans. The government in Washington simply wanted to maintain amicable relations with Spain, no matter who ruled.[1]

Both nations believed this goal could be achieved through greater commercial contacts and concentrated their efforts toward this end. *La Epoca*, a widely read newspaper in Madrid, reported a sharp increase in American investments in Spain between 1918 and 1920, editorializing that this boded good for both nations.[2] In 1919 Ameri-

---

1. Diana F. Todd, "The United States and Spain during the Regime of Primo de Rivera" (Master's thesis, Florida State University, 1967), 18.
2. *La Epoca*, May 14, 1920, p. 3.

cans purchased $26.14 million worth of goods and services; in the following year, they increased to $45.7 million, suggesting that the governments in Madrid and Washington were effectively encouraging trade.[3]

As a small symbol of their growing friendliness, they renewed their arbitration agreement of 1909 in 1919.[4] Diplomats then tried to negotiate an end to minor economic differences. For instance, the passage of the Eighteenth Amendment prohibiting the manufacture or consumption of alcoholic beverages in the United States made it illegal for Spanish ships coming into American ports to carry wine for their sailors. The Spanish wanted an exemption. The two governments failed to resolve the problem as negotiations abruptly ended in the confusion of Primo de Rivera's coming to power in 1923.

More serious economic problems faced them in the 1920s. The passage of the Eighteenth Amendment seriously damaged Spain's export trade to the United States since a significant portion of it consisted of wines. Many protectionist Spaniards, along with others in the wine industry, wanted to retaliate by not renewing the Spanish-American most-favored-nation commercial treaty, which would expire on November 5, 1923. They argued that to pass it not only allowed the injustice done to wine producers to go unavenged but would increase the imbalance in trade relations. At the time, the United States sold more to Spain than Spaniards to Americans, creating an unfavorable balance of trade for the Iberians, which threatened to deplete their foreign currency stocks and weaken the value of the peseta on the international monetary market.[5]

Economics diversified relations in the 1920s with the growth of tourism in Spain. Between 1924 and 1925, about 40,000 Americans visited Spain, spending their dollars freely.[6] Since most of this money

---

3. Shirley F. Jackson, "The United States and Spain, 1819–1918" (Ph.D. diss., Florida State University, 1967), 224.

4. U.S., Department of State, *Papers Relating to the Foreign Affairs of the United States, 1919* (Washington, D.C., 1919), 2:806–808 (hereafter cited as *FRUS* and year).

5. *The Literary Digest*, November 24, 1923, p. 22.

6. *New York Times*, November 5, 1925, p. 8.

went into the service sector of the Spanish economy—which did not rely on heavy capital investment—these dollars were a windfall that could be used to purchase American goods. The sharp increase in tourism after Primo de Rivera came to power also indicated American confidence in his ability to maintain peace within Spain. This became evident in other ways as well. In 1925 American banks bought Spanish bonds and businessmen negotiated with Madrid to establish a national telephone system valued at $18 million. American Telephone and Telegraph Company (ITT) eventually won the contract for service in Spain, undercutting a Swedish competitor. Also in 1925, the United States placed an embargo on Spanish grapes and oranges after receiving reports that they were infested with Mediterranean fruit flies, and the embargo remained in force throughout the 1920s.[7]

Business attitudes toward each other remained cordial. The dictator's economic reforms, coupled to Alfonso's continued expressions of affection for the United States, encouraged American businessmen. Spanish merchants and industrialists reacted similarly to the United States. But the amicable feelings about commercial matters changed in 1926 and 1927 when the American press reported political unrest in Spain. Minor revolts against the central government and criticism of Primo de Rivera's policies now scared American businessmen, boding ill for Spanish-American trade.[8] By the fall of 1927, Spain's domestic unrest had adversely affected commerce.

The commercial problems facing both Spain and the United States clearly suggested some of the reasons why their volume of trade was in danger of declining. American sales to Spain continued to rise steadily from 1926 through 1928, with only a slight decline registering in 1929. Spanish exports declined only after the onset of the world depression since domestic tranquility in the United States ensured sales until the economics of recession followed by depression became effective. Officials in 1927 and 1928, however, did not know what events taking place at the moment would do to trade, and they believed both faced potentially serious economic problems.

---

7. *FRUS 1925*, 2:714–724.
8. Todd, "United States and Spain," 52–63.

During the spring and summer of 1927, Primo de Rivera's minister of finance, José Calvo Sotelo, initiated a series of economic reforms, most of which came to fruition in 1928 in the form of revised tax scales and improved collection methods. In 1927, however, he proposed that the government form a national petroleum monopoly as a means of increasing revenues for the treasury, a suggestion that would affect the interests of American oil companies in Spain which, along with the automotive industry in the United States, sold Spaniards everything from cars to gasoline. In fact during 1925 alone, 6,384 American vehicles went to Spanish customers, and a great deal of the fuel to operate them came from American companies.[9] Oil officials worried that their properties might be nationalized; in 1927 the Spanish automobile industry had been taken over by the regime without proper compensation.

American businessmen tried to convince the Spanish that they (the Americans) could operate oil companies more profitably than the Spanish government. They disagreed that profits could be increased for both the government and industry by as much as one-third if under Spain's control. Making no headway, American oil men feared their holdings would be confiscated by the end of that summer. The American embassy reported that Primo de Rivera probably had advisers who recommended nationalization in order to profit personally by such a move and at the expense of Spain's international trade.[10]

Three large American companies believed their properties would be confiscated: Standard Oil of New Jersey, Vacuum Oil Company, and Atlantic Refining Company. On June 30, 1927, the Spanish government published a decree announcing it would take over the entire oil industry. Officials in these American companies tried to get what they considered to be adequate compensation when Spanish authorities began taking over their assets—only to run into serious opposition. They turned to the State Department, which tried to help, but with little effect. By the end of 1927, virtually all American

---

9. *Foreign Commerce and Navigation of the United States, 1925* (Washington, 1926), 1:158.

10. *FRUS 1927*, 3:656.

oil properties in Spain had been seized with little or no compensation. In 1928 they received some payments, but far less than the Americans hoped to gain.

These Americans claimed they were owed $200 million; but since the Spanish monopoly itself was capitalized at only $250 million, it could hardly make such large payments. Furthermore the Spanish refused to provide more funds. Another problem derived from the dictator's reluctance to pay out any more when it became apparent to him that the monopoly was not making as much profit from the oil industry as originally anticipated—a fact the regime tried to keep secret.[11] One American diplomat concluded from the episode that "foreign interests in Spain [were] absolutely at the mercy of the whim of an irresponsible Dictatorship."[12] Throughout the controversy, both governments exchanged notes highly critical of the other's behavior. The fact that the Americans were left unsatisfied made Washington wary about the regime after 1927.

The dictator's detractors blamed him for Spain's problems and demanded that he relinquish power. Opposition to his rule steadily grew, marked by student unrest and loss of clerical, political, and military support. Finally aware that no fundamental basis for his rule existed, Primo de Rivera resigned on January 28, 1930, at the request of King Alfonso. Despite the king's attempt to form new and stable cabinets, he found his efforts useless and finally left Spain in spring 1931; he had suffered the same loss of support experienced by Primo de Rivera and was guilty by association. The municipal elections of April 12, 1931, brought to local power all over Spain critics of the monarchy, leading previous supporters of the government such as the Count of Romanones for the monarchists and General José Sanjurjo for the military, to deny the king their effective support. In short, Alfonso concluded he could either step down from power or pose the threat of increased opposition to the government bordering on civil war; he chose the former. On April 14 the second Spanish republic came into being under the provisional leadership of Alcalá Zamora, head of the Liberal Republican Right party.

---

11. Todd, "United States and Spain," 65–74.
12. *FRUS 1927*, 3:719.

Both Primo de Rivera and the king fell from power because of increased opposition from the political left (regional groups such as the Catalans) caused by the decline in the peseta's value, the impact of the world depression on Spain, the dictator's lack of financial acumen, consequent repercussions of price and wage fluctuations, and unrest among agricultural and industrial workers. On the positive side, Primo de Rivera had extracted Spain from its difficult North African war, reduced the national debt by two-thirds from what it had been in 1923, took his government back into the League of Nations after a brief withdrawal, encouraged foreign commerce, and left Spain diplomatically free from major controversy. His successors under Alfonso were unable to maintain the monarchy in the face of widespread unrest, which threatened to explode into civil war. Along with the king, the monarchist cabinet relinquished power in the spring of 1931.

Because Primo de Rivera's exit from Spanish politics signaled the end of an era in Spain's domestic history, it would help to summarize Spanish-American relations of 1930–31. Americans generally had viewed him as a reformer, at least until 1926 and 1927 when he began losing control over the government. He never posed a threat to the democratic system to the degree that Spanish governments in the 1800s had in either the United States or Latin America. Both nations did well in their commercial exchanges (table 1). Throughout the 1920s, imports from Spain increased until 1930 when the depression curtailed demands on Spanish goods in North America (1924 was the only exception to an otherwise expanding demand for Spanish imports). Exports to Spain always exceeded imports. While the figures fluctuated yearly, commercial traffic to Spain remained about double Spanish exports to the United States, leaving the Iberian nation with an unfavorable balance of trade.

Spaniards bought consumer goods and machinery from the United States, while Americans continued to purchase such traditional items as fruits, cork, and luxury products. Sales of wine to the United States ceased, of course, but were quickly made up for by the exportation of other items. Until 1936 imports and exports generally were less than during the previous decade, reflecting both the worldwide decline in international trade caused by the depression and political

TABLE 1. **Commerce between Spain and the United States**

Year	Imports from Spain	Exports to Spain
	(*in millions of $*)	
1921	26.160	69.197
1922	28.669	70.901
1923	31.461	61.862
1924	28.992	71.163
1925	32.915	79.203
1926	41.369	68.206
1927	34.351	73.776
1928	35.018	86.613
1929	36.059	82.120
1930	25.362	57.507
1931	16.621	33.971
1932	11.406	26.688
1933	13.701	30.757
1934	18.903	38.029
1935	20.021	41.303
1936[a]	18.537	21.540

[a] The start of the Spanish civil war in July 1936 accounted for the sharp decline in exports to Spain that year.
Source: Annual editions of *Foreign Commerce and Navigation of the United States, 1921–1936* (Washington, 1922–1937).

unrest in Spain. These two trends upset normal business transactions, especially in the agricultural sector.

At the start of the 1930s, both governments realized that they faced difficult days ahead. The new Spanish republic hoped to gain speedy recognition from other liberal governments, looking toward Paris, London, and Washington. The United States wanted to determine if the new Spanish government controlled Spain, gave evidence of being able to survive, and would agree to honor the nation's previous national debt. Sympathy for a fellow republican government hardly influenced policy makers in Washington, although the American press welcomed its birth. The ambassador to Spain, Irwin B.

Laughlin, advised the Department of State not to recognize it. The conservative diplomat reflected his hostility toward the new liberal regime and its solution to Spain's political problems when he prophetically noted that "communistic falsities have captivated the seventeenth century-minded Spanish people. All at once they see a promised land which does not exist. Ultimately they will be disillusioned. Then they will grasp at anything within their reach. Should the weak restraints of their newborn regime collapse, they will easily be captured by the wide-spread Bolshevistic influences."[13] Yet on instructions from Washington, the ambassador extended recognition on April 22, 1931.

This new republic's political instability became apparent soon after its creation. American diplomats reported unrest in the country. The revolt of 1934 against the government confirmed what diplomats had been expecting since 1931 and would continue to see until July 1936. The republic hoped to shore up its problems at home with diplomatic events, such as developing publicized intimate relations with the United States and other republics. But the opposite took place. The Spanish republic's tendency to implement anticapitalist legislation not only reduced trade with the United States but threatened businessmen who complained to the State Department and newspaper editors at home. The American ambassador was also critical of the new regime and did little to foster better relations.

Things worsened in many ways. Between 1931 and 1933, Spain raised its protective tariffs to such levels that American exports were cut by half from what they had been in the 1920s. New banking regulations inhibited American financial dealings in Spain. The confiscation of American properties was always a fear, accenting the problems faced by businessmen in Spain. The increasingly left-wing, socialist image of the republic also frightened Americans at home who feared that a communist or anticapitalist system of government would seize power in Spain.

The republic had its criticisms to make of the United States as well. Officials objected to Laughlin's antiliberal position, which some believed discouraged better relations with Washington. They also

---

13. *FRUS 1931*, 2:986.

blamed him for negotiating a $60 million credit note with the monarchy just before it collapsed, yet he would not consider such loans to the new government. What the republic refused to accept was the fact that Laughlin's antipathy toward it had little to do with American banking policies. The republic denied itself access to such funds when it implemented laws restricting the financial activities of foreign bankers and simultaneously subscribing to autarkic tariff policies. After Laughlin was removed from Madrid by President Franklin D. Roosevelt in 1933, his replacement by Claude Bowers, a Jeffersonian liberal sympathetic to the republic, failed to improve relations, a fact indicating that more than just personalities was involved. During the last three years before the civil war, relations publicly appeared more amicable, but in reality they were just as poor as they had been during the previous twenty-four months.

The differences experienced by both governments from 1931 to mid-1936 focused on economic problems. The Americans requested the elimination of tariff discriminations against their products. The republic refused, fearing loss of support from the industrialized sectors of Spain, particularly Catalonia, which was a mainstay of the regime. Throughout these years, however, both governments talked about tariffs, terminating these discussions after the outbreak of the civil war. In an attempt to resolve the issue, they did tentatively agree on a treaty by the fall of 1935, but technical differences over quotas for specific items prevented a final settlement.[14]

Another problem concerned the American telephone company in Spain, which the Spanish considered nationalizing, citing poor service as its major reason. Unquestionably it had faltered, but the Americans hardly considered this legal grounds for confiscation. And although the two nations worked out their differences over the issue before the civil war, one can hardly escape the conclusion that throughout the 1930s, Spanish-American relations were fraught with problems.

The main source of this annoying friction stemmed from the economic philosophy of the new Spanish government, which proved far

---

14. These negotiations, which were of a highly technical nature, are in *FRUS 1931*, 2:955–1007; *FRUS 1932*, 2:527–560; *FRUS 1934*, 691–708; *FRUS 1935*, 2:687–738; and *FRUS 1936*, 2:785–795.

too liberal for the Americans. These ideological positions on economics came in an era (1931-33) when conservative business ideas prevailed in the United States. These conflicting philosophies also posed significant problems in a period when commercial issues dominated Spanish-American relations. And although the republic became more conservative in its philosophy and politics after 1933, its repution in the United States had been fixed.

Relations were not entirely monopolized by economics. The Latin American policies of both sometimes irritated each during the 1920s and 1930s. In this traditional area of conflict, the two competed less intensely than in previous decades. Even when joined with economic and political concerns, relations were less momentous than in earlier years. In fact when compared to previous decades, Latin America played a small role in Spanish-American relations. But this issue remained and could not be ignored. Spaniards continued to express concern for Latin America's peril in the face of the ever-growing North American power, and, as before, liberals and conservatives argued among themselves on the role Spain should play in the New World. Their arguments acquired greater meaning, however, since between 1918 and 1936, each group took turns running the Spanish government. The liberals generally dominated between 1918 and 1923 and again from 1931 to 1933 with more moderate forces in power from 1933 to 1936. The conservatives identified with Primo de Rivera and Alfonso's subsequent cabinets.

After World War I, Spanish liberals softened their hostility toward the United States for a number of reasons. They had favored the Entente, specifically France, the side Washington supported when it entered the war. Liberal observers recognized that the South Americans could hardly avoid extensive contacts with their powerful neighbor to the north. The material prosperity of the United States and the promise of a higher standard of living proved too tempting for Hispanic Americans to resist. Liberals also concluded that the United States did not want to destroy their Hispanic culture and would defend it against outside threats. This had become particularly obvious during Wilson's term as president and while organizing the League of Nations. Moreover they noticed that North American society was far more stable than Europe's. It did not indulge in revolution in 1918-19 like many European states, which suggested that the United States would be a strong and reliable asset for Europe and Latin America.

As early as 1916, a few liberals began recommending that Spain serve as an intermediary between the United States and Latin America in such matters as trade, cultural exchange, and diplomatic endeavors. They saw that Spain could thus shield Hispanic culture from exposure to the more disagreeable elements of the Anglo-Saxon power while satisfying Latin America's desire for economic development. Because they spoke the same language and understood the Latin American culture, Spaniards could perform a valuable service for North Americans who might otherwise fail to make significant progress with their southern neighbors. Such a role guaranteed that Spain would continue influencing the course of events in the New World—something it could not do in opposition to the United States.

Unfortunately for Spanish liberals, their timing was poor. During the 1920s Latin Americans experienced an upsurge of nationalism. They resented Washington's constant interference in their affairs and condemned anyone who suggested cooperating with the North Americans. Thus they were the main opponents of the liberal program outside of Spain. In fact by the late 1920s, many Latin Americans believed Spain had failed them by refusing to protest North American intervention into South America as Madrid had done in the 1800s. Spain, in short, betrayed them to Washington at a time when the United States intervened in their lives more than ever before. They rejected Spanish overtures in the belief that even Spain could not be trusted.[15]

Primo de Rivera's policies toward the New World reflected the conservative Spanish position on Latin America. He advocated using Catholicism as the principle medium for advancing *hispanismo*. The usual arguments about the threat of Protestant North American society reappeared again, along with concern about the corrupting influences of prosperity and materialistic values. With King Alfonso, the dictator launched a program to broaden contacts with Latin

---

15. Frederick B. Pike, *Hispanismo, 1896–1936: Spanish Conservatives and Liberals and Their Relations with Spanish America* (Notre Dame, 1971), 159–160.

America, involving increased trade, sending skilled diplomats to the New World, and exchanging professors. Moreover it meant criticizing the United States with propaganda and forming a Hispanic block in international affairs, an effort that failed. With considerable success, the conservatives were able to discredit the Spanish liberal position. How much of their success was due to their efforts rather than to general Latin American hostility toward Spain is difficult (perhaps impossible) to determine. Yet the key development in the years after 1918 seemed to be the general Latin American criticism of Spain as the betrayer of a common cause.[16]

Spain's attempt to expand its influence into South America during the 1920s and 1930s failed for other reasons as well. The Latins turned to the United States, Great Britain, and other European nations for economic and technological aid, which they believed Spain could never provide. As before World War I, the Spanish lacked adequate economic and scientific resources to satisfy the needs of South America. In cultural matters, the Hispanic Americans kept to themselves, seeking little from Spain and less from the United States.[17] In the important area of economic competition, Spain's trade with Latin America fell to figures far below Washington's volume with the southern hemisphere throughout the 1920s and 1930s.[18] And at the start of the civil war, the United States had South America to itself, never facing any threat from Spanish businesses.

In the 1920s, the Latin American policy of the United States was not directed primarily at blocking Spain's efforts. Spain's views on Latin America were not as important to the United States as were the views of North Americans on the Hispanic world to Spaniards. The North Americans simply conducted a policy geared at expanding their influence southward with little respect for the concerns of

---

16. Miguel Primo de Rivera, *El pensamiento de Primo de Rivera: sus notas, artículos y discursos* (Madrid, 1929), 74; José María Peman, *Valor de hispanoamericanismo en el progreso total humano hacia de unificación la paz* (Madrid, 1927), 30–34.
17. Pike, *Hispanismo*, 236–237.
18. Ibid., 228–229.

the Latin Americans. If some Hispanic nation failed to pay its debts or threatened North American lives and properties either by policy or revolution, Washington sometimes landed troops and seized strategic points. They marched into Santo Domingo several times during the early 1900s. In Nicaragua marines stayed for thirteen years, finally leaving in 1925. Two years later troops temporarily penetrated Mexico. President Herbert Hoover attempted to alter this state of relations between 1928 and 1933 by withdrawing some American soldiers from Latin America and encouraging trade and goodwill.[19]

His successor, Franklin D. Roosevelt, continued to foster better relations by launching his Good Neighbor Policy, which carried the essential ingredients of Hoover's program past 1933. Roosevelt realized that the most irritating action of the United States in Latin America was sending troops southward. Therefore he withdrew all remaining forces from South America (except at the Panama Canal Zone) and preached a policy of nonintervention. A number of factors motivated Roosevelt. He wanted to expand commercial ties with the southern hemisphere in order to ensure the constant flow of raw materials into the United States, which would help provide jobs for North Americans. He believed that with growing problems in Europe, which threatened to explode into another world war, one way to keep the United States out of it would be to prevent such a conflict from involving the New World. The failure of Spain's policy toward Latin America played into Roosevelt's hands and was not a direct product of it.

In the course of events, Spain and the United States discussed Latin American affairs. When, for example, in the early 1920s, Spain tried to form a Hispanic bloc in the League of Nations, the State Department discouraged such a bond. Its disapproval of Spain's effort reflected Washington's concern about keeping the New World separated from Europe. Its rhetoric about nonintervention in Latin America melted away in specific instances such as this one when U.S. interests were endangered. Another issue involved claims.

---

19. Alexander DeConde, *Herbert Hoover's Latin-American Policy* (Stanford, 1951), passim.

Whenever American troops marched into one of the Latin American republics, Spaniards invariably had their properties or rights disturbed, and they wasted little time in lodging protests and claims. Property damage caused the greatest number of difficulties since each government had to determine liability and negotiate the details of a settlement.[20]

No better proof of how quiet relations between them were during these years exists than in their cultural contacts. Literary or cultural views involved large numbers of people swayed by images. These years stood in sharp contrast to those immediately following the Spanish-American conflict and during Spain's civil war. Cultural relations, like economics and politics, were pleasant for the most part. Each displayed increased curiosity about the other's society. Tourism, publications, and literary borrowings indicated that cultural relations in the 1920s were not only extensive but followed the general pattern that existed between Europe and the Americas at the same time.

One way to test a nation's interest in another is by examining its travel literature. Spanish publications on the United States prior to the civil war were virtually nonexistent other than for periodic articles appearing in newspapers. American publications on Spain, however, appeared throughout the early twentieth century. With tourism on the rise in the 1920s, passing the 40,000 mark at one point, it was natural that some guides would be published. Americans came to Spain for the same reasons they always had—to explore a different culture. They continued expressing interest in the Spanish character, history, and culture. Others had heard of the excellent fishing in the Pyrenees or the bullfights in Madrid and Pamplona.

Most of the travel literature described various points of interest in Spain. Consequently a great deal of it was light, often with short essays and photographs on interesting towns, regions, and annual events. They generally lacked any depth of perception, however. There also appeared more serious volumes on Spanish literature, which served as guides for some travelers. There were, for example,

---

20. For examples see Sp/pol/USA/2445, Foreign Office Archives, Madrid, covering the years 1920–24.

the popular minor classics of Georgiana G. King, *The Way of Saint James* (1920) and *Heart of Spain* (1926). In most cases, authors presented a thumbnail sketch of the typical Spaniard or community, using a romantic motif that had about as much relation to the truth as the works of some Spanish writers who portrayed New York City as typically American.[21]

Spanish scholars rarely visited the United States or even wrote about it, but their counterparts in America continued visiting Spain. Historians such as Charles Chapman and Roger Bigelow Merriman were the outstanding examples of a group who joined tourists and businessmen visiting Spain. Their publications went far to encourage other scholars to study Spanish history.[22] This is not to suggest that Spaniards ignored the United States, not writing books or publishing translations of American works. Quite the contrary; monographic studies appeared along with lighter pieces. One of the standard histories of the Monroe Doctrine was written by a Spaniard in the 1920s.[23] Others wrote their recollections of working or visiting in the United States. They generally praised the vitality of American society, commenting on its stability and economic prosperity.[24] Books on its politics and economics betrayed the same respect for North America that Spanish visitors could not disguise.[25]

The most influential area of cultural exchange came in literature.

---

21. Stanley T. Williams, *The Spanish Background of American Literature* (New Haven, 1955), 76–82.

22. Ibid., 168.

23. L. Izaga, *La Doctrina de Monroe: su origen y principales. Faces de su evolución* (Madrid, 1929).

24. Alvaro Seminario, *El cónsul de España en América* (Madrid, 1935); Adolfo Bonilla y San Martín, *Viaje a los Estados Unidos de América y al Oriente* (Madrid, 1925); Eleuterio Abad, *Un viaje a Norteamérica. Sus bellezas y progreso agricola y pecuario* (Madrid, 1929).

25. Federico López Valencia, *Instituciones patronales de previsión en los Estados Unidos* (Madrid, 1918); Juan Leitch, *De hombre á hombre. Historia de la democracía industrial. Solución de los problemas sociales en Norteamérica* (Barcelona, 1920); Charlotte Lutkens, *El estado y la sociedad en Norteamérica* (Madrid, 1931).

The important works of the generation of '98, the majority of whom wrote after 1900, appeared either in Spanish editions released by American publishers or in English translations. They were used in thousands of classes in Spanish literature offered in high schools and universities, and occasionally a leading Spanish writer would visit the United States. Little evidence exists at this writing to suggest that American society influenced the nature of Spanish literature between the two world wars. However, Spanish society definitely affected American literature. One has only to think of John R. Dos Passos and Ernest Hemingway.

Don Passos became interested in Iberia's role in history and was fascinated by the contemporary Spanish peasants' struggles. Examining the friction between Spain's ruling order and agrarian society, he noted the dignity of its participants, their passions and actions. He tried to formulate a composite picture of the typical Spanish peasant of the 1920s, finding rich material for his writing as he watched liberals quarrel with conservatives. Through his works, the books of such modern Spanish authors as Pío Baroja, Machado, and Maragall were introduced to American readers along with his own views on the turmoil in contemporary Spain.[26]

Even better known to Americans was Hemingway, especially during the 1930s when he wrote continuously on the civil war. Some of Hemingway's classics reflected interests similar to Dos Passos's developed during the 1920s. In *The Sun Also Rises* (1926), Hemingway addressed himself to Spain of the 1920s. *For Whom the Bell Tolls* (1940) examined the Spanish character in war (his protagonists were on the Republican side). Hemingway also wrote a nonfiction account of bullfighting, *Death in the Afternoon* (1932), in which he reflected a sensitive appreciation of how the Spanish viewed a sport that most Americans considered brutal. In his novels and newspaper articles, he discussed the political struggles between liberals and conservatives in politics, their moral values, social behavior; like Dos Passos, he favored the forces of Spanish liberalism.[27]

To a lesser extent, Gertrude Stein came under Spain's influence.

---

26. Williams, *Spanish Background*, 1:237–239.
27. Ibid., 239–241.

Between 1913 and 1922, she explored the Iberian peninsula as did other expatriated American writers, painters, and musicians. On each trip she met Spanish intellectuals and painters. Stein called Pablo Picasso a close friend from whom she learned much about Spanish culture. Students of this period believe that the psychological or mental characteristics of the Spanish as she perceived them became imbedded in her own views toward European culture. She rarely described Spanish events or people, selecting instead to reflect their attitudes in her own publications.[28]

In its totality, economic, political, and cultural relations between Spain and the United States from 1918 to July 1936 were generally friendly because neither posed a threat to the other. Economically they failed to compete seriously. Politically they had few issues to debate. Their cultural contacts were extensive—far more so than in any earlier period, which undoubtedly contributed to the unusually amicable relations they experienced. But when the civil war began, old prejudices, conflicts of interest, and ideological battles borne out of different cultural heritages and new political movements in Europe proved how much the interwar period had been an exception to an often rancorous relationship.

---

28. Ibid., 241–244.

11
CIVIL WAR DIPLOMACY

During the spring and summer of 1936, American diplomats and newsmen reported increased unrest in Spain and predicted that violent revolutionary activity would follow. What surprised Americans and Europeans was the extent of the uprising of July 1936, which soon became known as the Spanish civil war. Previous military revolts in Spain had lasted for short periods of time and more often than not had involved only small dissident groups. The breadth, violence, length, and impact on European affairs of this new revolution caught policy makers on both sides of the Atlantic unaware. As the fighting increased, it affected an ever-growing number of governments. For three years the struggle continued, influencing the foreign policies of Britain, France, Soviet Union, Germany, Italy, Austria, all of Latin America, and the United States.

Several factors clearly played important roles in the outbreak of the war. The Spanish republic's policy of curtailing the power of the Catholic church in politics and education cost the government much support in the 1930s. Suppression of anarchists denied the regime approval from the left. The socialists, growing more radical during the 1930s as Spain's economic ills mounted, competed with the anarchists for labor's support. In the process they failed to uphold the republic, forcing it to turn to the right for some backing. Thus dissatisfied socialists launched a widespread revolt in October 1934, which failed. The use of forces drawn from Morocco to suppress them, however, irritated many other Spaniards who criticized the conservatives for supporting the government's actions. Liberal and left-wing factions now compromised, forming a "popular front" government early in 1936. Yet elements on the left still competed among themselves. Closer to the right, the army, disgruntled by republican measures that reduced its power and privileges, plotted, as did fascist groups, and other conservatives that spring. These peregrinations finally led to the outbreak of the military revolt in July led by General Francisco Franco, one of the most popular and highly respected army officers.

The republicans, known as Loyalists, and Franco's faction, labeled Nationalists, early in the fighting called on outside help to ensure their victories. By these actions the Spanish made their civil war an international event from its beginning. Neither side could implement foreign policies toward the United States or any other government as the republic had done prior to 1936 because of the new circumstances in Spain. For each, survival of their cause became an overriding goal.

The civil war attracted considerable attention in diplomatic circles, forcing governments to determine whether to interfere, assess their relationships with other powers, and develop attitudes toward events in Spain. American officials viewed the Spanish conflict as the most important international crisis in the late 1930s in Europe because of the potential impact on foreign relations and as an outgrowth of intense feelings about the fighting. Consequently it affected Washington's entire policy toward Europe. The revolt also raised the issue of what influence domestic politics might have on diplomacy. The American public as a majority wanted to remain aloof from the fighting. To a limited extent, the government succeeded in doing this, but many individuals could not. The Roosevelt administration observed events in Spain from the sidelines as much as possible by following the noninterventionist policies laid down by France and Britain from the earliest days of the war.

Spain, or one might argue both Spains, believed its relations with the United States were less important than Spanish events became for Americans. Each faction, however, could not discount the United States entirely because of the possibility that the Americans might intervene to aid one side. Spaniards realized that no other European event attracted more interest in the United States since World War I, that it colored American attitudes toward Europe, and that it affected domestic politics in the same manner as in European nations. Therefore, from both a Spanish and American perspective, relations between them from 1936 to early 1939 became complicated, significant for both Europe and the New World, and of greater importance to these two nations than at any other time since their war in 1898.

Washington's policy toward Spain followed the general lines established by Paris and London. Europeans quickly turned their attention southward, on July 17, 1936, when General Franco raised the cry of revolt. Leaving aside the philosophical questions concerning the political balance of power in Europe and the virtues of both factions for later contemplation, European authorities faced the immediate problem of how to react to the outbreak, since both the republic and the Nationalists asked for international assistance in suppressing each other within a matter of days. All governments found it difficult to determine the nature of the revolt and its extent. And each wanted to find out how other nations would respond to Spanish events.

The Spanish republic identified itself with the liberal governments of Europe politically and ideologically. France had a popular front regime and Britain a parliamentary system. The United States, a democratic power, was linked to Britain and France. Spanish republican diplomats believed their cause would receive more than mere sympathy from Europe's parliamentary regimes. They turned to France to purchase arms, asking for French support and aid. At first France agreed, but then it blocked all deliveries after learning that Germany and Italy planned to help Franco and that Britain disapproved of French involvement. Mixed feelings within French political circles further accounted for the ambivalent policy of Leon Blum's government. One thing was certain, however: French officials wished to avoid a major confrontation with Hitler and Mussolini in Spain.

The Spanish republic also turned to Britain for support, but London refused to become involved. The British pressured France to disengage itself from the war and, along with other European states, met in August 1936 to announce a collective policy of nonintervention. Most European diplomats wanted to localize the conflict by not aiding either side. To facilitate such a policy, they established the Non-Intervention Committee, headquartered in London. Madrid protested, arguing that the republic was a properly constituted government recognized by all the nations of Europe and therefore legally entitled to purchase arms with which to suppress a domestic revolt. While diplomatically correct, this argument carried little weight with Europe, which feared that the Spanish conflict might evolve into a general European war. This especially became obvious when the Italians and Germans finally decided to assist Franco.

The Nationalists turned away from republican Europe for support. Representing conservative Spanish society as reflected in the political beliefs of the Catholic church, army, large landowners, and neofascist and monarchist parties, Franco looked to Berlin and Rome for assistance. Using the Falange (Spain's fascist party) as a political tool to unite disparate groups into a unified front against the republic, which he labeled left-wing, communist, and contrary to Spanish religious and political traditions, he appealed to the fascist dictatorships as a potential ally in their struggles against liberal European regimes. Both Berlin and Rome saw an opportunity to check the French in Western Europe and the British in the Mediterranean. Limited aid would ensure continued political instability, which Germany, for instance, deemed useful in promoting Nazi interests in Eastern Europe. Hitler reasoned that by prolonging the war in Spain, France and Britain would be sufficiently distracted from Eastern Europe to allow him to break the French system of alliances there, which threatened to block further German expansion. The Italians reasoned similarly, although there is evidence to suggest that Mussolini wanted to terminate the war sooner than Hitler in favor of Franco's forces. Either way, both would be able to exercise their military forces and develop new weapons.

Moscow was the only major European power willing to provide the republic arms, diplomatic support, and advisers. Stalin believed that, by aiding the Spanish, he might draw closer to Britain and France and thereby discourage German expansion into Eastern Europe. Initially Stalin expressed little interest in imposing a communist government on Spain, which would frighten the British and French and thus work against the national interests of the Soviet Union. In short, the Russians decided to work for the evolution of a bourgeois parliamentary republic in Spain. As the war continued, Soviet influence grew within the republican zone, as did that of Germany and Italy in Franco's. This in turn led many Europeans and Americans to view the Spanish struggle as an international battle between the democracies and governments of the left and the fascist or dictatorial systems of the right for dominance in Europe.

Officials on both sides of the Atlantic were hardly imbued with such an ideological view of the crisis in 1936. They believed that the war threatened the political balance of power and the position of their individual countries within it. Already they saw Europe divided between the Entente and the Axis. The position of the Soviet Union remained unclear to both blocks throughout the 1930s since no one knew on which side of the balance of power Moscow aligned itself. Officials in parliamentary Europe generally sought to maintain the uneasy peace established after World War I. The Axis wanted to change all of this to increase their political and economic power within continental Europe. The Americans subscribed to British and French views by supporting their policy toward Spain. Questions of right and wrong, good and evil, as expressed in ideological terms and discussions regarding fascism versus communism failed to arouse officials except when they blended with domestic political issues.

One can best see the interrelationships of domestic and international politics in the United States as it passed through another presidential election year. The viewpoint of Americans and their officials toward diplomacy, communism, fascism, and European affairs in the late 1930s was clearly reflected in their reaction to the Spanish civil war. For this reason, events in Spain and Washington's policy toward them have always attracted the attention of American historians. At the start of the fighting, it did not seem that Americans would be so aroused by the issues at stake. The majority thought the republic was a legally constituted government and Franco a rebel. If they took sides—and few did in the early days of the war—they believed the republic was democratic and more attuned to the traditional liberal position of the United States, which supported popularly established governments.[1] Yet in these early days, the opinions of American citizens proved less important than the reaction and initial policies of their government.

During the summer of 1936, Roosevelt's administration watched

---

1. Allen Guttmann, *The Wound in the Heart: America and the Spanish Civil War* (New York, 1962), 3.

apprehensively as both Italy and Germany displayed growing aggressiveness in Europe, which Britain and France were reluctant to curb. In fact for over a year, events in Europe had disturbed American officials. In March 1935 Hitler announced that Germany would rearm in defiance of the Versailles Treaty. Later in the same year, Mussolini invaded Ethiopia. In March 1936 German troops moved into the Rhineland, meeting no French opposition. In each instance neither Paris nor London moved to block the two dictators from jeopardizing world peace. The American public, aware that Britain and France were not willing to enforce the Versailles settlement and fearful that war might erupt in Europe once again, expressed its collective desire to remain aloof from the problems of the Old World. Congress consequently passed neutrality acts in 1935 and 1936 to prevent American involvement in European politics. These measures prohibited arms from being sold to Italy or any other belligerents and restricted loans and credits to them.

The Spanish civil war broke out in July. During the same month, Ethiopia again appealed for help to the League of Nations, which refused to act decisively against Italy. It thus became clear to Washington that London and Paris would do little to stop the dictators. Moreover Americans noticed a growing friendship between Rome and Berlin as a result of a German-Austrian pact signed that month clarifying Italo-German policies toward Vienna—previously a sore point between them. During this same month, Berlin and Washington were on the verge of a trade war, and Americans watched political unrest in France, which threatened the stability of the Paris government. Throughout July Britain refused to take any diplomatic initiative in Europe. Furthermore, in regard to growing Japanese aggression in Asia, European parliamentarian regimes failed to take measures to protect even their own interests there while Tokyo grew more intimate with Berlin and Rome.

The American government did not want to take any strong position on the Spanish question or interfere in European affairs without the assurance and leadership of British and French cooperation. Since Roosevelt was running for reelection in 1936 and knew the isolationist mood of the electorate, he refused to jeopardize his political fortunes with a diplomatic initiative. At the same time, the British and French encouraged him to remain quiet on Spain; if he did not and then at a future date backed off after involving them, they would be left to face Berlin and Rome alone. Therefore the British urged Roosevelt to adopt what one historian has called an "ostrich-like" policy toward Spain.[2]

Secretary of State Cordell Hull initially reacted to the start of the civil war by urging caution in developing an American position and gathering whatever confusing facts he could on the fighting. Once he determined that Paris and London were going to remain uninvolved and that the American public wanted to follow suit, he suggested that Roosevelt cooperate with the Non-Intervention Committee. Hull also wanted the war kept in Iberia and imposed a moral embargo on any American intervention. He believed that Americans could stay out of it and not sell arms or supplies, thereby containing the danger of international conflict that much more. Hull urged other Americans not to express support for either faction and announced his government's neutrality. Thus the United States easily fell into cooperation with the British and French governments, following a policy they had already established.[3] During the rest of 1936, Washington kept its contacts with the Spanish limited virtually to the protection of American lives and properties in Spain.

The State Department notified its agents in Spain of American policy. Each of the governments in Europe, including the one in Madrid, received statements explaining Washington's neutrality. The Spanish embassy in Washington protested since the American stance meant the republic could not purchase arms and other supplies. Ambassador Luis Felipe Calderon y Martin, and his replacement who took office in October 1936, Fernando de los Rios, both argued that German and Italian intervention threatened the existence not only of the republic but of every other liberal government in Europe. Employing the logic of a domino theory, they reasoned that if such a catastrophe was not avoided early in Spain, it might eventually threaten the United States. However, their arguments had no effect on the American government.

---

2. Richard P. Traina, *American Diplomacy and the Spanish Civil War* (Bloomington, 1968), 13.
3. Ibid., 73–74.

There was no reason to suspect that the Spanish could have persuaded the Americans to change their policy. The public supported the moral embargo with little protest during the first four months of the fighting. Few Americans living in Spain were injured, and little could be done to protect property anyway since neither Spanish faction paid much attention to anyone's claims. Contacts with the Spanish republic declined in 1936, partially because of American policy but also as a result of conditions in Spain. In fact, the military situation proved so fluid that the American embassy had to move from Madrid to Valencia on the Mediterranean coast in the fall in order to maintain its lines of communication with the outside world and to protect American lives.

By January 1937 the American government realized that the civil war would last longer than it had originally estimated. At first Hull and others believed that Berlin, Rome, and Moscow would avoid major involvement but, by the end of the year, they knew the three had committed themselves extensively to the war. Moreover Franco had seized control of southern Spain, and he was laying siege to Madrid, which suggested that the conflict would not be over soon. Some American businessmen had begun defying the moral embargo late in 1936 by requesting export licenses to sell arms to the republic. Hull concluded that legal sanctions would be needed to preserve strict American neutrality.

Not taking into account how further neutrality legislation might restrict the president's power to formulate and implement foreign policy, the government rushed to create new legislation to stop arms shipments from leaving New York early in 1937. Passed on January 8, the Spanish Embargo Act extended the provisions of earlier laws governing neutrality to civil wars. It forbade the sale of munitions to either side, limited loans and credits, and made it illegal for Americans to sail on belligerent ships. Some goods of a nonmilitary nature could be sold to parties representing either Spanish side strictly on a cash-and-carry basis. This meant paying for items purchased in the United States and transporting them to Europe in non-American ships with foreign crews. In order to meet the immediate problem of arms sales to Spain, the government was saddled with more neutrality legislation, making it virtually impossible for Washington to consider deviating from Anglo-French policy, which President Roosevelt originally had supported more out of choice than necessity.

During the first seven months of 1937, the Americans remained clearly noninterventionist. Events strengthened this stance, despite protests from the Spanish republic. The United States refused to have any dealings with Franco, and discussions with the Loyalists simultaneously declined. Between April and October the Nationalists scored a series of military victories, bringing most of the northern portions of Spain under Franco's control, thereby tipping the balance of power to his side. The Americans were now more reluctant to support the republic, yet they hesitated to recognize Franco since a Nationalist victory might encourage Hitler and Mussolini to act elsewhere. Moreover the Russians had expanded their assistance to the republic, which increased the risk of converting the Spanish civil war into a general European conflict. American officials concluded, as the British and the French had, that the fighting was far from over. For Washington, nonintervention was still the best course.

Another event influencing Washington occurred in May when Neville Chamberlain, the growing symbol of appeasement, became prime minister of Britain. Immediately upon taking office, he announced that his government would not intervene in the civil war. The uncertain military situation in Spain encouraged the British prime minister to remain aloof from the conflict, fearing that participation might lead to direct confrontation with Hitler and Mussolini. He also knew that neither Washington nor Paris would challenge his policy. And as long as the situation in Spain remained about the same, Roosevelt saw no need to retract support for London's position. The president's position became more evident as a result of developments in the United States during the early part of 1937.

Laws establishing American neutrality were to expire in May, forcing both Congress and the State Department to consider whether to extend such legislation. For the first time since the start of the civil war, Nationalist and republican sympathizers lobbied vigorously for or against the proposed measure. These pressure groups represented a minority of the American public, but they were loud and articulate. Polls taken at various times during 1937 suggested that the majority of Americans were indifferent to either side. In fact this lack of commitment hardly changed in any substantial fashion until almost the end of the war.[4] Most Americans feared involvement, expressed their revulsion at the horrors generated by this war, and knew little of what was happening in Spain despite the extensive press coverage and partisan accounts. Yet lobbyists gave the appearance of representing many Americans.

Pro-Loyalists wanted to repeal neutrality legislation in order to facilitate the flow of arms and other supplies to the republic and eliminating an excuse for remaining neutral. With support from the Spanish embassy in Washington, sympathizers in the press and on lecture circuits talked of the dangers of another European dictatorship coming to power. They argued that such a new regime would help destroy the liberal powers, especially France and Britain, and eventually the United States. In April 1937 Nationalist forces bombed the republican village of Guernica, killing many citizens. This incident created a large stir among uncommitted Americans who now criticized Franco and the Germans. Antifascist feelings increased in the United States, which pro-republican elements exploited. To a far lesser degree, pro-Nationalists lobbied against repeal of neutrality because they did not want the republic to receive any assistance and knew the United States would never help Franco. A minority in the United States, they propagandized in favor of Franco's cause, calling his side Christian, responsible, and a bulwark against communism. This faction had little influence on public opinion when compared to the pro-republicans but, with its competitor, affected thinking within government circles.

Officials feared that increased concern over the civil war would threaten their nonintervention and force Washington into further involvement in Europe's troubles. To avoid this situation, Roosevelt and Hull decided to continue to support the British and accept other neutrality legislation. It became nearly impossible to consider alternative policies by spring since the precedent had been set, because the military situation remained unclear, and out of concern for the effect on domestic politics. The Neutrality Act of May 1937 easily

---

4. Hadley Cantril and Mildred Strunk, eds., *Public Opinion, 1935–1946* (Princeton, 1951), 807–809.

passed and stayed in force throughout the year with little objection from either the government or the public.[5]

Although the administration openly remained confident of its policy, certain developments during 1937 suggested to Roosevelt that his attitude might have to change. In July Chinese and Japanese troops clashed; by fall fighting in Asia had spread, threatening not only American concerns in the Pacific but peace in Europe since the liberal governments and the regimes of Mussolini and Hitler were taking more than a casual interest in the Pacific. The president concluded that appeasement might not prevent wars or the rise of other dictatorships. He hinted of this in public speeches and private conversations by October. Yet for the time being there was little he could do to change his policies, given the public's attitude and the nature of European diplomacy. Moreover the military situation in Spain during 1937 augured well for the Nationalists and their Italo-German allies. In fact, Franco broke a major Loyalist offensive by January 1938, leaving the republic's position uncertain.

By spring 1938 the republic had increased its demands that the American government jettison its neutrality and help the liberal regime from being overthrown. Pro-republicans stepped up their pressure in a frantic effort to gather supplies for the crippled regime. In April the Spanish embassy protested Roosevelt's policies; in Spain, Foreign Minister Alvarez del Vayo openly criticized American neutrality. The United States refused to budge. Although Roosevelt personally sympathized with the republic, he believed more firmly that the interests of the United States dictated neutrality. Retreating from that policy might encourage further appeasement of the dictators by Britain, thus risking the more important object of maintaining peace in Europe. The Germans and Italians could not be allowed to do as they pleased. Moreover Roosevelt's European policies were still too closely wedded to London's to break so easily.

Throughout 1938 the State Department rejected all suggestions that neutrality be abandoned despite differences of opinion within government circles. Roosevelt continued to study military developments in Spain and political events in Europe. Franco divided the

---

5. U.S., Department of State, *Papers Relating to the Foreign Affairs of the United States, 1937* (Washington, D.C., 1919), 1:98–102.

republican zone in half by June, and in December he launched a major offensive against the Catalan area in northeast Spain, which signaled the start of the final phase of the war. By March 1939 both Catalonia and Madrid were under his control.

Events taking place in Europe at the same time as Spain's civil war clearly influenced perspectives of various governments on developments in the Iberian peninsula. In March 1938 Hitler fused Germany and Austria into one nation. In August 1939 he neutralized Eastern Europe as a threat to him by signing a pact with Moscow that essentially recognized spheres of influence in the area. Earlier, in September 1938, Britain and France had allowed him to occupy the Sudetenland in Czechoslovakia, following the famous Munich conference.

Roosevelt knew by fall that he had to regain fuller control of American foreign policy from Congress in order to meet the growing threat that Germany, Italy, and the Soviet Union posed to Europe and, indirectly, to the United States. He wanted to retire embargo and neutrality legislation. Members of Congress and the public at large also worried about international affairs. Between late 1938 and March 1939, the embargo question became one of the most debated issues in the United States and, along with it, the related position of American policy toward Europe. With news of Franco's victories in February and March 1939, diplomats considered the need to recognize his government. The State Department wished to delay such a move until it could no longer be avoided. Officials also hoped that London and Paris could sway Franco away from Berlin's influence with promises of economic aid to reconstruct his crippled nation. Before such an effort could begin, Franco gained full control of Spain, forcing Washington to recognize him quickly in an attempt to gain some influence with the general.

Throughout the period of the civil war, non-European factors had also influenced Spanish-American relations. As in previous times, Latin America affected both governments. The civil war threatened to destroy Roosevelt's Good Neighbor Policy by alienating some regimes from the United States that wanted to support the republic more actively than Washington did. The Spanish crisis also created divisiveness among the Latin Americans and added the danger of drawing Hispanic America into the vortex of Europe's complicated and dangerous politics. President Roosevelt's policy of insulating the Americas from European problems generally received Latin American approval, yet many neighboring countries also expressed great interest in Spanish events. Roosevelt and Hull found in their desire to preserve friendly relations with all Latin governments further reason for remaining neutral. To have taken sides would have meant alienating at least a few governments.

Costa Rica and Colombia refused to recognize either faction. Mexico, on the other hand, staunchly supported the republic and continued to defy Franco throughout the war and for decades afterward. The Nationalists obtained recognition from El Salvador, Guatemala, and Nicaragua in 1936. Argentina strongly sympathized with Franco and exemplified how the war complicated relations between the Latin Americans and Washington since the Argentines competed with the United States for political influence in the Hispanic world, exploiting the civil war at times for this purpose.

South Americans occasionally suggested a unified policy toward the Spanish civil war. Several proposed that an international conference be held during 1937 to discuss collective hemispheric recognition of Spanish belligerency. Uruguay attempted to organize such a meeting in August 1937, but because of differences of opinion among the Latin American governments on how to deal with the Spanish, it failed. Chile wanted to join with the United States to complain about the Spanish republic's policy on political asylum, but Washington refused to do so. Paraguay sold some arms to the Nationalists in violation of Hull's appeal for hemispheric neutrality. Brazil praised Hitler, Mussolini, and the Nationalist position, and Cuba talked of hemispheric mediation.

Meanwhile both Spanish factions exerted intensive pressure on the Latin Americans for support. The republic used its embassies to issue propaganda and seek diplomatic assistance, and the Nationalists usually relied on either the Falange or other fascist groups to plead their case. Both sides hoped that with Latin American support they might win aid and recognition from either the United States or European governments. But the North Americans generally resisted any hemispheric effort to become involved in the civil war. In the fall of 1938, following the Munich debacle, Roosevelt considered using a Pan-American conference as a means of slowing the successes that fascist powers were enjoying in Europe. Yet after concluding that the Latin Americans were too divided on how to deal with Europe, he rejected the idea. Instead he continued to discourage Latin American involvement in Spain's affairs.[6]

One must also keep in mind the role played by American volunteers fighting predominantly for the republic. This aspect of the war received a great deal of publicity in newspapers, magazines, and newsreels in the 1930s and later from historians and memoir writers. In fact, the amount of effort expended in publicizing their role far outweighed their significance on either the military or diplomatic aspects of the war. Therefore it is essential to place in perspective their historical impact on Spanish-American relations.

Approximately 3,000 Americans bore arms in the Spanish civil war; 900 lost their lives, and an even larger number were wounded. The majority served with the Loyalists and only a handful under Nationalist command. Thus discussions of the volunteers usually refer to those who served the republic. They fought for a multitude of reasons: for democracy, against fascism and dictatorships, for rights of peasants over aristocracy, for glory, and for good over evil. In most cases, a combination of reasons prevailed. The majority of those who fought volunteered between January and fall 1937. After about October a combination of factors accounted for reduced enlistments: stories about the horrors of the fighting, disillusionment with the republican cause resulting from increased communist influence and its anticlericalism, sacrifice of ideals by the Loyalists, and eventually, defeatism generated by Franco's military victories.

The Loyalist's supporters in the United States recruited actively and openly for volunteers—experienced pilots, trained medical personnel, combat soldiers, and supplies. Although republicans recruited in the New World and Europe, they deemed the flow of American volunteers important since these might serve as a vanguard for future aid from Washington. The Abraham Lincoln and Washington brigades hardly proved to be militarily decisive although they served the republic well. By the end of 1938, however, their political and military role in the civil war was negligible. Washington discouraged

---

6. For an excellent summary of Latin America's influence on Spanish-American relations, see Traina, *American Diplomacy*, 144–157.

such enlistments although it helped repatriate them during the latter stages of the war by using funds provided by pro-Loyalists in America.

At no time did these volunteers affect Washington's foreign policy or create major problems with the Spanish republic. But they did irritate American diplomats in Spain and in the United States. They never jeopardized neutrality and hardly affected the attitude of the American or Spanish publics toward each other. Of greater influence were the political issues generated by the war. That the groups supporting the volunteers dispensed large quantities of propaganda in the United States cannot be denied. But this effort in itself hardly affected policy. More important to officials were the opinions held by most Americans on the civil war, views that grew less out of propaganda than from fears about the future and memories of World War I.

A survey of the partisan literature exposed the various opinions current in the United States that received considerable attention by historians. Defenders of both Spanish factions waged their propaganda war in newspapers, journals, books, on lecture circuits and radios, and in churches and universities. They talked to a broad range of people who reacted emotionally and intellectually, crossing religious, political and social classes, and ethnic boundaries. For many Americans the war symbolized all that was at stake in the twentieth century, and it led to emotional and ideological commitments.

The arguments put forth by contending factions can be limited to two sets. Many Americans supporting the republic considered themselves liberal. They generally believed the Spanish republic was democratic and parliamentarian, representing virtues close to their political beliefs. More leftist Americans of socialist or communist persuasions thought the republic was a modern, communistic, or at least socialistic regime, influenced by the political philosophy of nineteenth-century European socialism. Others of various political colorings supported the republic because it was the legal government of Spain, recognized by the United States and other world powers. Its supporters were also united in their disdain for fascism and the conservative political dictatorships typical of post-1918 Germany, Italy, and other European states.[7]

---

7. Guttmann, *Wound in the Heart*, 81–167.

A smaller element in American society supported Franco. Generally conservative, it included members of Catholic organizations and subscribers to Catholic magazines but was not limited solely to Catholic Americans. Supporters of the Nationalist faction argued that Franco was not a fascist and did not subscribe to the ideological beliefs commonly associated with Hitler and Mussolini. They pictured him as a strong ruler, a defender of Christianity against pagan Spaniards, and a supporter of the Catholic church. The religious metaphor constantly appeared in pro-Franco literature in which Christian Spain was often pitted against atheistic Spain. Also common were discussions about red scarces and the growth of communism or satellite regimes subservient to Moscow and, therefore, a threat to democratic and Western traditions.[8]

Relief organizations helped refugees, foreign volunteers, and Spaniards on both sides while dispensing propaganda. The only major relief institution that attempted to remain impartial and help each faction was the International Red Cross. Most groups were partisan. The Medical Bureau of the American Friends of Spanish Democracy and the Friends of the Abraham Lincoln Brigade circumvented restrictions imposed by the State Department in order to help the republican cause. Less effectively, pro-Nationalist elements established similar organizations, such as the American Committee for Spanish Relief. A few Catholics, including some members of the National Catholic Welfare Conference, aided Franco's cause with medical supplies, trained doctors and nurses, money, food, and clothing. Although the assistance offered to Spain by various groups was small, they helped many Americans to formulate opinions about the Spanish civil war. They also used their limited power to pressure Congress either to support neutrality by law or to cancel such legislation. They received much publicity, but they did not have a great influence on Spanish-American relations.

The confusing history of relations between Spain and the United States from 1936 to early 1939 can readily be summarized. During the first year of the war, Washington followed a policy of neutrality. With the passage of the embargo resolution in January 1937, the president could not turn away from the course set in July and August

---

8. Ibid., 29–53.

1936. Options were legally closed, but with Americans predominantly isolationist, it served the government's purposes to maintain neutrality even at the expense of seeing the Spanish republic succumb to Franco. The alternative of charting a policy different from the British and French was not viable. Paris refused to support the republic and thereby break with Britain; London was willing to pressure the French into remaining neutral. Neither wanted the United States to take a different stance since this would jeopardize their position. And Washington refused to take any stance on Spain without British and French support. In 1936 it seemed to most American and Spanish diplomats that the Anglo-French policy of noninvolvement would be adhered to by most Europeans. Washington, in short, refused to act without a combined European effort led by the British and the French.

Foreign policy had always been linked to domestic politics in the United States, as were the international programs of other nations to their internal affairs. The civil war was no exception. This applied clearly in the case of the United States. Widespread publicity, which in turn triggered the actions of various pressure groups and captivated the imagination of many articulate Americans, made it necessary for the administration to take into consideration public opinion and the political influence of lobbyists when formulating policies. The introduction of ideological factors, which led both citizens and some diplomats to view the civil war as a struggle between the forces of democracy and dictatorship, Christianity and paganism, good and evil, further complicated perspectives in both nations. Because of the complex domestic picture in Spain created by the fighting, Spanish public opinion toward the United States probably mattered less to the republic or to Franco than in earlier times when it could be monitored with greater accuracy. Yet even in Spain ideological and emotional concerns confused issues and befuddled authorities.

When writers on the 1930s discuss Spain and the United States, they generally comment more on the role of Americans than of the Spanish in international relations, since more information is available on the participation of the United States and because of a conviction that Washington's diplomatic position was greater than Madrid's. Yet Spain's foreign policy during the war was clearly defined by its diplomats. They constantly sought British, French, and American support yet never received it. Realizing at the start of the conflict that Washington would probably deny them aid, the republicans turned to indirect and more conspiratorial means of obtaining arms, soldiers, supplies, and public support. They waged a propaganda campaign on a massive scale throughout the Americas and in Europe and exerted diplomatic pressure on other governments to acknowledge their legal right to purchase supplies.

Franco carried out the same tactics to win approval for his cause. Yet he expressed greater interest in gaining the support of authoritarian governments, which proved more willing to help and discounted the possibility of being aided by a liberal power. Moreover, with massive support coming from Italy and Germany, he hardly needed to mount as intensive an international campaign as the republic, which received aid only from the Soviet Union.

Taking advantage of historical hindsight and the record of Spanish-American relationships prior to 1936, it became evident during the civil war that their relations appeared quite normal, reflecting the familiar pattern of friction. British and French policies were also important since they influenced both. Moreover neither Spain nor the United States could fully escape the broader problems of European international realities of which they were merely parts. In this short period, issues grew out of Hitler's and Mussolini's increasing threat to the republics of Western Europe and from the Soviet Union's to the east. Perhaps the intensity of ideological factors could be counted as a greater influence than earlier in the 1900s, but even national attitudes had always been a factor in Spanish-American relations.

No better example of how political and ideological issues blended together can be found than Latin America, which had always been important to both nations. Despite the fact that the two Spanish factions competed in Hispanic America, Washington showed its concern over their collective influence in the southern hemisphere. In fact Roosevelt became more irritated over Spanish meddling in Latin America than any other president since Abraham Lincoln. In contrast to earlier decades, diplomats in Washington in the 1930s at least recognized more openly that Latin America influenced their policy toward Spain. The Spanish never ignored their Hispanic cousins, not even in the midst of their all-consuming civil war. As in previous years, they sought to influence Latin American politics at the same time that they asked for their support. The new factor this time was the overriding Spanish need for military, economic, and diplomatic support. Yet Latin Americans continued to pay closer attention to what the United States wanted than to Spain.

For many Spaniards and Americans, the civil war clarified the great issues faced by the Western world, but the late 1930s saw only the start of renewed difficulties between them, problems that would continue unabated in the 1940s. The ideological and political turmoil of the 1930s mixed with the immediate concerns of World War II to make their relations of continued importance to both.

12
MORE WAR, MORE FRICTION

Scholars usually consider the period from September 1939 through May or August 1945 as a unified historical unit applicable to the course of most events of the 1930s and 1940s. Diplomatic historians are especially fond of imposing this periodization on their subjects, and one is hard pressed to find a topic that does not lend itself to such categorization. Relations between Spain and the United States provide one, however, since the principles governing their diplomacy remained virtually unchanged from 1939 to April 1947. The United States viewed Spain after 1945 as an unsolved problem of World War II; Americans saw Franco's regime as the last of the fascist dictatorships yet to be destroyed. Madrid's foreign policy evolved in response to this threat. It was not until 1947 that relations between Spain and the United States reflected the politics of the cold war.

To a large degree, the history of Spanish-American relations from 1939 to 1945 resembled the experience of World War I. In each conflict, the two nations declared their neutrality and later the United States entered the war while Spain did not. Initially the Spanish favored Germany and ended each war with an ostensibly pro-Allied position. In both cases, the United States supported Britain and France before and after its own active involvement. Similarly Spain became an economic battlefield between the two major groups, each competing for Spanish ores and products. Spain also served as a conduit for intelligence and refugees from either side.

There were some differences between World Wars I and II. Obviously the characters involved had changed, the second proved more expensive, and the fighting was worldwide. Spain's civil war restricted Madrid's diplomatic and military flexibility, making it less possible than before to acquire North African territory or resist any invasion of the homeland. Fortunately for the Spanish, no one forced them to defend the motherland with their weak army. Spain's economic prostration during the 1940s also stood in sharp contrast to the prosperity it had enjoyed earlier. During the second war the Spanish could not make as much profit because they had less to sell and were in need of such basic commodities as fuel and grain, not to mention industrial and agricultural machinery. The economic problems Spain faced in the 1940s continued beyond 1945 and past 1947, making it important for the nation to establish normal relations with the United States.

Spain's foreign policy in 1939 evolved in response to conditions existing at the time. For instance, when Germany invaded Poland, many Spaniards criticized Hitler for attacking a Catholic country. They could take such a position since it did not appear at the moment that Hitler would soon dominate Western Europe. When it became more evident in the fall that Britain and France were determined to resist Germany, Franco decided to declare Spain's neutrality. After France fell to the Germans in June 1940, he no longer questioned Hitler's military strength. Although Spain announced its neutrality in September 1939, it became obvious to Franco by June that he would have to favor whichever side happened to be winning the war. In 1940 that was Germany. The Spanish reasoned that with the country badly damaged by civil war and hardly in a military position to participate in a new struggle, it had to remain at peace. Therefore, during the first three and a half years of the war, while German troops remained stationed in southern France, Franco favored the Axis. Yet he would not allow the Germans to violate his neutrality either by involving Spain in the war or by sending troops through the peninsula to North Africa.

Once it appeared to Franco that Hitler could never invade Spain from either Africa or France and that pro-German elements in his regime were weakened, he changed Spanish policy, making it friendlier to the Allies. This conversion became apparent by the start of 1943 and grew increasingly obvious as the months passed. Franco moved cautiously in diplomatic matters, thus often frustrating both the Allies and the Axis. Yet his foreign policy kept Spain out of war and consequently gave it time in which to recover from the civil war.

Many Americans lost sight of this obvious fact after World War II when they criticized Franco for being pro-German. In fact he was pro-Spanish and did not hesitate to irritate either side in order to serve Spain's best interests.

The American public failed to understand fully Franco's position, and some officials in Washington also confused political realities with their own ideological and emotional reactions to Spain, all of which grew out of their experiences with the civil war. Frustrated American diplomats generally knew what Madrid attempted to do, yet they never failed to mistrust the Spanish and always feared that Franco might join Hitler in the war. The British, more aware of what Franco wanted to accomplish with his foreign policy, constantly impressed upon the Americans the need to preserve Spain's neutrality—as biased as it seemed at times to all involved.

London worked carefully with Washington in implementing a foreign policy toward Madrid designed to keep the Germans out of the peninsula. Throughout the war, Britain and the United States competed with the Germans in Spain for the purchase of such items as tungsten by means of economic warfare. The Allies used Spain as a place to gather military intelligence, especially regarding the Mediterranean. Spain's neutrality provided a secure back for Gibraltar's defenses and offered an avenue of escape for refugees and downed pilots moving across military lines.

Britain, the United States, and Germany expressed considerable economic, military, and diplomatic interest in Spain because of its geopolitical position in Europe. Both sides were attracted to Spain, allowing Franco some leverage in conducting his diplomacy. Because of the concern expressed about this neutral country, Spain's international importance remained as high in the 1940s as it had in the 1930s. This applied to its relations with each power involved in the war. In fact, its significance for Washington far outstripped that which it had enjoyed in World War I.

Relations between Spain and the United States, following Franco's last military victory and the start of World War II in September 1939, reflected the impending dangers facing Europe. Both Madrid and Washington anticipated war. To many Americans it seemed obvious that Franco would join the Axis. Officials in Madrid discussed whether to take such a step. In both capitals, diplomats and domestic policy makers assessed relations between the two countries in light of Europe's political situation. Once war came, they favored that side which each considered vital to itself: Spain the Germans, the United States the British.

From September 1939 to June 1940 in Spanish-American relations was a twilight period in which no fundamental issues were raised since each wanted to study the other's international policy. They obviously had problems remaining from the civil war to discuss and used these issues as an excuse not to raise important questions. For example, the Americans negotiated the reestablishment of the National Telephone Company as Spain's system under the ownership of ITT, succeeding in returning it to its pre-1936 status by August 1940. Another group of problems grew out of unsolved claims from the civil war.

By summer 1940, they no longer could avoid facing major issues. German troops occupied France and patrolled along the Pyrenees, forcing Madrid to take a friendlier attitude toward Berlin. The British—and to a large extent the Americans—now worked hard to keep Spain out of the war against the Allies. Despite the fact that the United States was officially neutral, it began acting as if it was at war against the Germans. The Americans considered it vital to their security to support the British. Washington therefore viewed its role in Spain as a brake on any Spanish impulse to hurt Britain's war effort. American officials hoped to use economics to persuade Franco to remain neutral. By controlling the sale of such key items as fuel and grains and dangling before Franco the promise of economic aid to rebuild his nation, Roosevelt believed he could reduce German influence in Madrid.

Despite such hopes, Spain's changed foreign policy became evident to all in September when Rámon Serrano Suñer, a leading member of the Falange and an in-law of Franco, visited Berlin and Rome. His widely publicized trip hardly had become old news when in October Franco appointed him foreign minister, signaling to the Germans Madrid's favoritism toward them. During the same month, Franco met with Hitler at Hendaye on the northern Spanish border where, unknown to the United States at the time, the general turned down the German's request that Spain enter the war. Franco told him that in order to participate he would need vast quantities of fuel and war materiel, which he knew Hitler could not supply. Moreover he wanted French North Africa as reward, which he also believed Hitler was reluctant to surrender, thereby delaying Spain's entry into the war.

Secretary of State Cordell Hull soon heard of the visit between Hitler and Franco but little of their conversations. Fearing the worst, he concluded that Spain would soon enter the war on Hitler's side.[1] He decided not to extend economic aid to Spain since this would be the same as helping the Axis, and he ordered all negotiations for assistance terminated. Spain, in need of wheat, urged the United States to renew talks, assuring the embassy in Madrid of its intention to remain neutral. Hull rejected Spain's request again in December.[2] During the winter, famine occurred in various parts of Spain, especially in the south. Both the Spanish foreign office and American Ambassador Alexander W. Weddell prevailed upon Washington for some supplies of grain, which arrived in February 1941.[3] The concession came less for humanitarian reasons than out of fear that, in desperation, Franco would bargain away his neutrality for German wheat.

The Germans renewed their pressure on Franco to enter the war. He met these efforts with more delaying tactics, again demanding that supplies of fuel, arms, grain, and machinery be made in order to operate the army, which had worn out its weapons. The Germans were unable to satisfy such demands since their resources were needed to maintain Nazi armies in Europe and in the Mediterranean. Franco also revived his request for territorial compensation, even adding Gibraltar to the list. Gibraltar posed a problem for Berlin, which wanted the British naval station for its own use. Aware of the German pressures on Spain, the United States simultaneously warned

---

1. U.S., Department of State, *Papers Relating to the Foreign Affairs of the United States, 1940* (Washington, D.C., 1940), 2:826–827 (hereafter referred to as *FRUS* and year).
2. Ibid., 827–839.
3. Charles R. Halstead, "Diligent Diplomat: Alexander W. Weddell as American Ambassador to Spain, 1939–1942," *The Virginia Magazine of History and Biography* 82 (January 1974): 23.

Franco to remain neutral although officials privately worried that Hitler might invade the Iberian peninsula that spring.

Relations between Washington and Madrid deteriorated sharply during early 1941. The general mistrust for Franco evident in Washington contributed enormously to poor relations with Madrid. The fascist facade, which the Spanish maintained both domestically and in its dealings with other countries (notably Latin American), also created friction. To make things worse, Foreign Minister Serrano Suñer and Ambassador Weddell irritated each other. Their personality clash restricted communications between the two governments, frustrating policy makers in Washington. By April the two men were hardly on speaking terms and at a time when the Spanish increased their praise of Germany's cause and anti-American propaganda. While the Americans wished to reduce tensions, Franco searched for ways to maintain them to ensure good relations with Berlin. Exploiting the Serrano Suñer–Weddell problem, for example, Franco conveniently limited discussions with the United States regarding Spain's neutrality.[4]

Despite these and other difficulties, both nations remained neutral during the summer. In December the Japanese attacked Pearl Harbor, forcing the United States into the conflict. Since the Germans soon declared war on Washington, the Americans were now involved in Europe's struggles, placing increased strain on Spanish-American relations in much the same manner as in the spring of 1917. Yet both wished to settle some of their differences and obtain concessions from each other. In May 1942 they signed a commercial agreement that permitted the flow of American grain to Spain in exchange for Spanish tungsten, fruits, and other items. The British had earlier concluded a similar agreement with Madrid. Moreover the three governments worked out an arrangement for the exchange of dollars and pounds for pesetas with which to conduct preemptive buying of tungsten.

The American commercial agreement was essentially an extension of the British economic program in Spain. Britain already had developed a system of commercial policies designed to reduce German

---

4. Ibid., 26–33.

purchases while slowly making the Spanish economy dependent upon the Allies. By this means, the British hoped to keep Spain neutral and, possibly later, win its support against the Axis. In exchange for Spanish products, the British traded fuel, which Spain needed and could not obtain in sufficient quantities from the Axis. The Americans contributed more supplies of oil and shouldered the responsibility for controlling its flow to Europe. Franco now faced the delicate problem of his economy's being influenced considerably by a combined Allied plan, making it more difficult for him to preserve his freedom of action in foreign policy.

During 1942 the military situation in Europe worried both Washington and Madrid. Germany occupied much of the Atlantic seaboard and those territories westward toward the Soviet Union. Switzerland and Sweden became neutral islands in an otherwise German-dominated Europe. The Nazis also pressed the British in the Middle East and had large numbers of troops in North Africa. The Italians were heavily involved in North Africa and elsewhere in the Mediterranean. The Germans laid siege to Britain itself before the Americans could join the fight. Most important to Spanish-American relations, German troops patrolled the southern French border, worrying Spanish officials about a Nazi invasion of their homeland. During the spring Weddell resigned his post, leaving open the option to both governments to either increase or decrease tensions between them as the military situation dictated. In Washington, relations with Spain were viewed as grave since Hull momentarily expected to hear that Franco had declared war on the Allies.

More optimistic and patient than the Americans, the British persuaded Washington not to give up hope on Franco's neutrality. London invited the Americans to renew efforts at persuading him to remain out of the war by promises of economic aid to rebuild Spain. Such commitments mixed with the Allied policy of buying everything they could that the Germans wished to purchase. This led to heated economic warfare in the Iberian peninsula, spilling over into Portugal, which also attempted to remain out of the fighting.

In June 1942 the United States decided to continue implementing Britain's policy toward Spain. The new American ambassador, Carlton J. H. Hayes, received instructions to withhold fuel to Spain if the Germans purchased too much tungsten and other supplies. The

State Department also wanted him to compete on the open market with Germany for such commodities. Upon his arrival in Madrid, Hayes urged the Spanish to trade less with Berlin while assuring them that the Allies would soon defeat the Axis.[5] The Spanish, however, still feared a German invasion and continued to display open favoritism toward Germany, even to the point of sending a group of volunteers, known as the Blue Division, to serve under Germany on the eastern front. Despite diplomatic complaints and outcries in American newspapers, the Spanish refused to change their policy.

The Spanish had no alternative until the military situation changed in favor of the Allies. To have maintained a strict neutrality would have invited invasion by Germany, which Franco knew he could not resist. Openly declaring for the Allies guaranteed a German-Spanish war—the last thing he wanted. In September, anticipating a major Allied offensive in North Africa and also as a result of domestic political conditions, Franco modified his position slightly: he changed his cabinet and decreased anti-Allied propaganda. He replaced Serrano Suñer, who had become the symbol of Spain's pro-German foreign policy, with Count Francisco Gómez Jordana, known for his admiration of the British. Other pro-German officials, including some members of the Falange, also lost their positions to less controversial individuals. The Americans quickly viewed these changes as an alteration in Spanish foreign policy but did not comment publicly for fear of arousing German anger at Madrid, which the British emphasized would threaten Spain's neutrality.[6]

This adjustment in Spanish policy became more evident when Count Jordana took office. The British and Americans invaded North Africa, leading him and other Spaniards to conclude that the Allies were finally on the offensive with the strong possibility that the military balance of power in the Mediterranean might change. Moreover the Spanish expected the United States to increase its pressure on them to stop selling tungsten to the Germans. The Americans did and also requested that anti-Allied propaganda be curtailed. The Germans reacted to the Allied invasion of North Africa by asking Franco for permission to send reinforcements to General Rommel

---

5. *FRUS 1942*, 2:611–612.
6. Hayes to Hull, September 4, 1942, National Archives, 852.00/10072.

through Spain. Hayes assured the Spanish that the Allies would not invade the peninsula or seize any of Spain's land in North Africa.[7] September thus proved a critical month to the Spanish; on the one hand, they feared what the Allies might do to the Spanish since any invasion of their territory threatened the existence of the regime and on the other, refusal of German passage through Spain brought the risk of Nazi invasion.

Some American officials and articulate politicians and journalists believed Franco would modify his attitude toward the Allies after the start of the new year to take into account British and American victories. Yet many other Americans continued criticizing Franco, forcing the administration to press Spain to reduce its economic ties to Germany. In fact the volume of Spanish business with the Germans steadily increased by millions of dollars throughout 1942 and early 1943. Washington feared Madrid was selling American oil to the Germans because Spain could not account for the consumption of all supplies of fuel; therefore officials advocated curtailing all shipments to the Spanish, arguing that stopping the oil might also make Franco more neutral.[8] In March 1943 the United States reduced fuel shipments to Spain, more out of fear that Germany might be planning an invasion of the Iberian peninsula in order to help its forces in North Africa than in an attempt to make Spain cooperate more fully with the Allies.

While the measure won the administration some support at home, the public was more militant in its demands that Roosevelt take a hard line with Franco. The Spanish protested both the oil curtailment and anti-Franco comments in the American press. They talked about how such measures would hurt the Spanish economy and make it more difficult for Spain to remain neutral. Hayes feared Washington's policy might force Franco to join the Germans and Italians in order to save his economy from total collapse. The British agreed, pressing Hull not to bow before public opinion.

The most heated period of activity in Spanish-American relations

---

7. *FRUS 1942*, 3:306.

8. Fuel did go to the Germans; see Charles W. Burdick, " 'Moro': The Resupply of German Submarines in Spain, 1939–1942," *Central European History* 3 (September 1970): 256–284.

during World War II came between autumn 1943 and May 1944, when the controversy over tungsten raged; perhaps it was the most intensive episode in Allied economic warfare against the Axis in Europe. Spain had been selling thousands of tons of ore and making enormous profits. The heavy tax on tungsten permitted the regime to acquire stocks of foreign currency vital for the purchase of oil and other commodities. These revenues also financed the reconstruction of municipal facilities all over the country. Politically the sale of tungsten on a competitive basis gave the Spanish a means with which to play one side off the other. The Allies could obtain their supplies in the New World, but they wanted to keep European stocks from the Germans. Germany could find the ore only in Portugal and Spain. The other major European deposits were in the Soviet Union, with whom the Germans were at war. Thus by the summer of 1943, Allied-Axis competition for tungsten was costing each more millions of dollars than they cared to spend. Washington decided to use oil as a way of reducing sales to the Germans.

The Americans hinted that if the Germans kept buying large quantities of tungsten, Spain might lose U.S. oil. In October the Spanish again emphasized their determination to remain neutral, inferring that their cooperation with Germany would slacken as a result of Allied military victories. Although London and Washington were encouraged, Roosevelt determined to press his demands further. In October the United States again asked Spain to stop selling the ore to Germany but without offering a quid pro quo.[9] Then in early November, the Americans repeated their request and added pressure by demanding that Madrid remove German agents who were spying on Gibraltar from Tangier.

Throughout these difficult months, Spain maintained its inflexible stand, refusing to bow to the Americans. By January 1944 Spain's reluctance to curtail relations with the Germans seriously disturbed Washington. The Americans knew that the Allied invasion of France at Normandy was only a few months away—just enough time for a large shipment of Spanish tungsten to be converted into German bullets. Spanish production continued to rise as did Berlin's ability

---

9. *FRUS 1943*, 2:643–644.

to pay for it. The Spanish still were wary of German might in France, which could be used against them so they resisted the Americans. In mid-January the United States reduced the Spanish oil allotment. Madrid immediately protested and then ordered strict rationing because any concession to the Americans might cause the Germans to invade Spain or, just as bad, encourage domestic enemies of the regime to plot Franco's overthrow.[10]

To complicate matters during February and March, Britain and the United States argued about how to deal with Spain. Spanish officials, aware of this divided Allied opinion, exploited it as a delaying tactic. Briefly, the issue between the Allies concerned whether Washington was too uncompromising regarding Spanish sales of tungsten. London wanted an embargo but not as badly as the Americans did. Each recognized that Spain believed it had to sell tungsten to the Germans to appease them sufficiently to keep them from invading Iberia. How much Spain could sell Berlin created the differences of opinion. Also neither wanted to do anything to disturb Spanish neutrality on the eve of the Normandy invasion. The Spanish realized that the Allies would insist on some curtailment of sales and that they would soon mount a major offensive against the Axis in Western Europe. Therefore Madrid agreed to a temporary embargo, pending a final solution of the problem.

The embargo did not come about, in large part because Washington's hard line had moved the Spanish. Following the insistence of the British that Roosevelt make some compromise, the embargo became possible. During April a final settlement on the quantity to be sold Germany was reached, and at the end of the month, Washington and Madrid exchanged letters of agreement. Their understanding allowed some sales over the next few months. Oil again flowed to Spain, and Madrid made more pesetas available to the Americans for the purchase of tungsten, which could no longer be sold to the Germans. For both, the settlement was good: the Allies cut supplies to Germany and Spain preserved its neutrality, or at least noninvolvement in the war.

---

10. José María Doussinague, *España tenía razón, 1939–1945* (Madrid, 1949), 301–315.

The subsequent period (May 1944–spring 1945) proved anticlimactic for Washington and Madrid. Tensions declined, although they did not vanish completely. The Allies, now winning the war, roared across France into Germany. Franco grew colder toward Berlin. In short, the major war effort in Spain had ended by late summer 1944. Yet problems remained. After the Allies invaded France, public pressure on Washington, coupled with official displeasure over Franco's regime, led the administration to consider harsher policies toward Spain. Secretary Hull wanted Franco to be completely neutral and then to sever his ties to Germany and Italy. Some even wanted to destroy the general's regime once the war against the Axis ended.

During World War II, considerations other than geo-politics, economics, and military campaigns influenced relations between Spain and the United States. They help to explain further why their diplomacy proved bitter and rancorous. One of these complicating factors was the American public's general hostility toward Franco, whom they viewed as a fascist no different from Hitler or Mussolini. Those who had supported the republic during the Spanish civil war continued to criticize the Nationalists. Many others joined this protest after the United States entered the war, and, in fact, criticism increased with each Allied victory in Europe. Although Roosevelt's policy toward Spain was anything but amicable, some Americans often complained of his friendliness toward Madrid.

A second factor grew out of Latin America's role in the war. As during the Spanish civil war, the United States attempted to keep South America out of the German sphere of influence and, after Washington entered the fighting, to support the Allies. Franco renewed the traditional Spanish policy of drawing closer to Latin America politically and culturally. Franco and especially the Falange wanted to advance Spain's international position by a program they called *hispanidad*. Essentially *hispanismo* with an element of fascist ideology and rhetoric, it was hardly different from earlier manifestations of the same spirit.[11] The Falange propagandized in the Americas

---

11. Bailey W. Diffie, "The Ideology of Hispanidad," *The Hispanic American Historical Review* 23 (August 1943): 457–482.

to develop sympathy for the new regime, help the Germans, and aid in Spain's economic recovery. Washington worried, fearing Nazi encroachments into the New World. Besides expending a great deal of effort monitoring these activities, particularly in Argentina and Cuba, the Americans formally protested to Madrid.[12] Because Franco's Latin American policy reflected that of previous Spanish rulers (it did not jeopardize Washington's plans for the Americas), Spain failed to influence Hispanic Americans who continued paying closer attention to Washington.

By the time the Allies defeated Germany in late spring 1945, both Spain and the United States were reassessing their policies toward each other. Franco hoped to survive by fostering closer relations with the victors while implementing domestic political reforms to give his regime a more democratic appearance. The government defended its wartime policies as necessary to preserve Spain's neutrality. Franco talked about closer ties to the Allies during World War II than either London or Washington would admit. Spain wanted economic assistance, particularly from the United States, in order to improve conditions, which had further declined in the last year of the war. Once again starvation and economic misery haunted the Spanish countryside and with it came the threat of internal revolution. Unfortunately for Franco, the United States took a different position. In April President Roosevelt died and was succeeded by Vice-President Harry S. Truman, a staunch critic of Franco. He refused to help the general and wanted the Spanish to change their form of government. Many Americans believed that with fascist Germany and Italy now crushed, Spain's dictatorship should be destroyed.

In an attempt to appear less dictatorial in an age when dictators were no longer fashionable, Franco issued a constitution on July 16, 1945, containing a Spanish bill of rights. This document outlined a series of rights subject to the government's control, but it gave the appearance of some liberalization. American diplomats saw it for what it was and reported that Franco remained as domineering as ever. A few days later (between July 20 and 25) Franco changed

---

12. Allan Chase, *Falange* (New York, 1943), passim.

his cabinet, replacing falangist ministers with individuals giving the appearance of having broad national support. The new foreign minister, Alberto Martín Artajo, had strong ties to the defunct Christian Democratic party. Franco followed these changes with another in February 1946 when he declared himself a monarchist and hinted that Spain one day might be ruled by a king. Then on March 31, 1947, he announced the restoration of the monarchy—but without a king.

The Spanish Foreign Office mounted a propaganda campaign to convince Europeans and Americans that its policies toward the victors were much more cooperative during World War II than Washington and London would acknowledge. The campaign failed to convert either diplomats or citizens, especially in the United States, and most governments reduced its relations with Spain to a minimum. Only Argentina and Portugal remained friendly with Spain during the first three years following World War II. In October 1945, Argentina loaned Spain money with which to buy badly needed food. Other than this gesture of friendship, Franco faced a battery of critical European and American governments that refused to have amicable relations with him.

The United States, although critical of the Spanish, moved cautiously in 1945. Washington did not want Spain to join the United Nations but beyond that did not know quite what policy to follow. American diplomats consulted with the British and the French since they were not willing to initiate any new policy without their approval and cooperation.[13] The Spanish complained repeatedly in 1945 and early 1946 about anti-Franco publications in the United States. The Spanish embassy, for example, protested on January 5 that the harder Spain worked to liberalize its government, the more the Allies complained.[14] Meanwhile American authorities discussed Franco's removal from office and indicated to Europeans that their government wished to see Franco ousted. Truman undoubtedly encouraged such an attitude, which received wide public support. The French agreed with Truman because of similar public pressure in France to remove Franco. Paris made clear, however,

---

13. *FRUS 1946*, 5:1023.
14. Ibid., 1030.

that it wanted the Allies to act against Spain through the United Nations rather than unilaterally.[15]

On February 6, 1946, the United Nations passed a resolution calling on its members to remove their ambassadors from Madrid and to sever diplomatic relations with Spain. The Americans complied along with the others. The Spanish lashed out in protest, declaring that it would not be destroyed by such actions. The regime also criticized various nations for interfering in Spain's domestic affairs. Other Spanish commentators said the action taken by the United Nations would draw domestic support to Franco since the world's hostility to the regime insulted all Spaniards.[16] On April 6 the United Nations passed another resolution condemning Franco's government. Finally on December 12, it prohibited Madrid from applying for membership to any of its agencies, even those acquired from the defunct League of Nations to which Spain had subscribed. Despite some minor participation in the United Nations' activities by individual Spaniards, the resolution proved useful to Franco in winning support within Spain for his government. Yet his critics viewed the actions of the United Nations as initial steps toward his downfall.

Spain defied the United States and Western Europe in seeking membership in the United Nations and renewed diplomatic contacts with other governments. These two goals were important; they would add luster to Franco's authority and would open avenues of assistance necessary to rebuild the Spanish economy. During this period, numerous publications emerged from Spain defending Franco's policies in World War II. They generally cited Franco's anticommunist record, which was impeccable, considering that he led the Nationalists in their fight against Soviet influence in Spain during the civil war.[17]

---

15. Ibid., 1043-1044, 1062.
16. Ibid., 1045-1046.
17. For example, Pascuel Galindo Romero, *La diplomática de la historia contemporánea* (Madrid, 1945); Ministerio de Asuntos Exteriores, *Tangier under the Protective Action of Spain during the World War: June, 1940-October, 1945* (Madrid, 1946), and Augustín del Río Cisneros, *España, rumbo a la post guerra* (Madrid, 1947).

Such publications, however, had little effect on the foreign policies of any government. The British and American foreign offices reconsidered their Spanish policies in early 1947, though for other reasons. They concluded that their hostility toward Franco did not lead to his removal and in fact may have strengthened his position. Moreover reliance on the ideological and political concerns of World War II as the basis for their Spanish policy when the issues of the cold war already made those of the early 1940s seem ancient history, dictated a reassessment. Fascism, in short, was a dated issue. Both London and Washington discussed alternative policies in response to economic and political issues growing out of the continued instability in southern Europe.

Using Spanish-American trade as an example to indicate the ineffectiveness of Washington's hostility toward Spain shows why the United States needed a new policy. Along with the rest of Western Europe, the United States in 1945 imposed economic sanctions on Spain. Washington hoped this would create a situation in the Iberian nation leading to Franco's overthrow. Spain suffered enormously from such a world policy, but trade with the United States declined only slightly. Imports from Spain during 1945 and 1946 were respectively $57.417 million and $48.327 million, hardly a significant drop. Exports from the United States to Spain for the same years were more illustrative: $40.759 million and $42.272 million.[18]

More important were the effects of Spanish-American relations on the politics of the cold war. Throughout 1945 and 1946, the Russians and their allies in Central Europe (such as Poland) practically led the United Nations in passing various anti-Spanish resolutions. The United States and Britain, desiring political and economic peace in all of Western Europe, found the Soviet policy toward Spain disturbing for two reasons. First, it did not result in the overthrow of Franco's government and replacement with a more democratic one and second, such agitation delayed political and economic stability in southern Europe and the western Mediterranean. In other words, London and Washington realized that Moscow was

---

18. Drawn from the *Foreign Commerce and Navigation of the United States* for 1945 and 1946, passim.

exploiting the Spanish problem to her advantage. Furthermore Madrid talked about becoming a partner against Moscow while Washington was criticizing both the Russians and the Spanish. Because of these contradictory actions, policy makers had to reconsider their relations with Spain.

The first real evidence of the change came on April 7, 1947, when acting Secretary of State Dean Acheson wrote to the British explaining his Spanish views. Acheson's ideas presented in this memorandum contained the germ of a new American policy, which led to more intimate relations with Madrid. He argued that as long as Franco remained in office, Spain posed a threat to the Allies. He saw "that Moscow not only is interested in keeping Franco in power until political and economic distress in Spain reaches the point of revolution" but also used the Spanish case for purposes of propaganda against the West. He reasoned that the Soviet Union's policy placed "the Western powers on the defensive as defenders of fascism and reaction." He also feared the United Nations might soon vote further measures against Spain, which would involve the United States and Britain in domestic Spanish affairs—something both wished to avoid. Acheson suggested that London and Washington encourage dissident Spanish elements in Spain to overthrow Franco and replace him with a more liberal government, which the Russians could hardly criticize. After this had been done, London and Washington would find it easier to aid Spain and thus stabilize the political and economic situation in the Iberian peninsula and in the western Mediterranean. By mid-April the British informed Acheson that they concurred with his reasoning.[19]

By the end of 1947, the United States had gone beyond Acheson's original idea and adopted the British view that Franco could be accepted as ruler of Spain, despite their objections to him. The change came in order to draw Madrid into the web of Western defense. What is important to realize is that previously historians believed the change in policy occurred in 1948 rather than a year earlier. Yet the exigencies of the cold war forced the two nations into closer contact than they had known for over ten years. The

---

19. *FRUS 1947*, 3:1066–1069.

United States was not the only government that had to swallow its pride, change position, and forget the bitterness of recent relations. Madrid had to accept American and European friendship to prevent economic chaos at home and ensure the continuance of Franco's regime. Once again each nation saw the importance of closer ties to the other.

13
DIPLOMACY IN MODERN TIMES

The Pact of Madrid became the basis of diplomacy between Spain and the United States for over a generation. Concluded in 1953, it provided for the establishment of American military bases on Spanish soil in exchange for sizable amounts of economic aid. The agreement did not grow simply out of the needs of the cold war, although that proved to be the main reason from Washington's point of view. Spain saw closer military ties to the United States as the way to gain badly needed economic assistance and support for integration into Europe's affairs. The dramatic effect such an arrangement would have in consolidating Franco's control over Spanish political life made it imperative that he draw closer to the Americans. Washington struggled with the issue of defining Spain's value to the United States, finally leading to the base agreement. The negotiations were long and complicated. The pact significantly increased the presence of the United States in the western Mediterranean and simultaneously augmented U.S. impact on Spanish society. For Spain, it furthered international acceptance of Franco's rule. The pact thus proved to be of great importance to both nations.

The United States took the first steps toward starting negotiations when it changed its opinion about Madrid's role in postwar politics. The decision to establish normal relations came in spurts since authorities never fully agreed on Spanish issues. The first signs of changing opinion came from lower-ranking diplomats and military officers. Members of the State Department had suggested friendlier contacts with Spain in April 1947. At the same time, the Joint Chiefs of Staff, representing the collective opinion of the military hierarchy, agreed, arguing that Spain's geographical position and hostility toward the Soviet Union made its sympathy for the West useful to the security of the Mediterranean sea lanes, which were the "shortest route[s] to the oil and processing facilities of the Middle East."[1]

Along with American diplomats, The JCS believed previous policy had reinforced Franco's authority in Spain. These Americans rejected the notion that Washington should not deal with the general because of his earlier ties to Hitler and Mussolini (a charge, one might add, that could be leveled against other countries with which the United States maintained diplomatic relations). In short, members of the Department of State and the military services urged the president to throw out the ideological and emotional leftovers from World War II in his Spanish policy. They recommended that economic sanctions be dropped in order to encourage stability in Spain, which they deemed useful to the security of the West. This could be done quietly in phases without any public announcement. Moreover the United States should block any proposal in the United Nations directed against Spain.[2]

During the ensuing months, these views gained currency within the government. Even those who had been publicly hostile to Franco, such as Dean Acheson, converted to the new thinking. The greatest opponent continued to be Truman, even though he felt enormous pressures from diplomatic and military advisers to change his policy. Privately he hardly bent them; publicly he did because the United States shifted its position. In December the embassy in Madrid was notified that the State Department now considered it U.S. policy to establish normal "relations, both political and economic." Although Washington still wanted Spaniards to modify their government (probably to make changes in American policy toward Spain more palatable to the public at home), the United States would not turn its back on the current regime. The department also announced that economic sanctions were being relaxed.[3]

The Spanish realized that new winds were blowing in the halls of

---

1. U.S., Department of State, *Papers Relating to the Foreign Affairs of the United States, 1947* (Washington, D.C., 1947), 1:742.
2. Ibid., 3:1092–1095.
3. Ibid., 1096–1097.

the American government and determined to encourage this trend. Franco took advantage of rumors to enhance his own international position by publicly speculating on improved Spanish-American relations, giving currency to the stories circulating about Truman's new policy. In July 1947 Franco told an American reporter that the United States might convince him to lease territory for bases with which to defend Western Europe against Soviet aggression.[4] Throughout 1947 and 1948, Franco hinted that Spain wanted a bilateral agreement parallel to the Marshall Plan, and other Spanish officials talked more often about their willingness to resist the growth of communism.

The Spanish were busy in other ways as well. The American embassy occasionally asked for clarification of Spain's position on Western European defense, bases, economics, and Mediterranean politics, which the Spanish responded to often. Spain, in fact, mounted a diplomatic offensive in 1948 designed to break down American resistance to closer economic and political ties. The moment seemed ripe for such a campaign since the Americans were in the midst of another presidential election. Madrid dispatched José Felix de Lequerica, one of its most skilled diplomats, to Washington as inspector of ministries to launch the assault. He wasted no time in organizing a Spanish lobby in Congress, making this a strong force by adding other members of the government and some newspaper editors. He could also count on the support of various Catholic groups, anticommunists, naval officers interested in bases, Truman's critics, and business people (such as cotton merchants). The first test for his lobby came in March when the Economic Cooperation Act to place the Marshall Plan into operation came up for a vote in Congress. Pro-Spanish members added a rider to include Spain. Although the bill was killed in committee conference, the initial vote for the Spanish clause was in ratio of three to one, indicating Lequerica had been busy.

The trend toward a closer bond continued in the following year, but in different form. In January 1949 Franco devalued the peseta

---

4. Arthur P. Whitaker, *Spain and the Defense of the West* (New York, 1961), 36.

in order to encourage American tourism and trade with Europe and the United States. In February the Chase National Bank announced a loan to Spain of $25 million. Truman refused Spain federal dollars or credits, despite pressure from within his own administration. To protect Spain's economy primarily in the face of continued resistance from Truman, Franco ordered another devaluation of the peseta in October. Without foreign aid from Washington, the Spanish had to curtail their foreign purchases—hence the new devaluation.

At the same time, Madrid launched a program to become further integrated into European affairs as another means of improving relations with Washington. It should be noted, however, that friendlier contacts with the United States did not solely motivate Spain's activities in Europe. In fact, Spanish officials viewed revived relations with Washington as a prerequisite to closer associations with the rest of Europe. The results of Madrid's campaign were mixed. In April 1949, Portugal recommended that Spain be admitted into NATO, using much the same logic employed by American military strategists. NATO's members rejected this proposal on the ground that Franco's regime violated the principles of representative government as defined in the charter of the alliance, but Lisbon's gesture signaled some change in Europe's opinion. Other events further confirmed the new tide. In May the United Nations voted to allow its members to send ambassadors to Madrid. During the discussion of this measure, most of the Latin American representatives supported Spain. Already France had opened its border to Spain for commercial purposes and talked of returning an ambassador to Madrid.

Despite these qualified Spanish successes, Truman and Secretary of State Dean Acheson still criticized Franco. Acheson, traditionally labeled anti-Franco for many of the same reasons as Truman was, however, played an important role in changing American policy as early as April 1947, thus discrediting any charge that he did not want improved relations with Spain. The reason for his hostile public stance probably grew out of the official position of the administration as defined by Truman and from his personal dislike of Franco. He repeatedly stressed that Franco's regime retained fascist qualities yet refused to support any anti-Spanish measures in the United Nations. The same could be said about Truman, despite his well-known antipathy for Franco. The double attitude of the American government became more obvious during the summer when a wave of anticommunism in the United States made Spain more attractive to officials and the public in general. This change was reflected in policy when, in September, Truman allowed Admiral Richard L. Conolly to talk with Franco.

American officials took the initiative away from Spain in working toward more intimate bonds during the following year. Truman, probably more concerned with the moral questions posed by the regime's political characteristics than with diplomatic and military realities, remained hostile toward Madrid yet he allowed closer Spanish-American relations than in the past. A major reason for increased American interest in Spain came from the outbreak of the Korean War in June 1950, an event accenting the threat that communism posed all over the world. With the United States now more involved in Asian problems, Washington feared increased Soviet activity in Europe. Thus Franco's anticommunist stance interested Americans more than ever before. Congress voted Madrid a loan in August by a substantial majority. Truman signed the bill on September 6 because it provided appropriations for other projects he wanted. Yet he warned that the Spanish funds would be denied Franco until they served the best interests of the American people. In short, no money would flow to Spain without a quid pro quo.⁵

Part of Truman's reluctance to deal with Madrid grew out of objections to Franco's rule raised by members of NATO who still refused to include Spain in their alliance.⁶ Although particularly irksome to the United States during the Korean War, there was little the Americans could do to change this situation. The European factor, along with domestic considerations and opinion within the administration, encouraged Truman's coolness toward Madrid. Yet Congress and the State Department still urged closer ties to Spain. Truman relented slowly to the rapprochement, and by fall it was in full swing. In the September session of the United Nations, the Americans introduced a resolution allowing Spain to join some

---

5. Quoted in Theodore J. Lowi, *Bases in Spain* (Indianapolis, 1963), 14.
6. Whitaker, *Spain and the Defense of the West*, 36–37.

agencies of the world organization. Washington also supported the return of ambassadors to Madrid. Spain now entered a new period of international acceptance because of Washington's tacit support. By the end of the year, various other governments were sending ambassadors back to Spain.

Spanish policy changed as a result of these developments. It appeared obvious to Europeans, especially Spaniards, that the United States sought more intimate relations with Madrid. Franco therefore switched his tactics. Up to 1951 he had initiated most of the efforts to establish normal relations with Washington. Now he maintained his reserve for two reasons. First, he wished to place himself in a good bargaining position. Franco wanted to ask for large sums of foreign aid, military guarantees, and greater participation in international affairs as the price for bases. Thus, to gain as much as possible it made sense to modify his earlier tactics.

A second consideration grew out of domestic conditions. There existed within his government and in nonofficial circles widespread opposition to a base agreement. Some nationalists objected to the idea of foreign troops being stationed in Spain. The last time that happened (1823), France had practically overrun the country. The proposal thus wounded national dignity and seemed to pose a potential threat to Spain's territorial integrity. Others believed such an arrangement would destroy Spain's neutrality in world affairs, a stance that had kept it out of World War II and might prevent involvement in another war. Staunch Catholics, led by the outspoken Cardinal Segura of Seville, feared Spaniards would be contaminated by Protestantism and corrupted by American dollars—shades of the conflict between the Anglo-Saxons and the Hispanic race of the nineteenth century. Franco could not afford to alienate a large block of his supporters by giving the impression that he had sought the agreement. He therefore wanted the Americans to come to him. Moreover, this tactic would give him considerable leverage in delaying ratification of such a treaty until his government had won domestic support for rapprochement by means of persuasion and propaganda. Along with the usual delays inherent in any complex diplomatic negotiations, these domestic considerations explained why the talks dragged on for two years before reaching a settlement.

This is not to say that Franco discouraged Washington; he simply wanted progress to come at a regulated speed. He hinted of his interest in a treaty on numerous occasions. In January and again twice in August, Franco told American reporters that Spain welcomed the opportunity to defend Western Europe from Moscow.[7] At the same time he fostered renewed commercial relations with Britain and the United States—traditionally two of Spain's largest customers. Imports from the United States, which had averaged about $39.464 million between 1946 and 1950, nearly tripled in the next five years. Exports from Spain almost doubled from an average of $36.918 million to $61.843 million.[8]

The United States also wished to move slowly toward a bilateral treaty for many of the same reasons as Spain. Truman did not want to give the impression that Franco had wrung a great deal out of him for bases. He needed to prepare public opinion and NATO to accept an American presence in Spain, which virtually guaranteed Franco would remain in power. The United States also faced the complex problem of determining what offer to make for the bases since the administration wanted to tie foreign aid and rental fees to a system that would ensure economic stability in Spain. Without such peace, the bases would become a liability and serve no purpose in defending the Mediterranean.

On March 1 Ambassador Stanton Griffis presented his credentials to the Spanish government. Earlier, on January 17, 1951, Lequerica had begun functioning as Spain's envoy to Washington. Negotiating teams for both started preliminary talks on a bilateral agreement in July. Meanwhile American diplomats in Spain took up the massive task of assessing Spain's economy, military power, and strategic importance to the United States in order to make a series of proposals to Madrid consistent with American interests. Also the costs had to be determined before Congress would appropriate funds. Franco initiated similar studies so that he too might know what to ask of Washington.

The complicated negotiations, which led to the signing of the Pact

---

7. Francisco Franco, *Discursos y mensajes del Jefe del Estado, 1951–1954* (Madrid, 1955), 21–24, 86–95.

8. U.S., Bureau of the Census, *Foreign Commerce and Navigation of the United States, 1946–1963* (Washington, D.C., 1965), passim.

of Madrid on September 26, 1953, were marked by skillful bargaining. The delay in concluding the talks could be attributed to each government's efforts: Truman hesitated for a long time to aid a regime he disliked; Franco proved equally determined to obtain what he wanted. In fact Franco delayed the final settlement even in the face of rapidly deteriorating economic conditions in Spain, gambling that Washington would grant him the bulk of his demands. After the inauguration of Dwight D. Eisenhower as president in January 1953, negotiations rapidly drew to a close.

The final arrangement was really a series of three executive agreements, which have served as the bases of Spanish-American diplomacy for the last several decades. One concerned defense, another involved aid for mutual defense, and a third stipulated economic provisions. The combined package stated both countries would use the bases for the defense of Western Europe. The United States would construct them. Spanish officers would command each installation. Washington agreed to pay an initial sum of $226 million for the bases. The defense pact stated that they would remain under Spanish sovereignty, although both nations had to agree on their use in war, a clause that allowed Franco some leverage in influencing American military policy in the Mediterranean. Franco considered this crucial in order not to jeopardize Spanish policies toward Europe and the Middle East should they conflict with Washington's. As it turned out, the two governments occasionally disagreed on Arab policies in the 1960s and early 1970s.

The initial agreement would be in force for ten years and be renewed automatically twice for periods of five years each unless altered by prescribed means. It called for American protection of Spanish air space while Spain promised to participate in the defense of Europe. In effect, the United States linked Spain to NATO and itself, virtually duplicating Bismarck's effort of involving Madrid in Europe's system of alliances in the 1880s. London and Paris found this arrangement more palatable since now neither had to face public criticisms and each gained a new ally at no cost.[9]

---

9. Whitaker, *Spain and the Defense of the West*, 44–49; for the text of the Pact of Madrid, see J. Lee Shneidman, ed., *Spain and Franco, 1949–1959* (New York, 1973), 102–103.

Following these understandings came the construction of the bases over the next few years. The United States built air force facilities at Torrejon (near Madrid), Zaragoza, and Moró de la Frontera. A large naval base at Rota emerged as a submarine supply and repair center. The air force established storage facilities at Seville and the navy at El Ferrol de Caudillo, Franco's home town. Seven radar sites and twenty other smaller installations appeared over the years.

Spain gained the most from these agreements. The leading defender of the West had accepted Franco's government as a member of the alliance directed against the Soviet Union. Over the objections of many Europeans, the United States brought Spain into closer contact with them. The confidence that Washington placed in Franco's regime indicated to many Spaniards that their country would enter a period of political stability and economic prosperity guaranteed by the United States. Many who had been apprehensive of the future reconciled themselves to Franco's rule. Support also came from the business community and those advocating closer ties to Europe. The added prestige enabled Franco to govern with a greater sense of security. Spanish officials also knew they would receive the necessary assistance to revitalize their nation's economy. In a press conference held in November 1953, Franco commented that the pact meant a rapid "economic mobilization" in Spain.[10] Coupled with his concordat with the Vatican (concluded in August stabilizing relations with the Catholic church), it had been a good year for him.

The Pact of Madrid also served the interests of the United States. It ensured the political and economic stability of the western Mediterranean, which Washington deemed vital to the security of noncommunist Europe. The Americans had their bases at a relatively cheap price since the number of dollars to be poured into Spain fell far short of what was being spent in other parts of Europe. Washington strengthened NATO by extending its effectiveness to the southernmost tip of Western Europe. Its policy of containing communism behind its existing borders thus progressed in 1953.

---

10. Franco, *Discursos y mensajes*, 421.

Relations during the rest of the 1950s centered around the implementation of the base agreement. The main effort, besides the actual construction of the bases, was economic. Washington urged Madrid to stabilize its currency, cut government spending, and free the economy from a jungle of regulations. The Americans encouraged Franco to develop economic competition and discourage monopolistic practices. During 1954 and 1955, Americans also urged Spain to welcome substantial foreign investments in Spanish enterprises. Franco recognized the basic outlines of his economic problems and made no effort to hide the fact that he needed American assistance.[11] Indeed he could hardly avoid the issue throughout the 1950s and early 1960s because American aid was massive—nearly $1 billion in nonmilitary funds and approximately another $400 million in military appropriations from official and private sources. These figures did not even include the expenses of constructing the bases, which also ran into the millions of dollars. All of these funds prevented a large unfavorable balance of payments for Spain, which proved serious during the 1950s.[12]

Simultaneously on the steps of increased economic pump priming and rearmament of Spain's military forces came further Spanish integration into world affairs. The main development occurred when the United Nations accepted Spain as a member. Until December 1955 the Soviet Union had vetoed Spain's membership along with the applications of other noncommunist governments. At the same time, Washington and its allies had refused to allow any more communist nations to join. In 1955 the United States announced it would support Spain's application. Moscow and Washington had struck a bargain earlier that fall whereby a group of countries friendly to each would be admitted. By this means, Spain became a member of the United Nations.

During the same decade, Spain and the United States faced various international problems. One was the Suez crisis in the fall of 1956, when Washington pressured Madrid into backing the American position. That meant Franco had to curtail his support of Egypt against

---

11. Ibid., 29.
12. Richard Herr, *Spain* (Englewood Cliffs, 1971), 244.

France, Britain, and Israel. Since Franco had been developing close ties to the Arabs, his actions in 1956 suggested the value he placed on continued American friendship. NATO and Europe provided yet another example. Consistently throughout the 1950s, the United States tried to persuade other European governments to accept Spain as a full partner. Although U.S. attempts failed, Madrid won membership in various international economic and cultural organizations.

The one issue that continuously attracted the greatest amount of attention from the two governments was Spain's economic ills, which by 1957 were causing increased friction between them. Briefly Spain's trade deficit grew from an annual average during the early 1950s of $100 million to about $400 million during the second half of the decade. This was caused primarily by Spain's need to import supplies and machinery. During the mid-1950s, inflation increased rapidly, and it led the regime to near bankruptcy by early 1957. The general economic crisis caused Spain to ask for increased economic assistance from the United States. Obviously the situation threatened to upset Washington's power in the Mediterranean. The Americans also faced the unpleasant possibility of having to spend more money in Spain than originally planned.

Even before the spring of 1957, when American officials worried continuously about the collapse of Spain's fiscal policies, danger signs had appeared. The year before, Foreign Minister Alberto Martín Artajo had called on Washington to resupply the Spanish army and increase its economic assistance. In a speech delivered at Fordham University in New York on April 16, he also encouraged American capital investments in Spanish industry. Washington preferred the latter suggestion since the administration did not want to increase economic aid to Spain. Some officials believed the bases were not as necessary as before anyway. In a press interview on August 7, 1957, Franco countered such reasoning with a catalog of arguments for them and expanded American involvement in his economy.[13] The Spanish asked Washington for more loans during 1957 and 1958 in excess of $400 million. The United States hoped

---

13. Franco, *Discursos y mensajes del Jefe de Estado, 1955-1959* (Madrid, 1960), 349.

to avoid granting the aid by bringing Spain into NATO. Washington reasoned that if the Spanish were more closely involved in Europe's affairs, this would offset the need for additional American aid. Yet this effort failed, forcing the Americans to extend more assistance to Spain.[14]

Inflation continued to increase steadily in Spain during 1959. The Spanish clearly lacked plans for economic development as well. Their deficit in international trade grew and the regime's expenses still exceeded tax income. The United States therefore insisted on major economic reforms before more foreign aid could be granted. The regime hardly needed American pressures to recognize that its economic policy, much of it the by-product of outmoded syndicalist and neofascist theories, had failed to revitalize the economy. Along with the International Monetary Fund, the United States recommended that Spain dismantle state regulations that restricted trade and capital investments, devalue the peseta, curtail government spending, encourage industrial growth, and attract foreign capital. The two further urged Franco to orient Spain's economy toward greater integration with Europe's and away from its autarkic basis. These proposals squared essentially with the recommendations of the Spanish government's own economists. Therefore when Spain adopted its stabilization plan of 1959, it included many of the suggestions put forth by the IMF and Washington.

The effects of this and subsequent economic plans were spectacular. General industrial production during the period 1959–63 jumped by 42 percent and food supplies increased by a third, giving Spain the highest rate of industrial growth of any European country, although agricultural problems still persisted, as they had for hundreds of years. Various other nations contributed to Spain's rapid economic growth in the early 1960s. Washington, for instance, encouraged American banks to loan Spain millions of dollars and the government extended credits. The Export-Import Bank in 1960 alone contributed $30 million toward the implementation of the stabilization plan. At the turn of the decade, American foreign aid totaled $543.3 million since the initiation of massive assistance. By 1967 Americans had contributed another $500 million to Spain's economy from govern-

---

14. Shneidman, *Spain and Franco*, 193–197.

ment sources. Private investments in Spain at the end of the 1960s ran into the hundreds of millions of dollars, standing in sharp contrast, for example, to the $68 million that had gone into the Spanish economy in 1958.[15]

Formal political and economic relations between the two governments proved equally impressive. On December 21, 1959, President Eisenhower stopped over in Spain while visiting Europe to talk with Franco. The significance of this visit could hardly be lost on the Europeans. It reaffirmed Washington's commitment to support Spain and maintain it as a member of NATO's defense system. Undoubtedly for Franco, the event went far to soothe any ruffled feathers caused by Washington's insistence on Spain's rapid and dramatic economic reforms while increasing his standing in Europe and at home. Following the president's visit, political and economic relations improved, matching the intimacy of the 1920s. During the Vietnam War Spain officially maintained a quiet profile but unofficially supported Washington since the conflict involved the defeat of communism in Asia and a battle between European culture and what it considered a more barbaric Oriental society. Madrid joined other European governments in privately urging Washington to disengage from the protracted war because it diverted American resources and interests away from Europe, thereby weakening NATO and the defense of the West.

During the 1960s their cordiality could also be seen in trade, which grew from an annual average of several hundred million dollars in the early 1960s to over $2.5 billion in the early 1970s.[16] In large part increased commerce could be accounted for by the continued economic expansion of production and sales in both countries. Despite inflation in the two, commercial ties remained firm. The base agreements were renewed in 1963 and again in 1969. Each time American assistance to Spain and rent for the bases went up. By 1969, total aid to Spain since 1946 amounted to $1,342 million in loans and credits: $383 million of these were surplus

---

15. Herr, *Spain*, 23.
16. For figures through 1967, see U.S., Bureau of the Census, *Foreign Commerce and Navigation of the United States, 1946–1963, 1964, 1965* (Washington, D.C., 1965–1968), passim.

agricultural products, $319 million in loans came from the Export-Import Bank, and military assistance amounted to $640 million.[17] Throughout the 1960s, a series of treaties, conventions, and notes broadened Spanish-American relations. They concerned the exchange of technical data, the bases, economics, cultural affairs, space programs, atomic energy, and extradition.[18]

During the same decade, tourism became an important factor in their relations. The number of Spaniards who visited the United States on business or for pleasure remained small, Americans visited Spain by the millions, reflecting the same pattern of increased tourist traffic as to other countries. Tourism became big business for the Spanish. Aside from the obvious increase in prosperity in the United States which made possible travel to Spain, other factors of a domestic Spanish nature were also responsible for this growth.

Following the devaluation of the peseta at the start of the decade which came on the heels of European and American prosperity, tourism grew. Americans found Spain inexpensive when compared to Germany, France, or the Scandinavian countries. In 1958, for instance, only 3.5 million tourists from all over the world went to Spain. In 1962 this figure rose to 8.6 and to 14.1 in 1964. At the end of the 1960s, tourists practically outnumbered Spain's population by doubling 1964's figure. The money these people brought into Spain went far toward eliminating the Spanish trade deficit of the 1950s and reinforced the peseta's strength. By 1965, for example, tourism attracted over $1 billion to Spain from all sources.[19] In 1959 Spain earned $296.7 million. By the end of 1968, the annual sum had risen to $1,178.9 million. Tourism brought even more money into Spain during the early 1970s.[20]

The number of American tourists grew steadily throughout the

---

17. U.S., Department of State, *Background Notes: Spain* (Washington, D.C., April 1969), 4.

18. For a list of these, see Carlos M. Fernandez-Shaw, *Presencia española en los Estados Unidos* (Madrid, 1972), 672–673.

19. Charles W. Anderson, *The Political Economy of Modern Spain* (Madison, 1970), 219.

20. Manuel Roman, *The Limits of Economic Growth in Spain* (New York, 1971), 41.

1960s. By 1967 over 600,000 Americans visited Spain. In 1968, 700,000 arrived and in 1971, 1.3 million.[21] Such a massive influx of Americans into a popular tourist area fostered closer ties between the two societies. The large tourist trade also indicated continued confidence in the political stability of Spain and acceptance of Franco by Europeans and Americans. Still all was not well in Spain. Basque terrorist activities, the assassination of President Luis Carrero Blanco in December 1973, unrest among labor, and open friction between the regime and the Catholic church were serious signs of future disturbances in Spain. Coupled with rapid inflation in both Spain and the United States, they suggested that the delicate tourist industry might be crippled in the 1970s with a simultaneous drop in the number of Americans visiting Iberia. These factors bothered officials in the Ministry of Tourism and Information in Madrid (while delighting some economists in Washington who wished to see fewer dollars leave the country). In the 1970s, Americans experienced serious deficits in their balance of trade. Thus curtailing tourist travel to Europe appeared as one way to reduce this problem.

The economic spinoffs of American tourism presented other complications for both nations. Americans spent more dollars per capita than French, British, or German tourists. They therefore encouraged tourism to become Spain's fastest-growing industry during the 1960s. Hotels, restaurants, shops, and entire international communities (particularly along the Costa Brava and Costa del Sol) dotted the peninsula, making it seem less Spanish and more American and West European at times. By the end of the 1960s one could purchase in Spain American beer, fried chicken, and hamburgers, ride in automobiles designed by Detroit, eat in restaurants with such names as the California and Reno, which catered to Americans and affluent Spaniards, watch movies made in Hollywood, and listen to country western music. The Americanization of certain aspects of Spanish business coupled with the large influx of dollars contributed to Spain's inflation in the early 1970s.

Ironically American tourism facilitated Spain's integration into European affairs quicker and more efficiently than all of Washington's

---

21. Fernandez-Shaw, *Presencia española en los Estados Unidos*, 22.

efforts. Inflation raised the cost of living to where it equaled or surpassed that of Western Europe—an economic prerequisite for membership in the Common Market. The influx of 200 million tourists into Spain between the early 1960s and the mid-1970s meant exposure to European attitudes toward politics, economics, culture, education, and morals. Although difficult to measure precisely, Spaniards have been more Europeanized in the mold of France, Britain, and West Germany. The increase in the standard of living, particularly in such urban centers as Madrid and Barcelona, led to a rapid expansion of a conventional middle class identified by automobiles, apartments, television sets, refrigerators, mortgages, and credit cards. This in turn contributed to some stability in the country although the question remains for how long this segment can continue to ensure solid economic growth and political peace. Yet the influence of American tourists and an expanding middle class in Spain resulted in those developments, which Washington set as goals for its policies in the 1950s but which failed to come about until the 1960s.

By the mid-1970s, American and European influences on Spain had grown to such an extent that some Spaniards began suggesting curtailing the number of tourists coming into their country. They wanted the standard of tourism raised, thereby encouraging only affluent visitors. Some argued that quality rather than quantity would save Spain from overcrowding, pollution, and a loss of national identity. The problem of numbers worried even the Ministry of Tourism and Information. In 1973, Spain had a population of just over thirty-five million people. In the same year, more than thirty million tourists visited the country.[22] American tourists were still welcomed, since they spent more per capita than most Europeans. Further expansion of tourism would accelerate Spain's cultural and economic tensions in the 1970s. (In fact, this is an issue Spaniards are discussing.) From an economic point of view alone, many Spaniards realize that the tourist industry is a delicate one subject to problems caused by political and economic unrest, rumors of such distress, or bad weather. An overreliance on this industry to the neglect of others would be as foolish for the Spanish in the twentieth

---

22. *Washington Post*, November 11, 1973.

century as it was in the sixteenth and seventeenth centuries in spending gold and silver on armies to the detriment of more stable capital-producing domestic industries.

Since tourism brought with it a mixed collection of problems, relations between Spain and the United States were not free of worries in the 1970s. Obviously old memories of the civil war still influenced some opinion about Spain in the United States, particularly among self-styled liberals who reached adulthood in the 1940s and 1950s. In Spain, ultranationalist and conservative elements continued resenting American military presence. Incidents, such as fights in bars or traffic-related arrests, involving members of the air force and navy or tourists further accented friction.

Other events also hinted of difficulties. In January 1966, off the southern coast of Spain, an American air force plane carrying several atomic bombs crashed into the Mediterranean. One bomb landed on Spanish soil without exploding and another was recovered from the sea floor after several months of searching. It reminded Spaniards of the dangers of having American military bases in Spain, particularly since the Spanish government had understood that no nuclear weapons were to be kept on its territory. Spaniards were generally furious that their country had been so threatened. Critics of the air and naval installations pointed to the incident as an example of the negative influence of the United States on Spain. The Americans apologized and presented the village of Palomares—where the incident occurred—a water desalination plant in 1968 as a gesture of goodwill.

The episode brought home once again to both governments how quickly the bases could stir public opinion. Some Americans believed they were too expensive to maintain in the late 1960s and certainly during the 1970s when intercontinental missiles could destroy both the Soviet Union and the United States before the military at these bases could react. In fact, they had become repair centers for American equipment located in Europe rather than points from which airplanes and ships could be sent out to attack Soviet forces—the original reason for them. Reaction to the bases in Spain was stronger since the Spaniards lived close to them. Some, critical of intimate ties to Washington, feared Spain might be the target of Soviet aggression should Moscow and Washington go to war. Spaniards also resented the fact that the United States spent less money for these installations than it did on NATO. They cited the wealthier governments of Britain and West Germany receiving more for contributing less to Europe's defense.

Yet at the end of the 1960s, Spanish authorities still wanted to keep the bases, despite the incident of the atomic bombs. The Foreign Office pushed for increased American rent each time negotiations for treaty renewal started. For both, the bases seemed a viable alternative to Spain's membership in NATO. Britain particularly objected to Madrid's inclusion in NATO, more because of its own difficulties with Spain over Gibraltar than out of any criticism of Franco's regime, although the British public still objected to the nature of the Spanish government. Spain asked for a formal alliance with Washington before renewing the base agreement in 1970, which the United States refused. The continuing friction between London and Madrid growing out of Franco's efforts to regain control of Gibraltar suggested that Washington could not accede to Franco's demand. Moreover, such a treaty would have been rejected by the Senate because of Franco's image as a dictator.[23]

In spite of these problems, the Nixon administration, which came to power in January 1969, reaffirmed American interest in maintaining the bases. For various reasons, the United States turned its interest back to Europe in the 1970s. With the end of the Vietnam War, Americans could concentrate on solving other major problems, such as the rivalry between Israel and the Arab states, which threatened to involve the United States and the Soviet Union in a major confrontation. The Arab-Israeli conflict also endangered the stability of the Mediterranean world. Increased Soviet political and military influence there made the Spanish bases more important to Washington than in the 1960s. Madrid's close ties to the Arabs meant that Spain might support American efforts to bring peace to the Middle East, particularly after the October 1973 war. Thus growing problems in the Mediterranean of mutual concern drew both governments into a more intimate bond.

Public events illustrated the basic direction of Spanish-American

---

23. Fernando Prieto, *España política 1969* (Bilbao, 1970), 139–147.

relations. In August 1970 they renewed the base agreement at a minimum cost of $300 million to the United States. Spain announced afterward that the new settlement linked it to NATO, perhaps a ploy designed to gain a defensive alliance from the United States. In October 1970 Foreign Minister Gregorio Lopez Bravo met with Nixon and Secretary of State William Rogers to discuss the balance of power in the Mediterranean and in the Middle East. The Americans asked Spain to use its influence in cooling the political crisis in the Arab world, while each determined the best way to checkmate growing Soviet naval strength in the Mediterranean. In fact, this exchange continued in the same manner for similar purposes after Jimmy Carter became president of the United States and while Adolfo Suarez served as prime minister in Madrid.

Another area of increasing concern to Europeans, Spaniards, and Americans was Spain's future after Franco's death. The issue became a diplomatic one by the mid-1960s and even more so in the 1970s. Washington worried about the political stability of Spain at the end of Franco's rule and during the transitional period to a new government. The assassination of President Carrero Blanco in December 1973 reminded officials that dangers lay ahead. Nixon signaled American allies that the United States still supported the present Spanish government. By inference this meant the regime after Franco. During the 1970s, the United States joined with various Spanish elements in urging Franco to smooth the transfer of power should he become incapacitated or die.[24] Franco did so by reaffirming Juan Carlos as heir to the Spanish throne and through investing greater power in the office of the president. The American government emphasized to its European allies the importance of the bases and the need to ensure Spain's political stability. As in previous years, Washington sought still further Spanish economic and political integration into Europe's affairs. American support for the current regime explained why a string of officials visited Spain to talk with both General Franco and Prince Juan Carlos. In October 1970 President Nixon stopped in Madrid. In January Juan Carlos came to Washington to repay the call. Vice-President Spiro Agnew arrived

---

24. *New York Times*, July 31, 1970, p. 2; *Washington Post*, July 27, 1971.

in Spain in July 1971 and Henry Kissinger in December 1973. Also lesser officials of both governments shuttled back and forth to discuss diplomatic, economic, and military issues throughout these years.

After Franco's death, the basic lines of foreign policy of both governments remained fundamentally unchanged. The new treaty on the bases was signed at the start of 1976, and both the regime of Prime Minister Adolfo Suarez and the administration of President Jimmy Carter carried on as before. Both Suarez and King Juan Carlos visited the United States while Vice-President Walter Mondale arrived in Madrid for talks during mid-May 1977.

Yet all was not always well. Besides the objections to the bases, other problems existed. Some senators critical of both the Nixon and Carter administrations objected that the base agreement did not always go to the Senate for examination, and in the case of the Nixon years, it had not been subject to the Senate's formal approval as a treaty. Others thought the bases were not worth the money spent on them. Conservative Spaniards believed the opposite and also objected to the lack of American support in Spain's bid to regain possession of Gibraltar. Criticism of Madrid's American policy, for instance, played an important part in the removal of Lopez Bravo from the Foreign Office in June 1973. He had also improved relations with communist countries by negotiating trade agreements with East Germany and the Soviet Union, which further irritated some of Franco's supporters. A more distant relationship seemed in the works after June 1973, at least for domestic Spanish purposes, because a new foreign minister, Pedro Cortina Mauri, reflecting the growth of political conservatism in the cabinet in the mid-1970s, came into office in January 1974.[25]

During 1974 American officials watched Spanish developments carefully.[26] The swing to the political right and more conservative Spanish policies did not suggest that the bases might be lost. Members of the Defense Department in Washington anticipated Madrid's asking for a security treaty as part of the price for continued American presence in Spain. Some American military observers thought it

---

25. *New York Times*, June 12, 1973, p. 7.
26. Ibid., November 26, 1973, p. 6.

worth paying since the concession would simply formalize the already existing de facto alliance. Others, agreeing with the State Department, objected since they did not expect Congress to fund the bases under that condition. Thus the very existence of the installations appeared threatened if the Spanish insisted on a formal defense treaty. Madrid stressed Spain's importance in the defense of Western Europe. Spaniards continued rearming their military forces, which they had started to do in the late 1960s, by purchasing large quantities of equipment from American manufacturers. They cited their rearmament as proof of their commitment to protect the Mediterranean and thus of Spain's value to the United States.[27]

As in previous decades, friction caused by conflicting political and military objectives complicated relations in the three decades following World War II. The objections to the Spanish raised by liberal European governments frustrated American attempts at integrating Spain and Europe militarily and economically while Spaniards expressed their annoyance with the same problems. Before making an assessment of their relations in the late 1970s, however, a brief survey of cultural affairs during the past generation is in order.

---

27. Spain observed carefully the changes being brought about by the United States in the 1970s and Madrid's role within that process. For some details, see Carlos de Luxán, *Henry Kissinger (una visión de la política exterior americana)* (Madrid, 1973), passim.

14
RECENT CULTURAL RELATIONS

Cultural issues are difficult to summarize, quantify, analyze, or document in Spanish-American relations. At best they can be presented only in some impressionistic fashion, particularly for the recent period. The vastness and complexity of cultural contacts between Spain and the United States becomes evident by examining the current influx of millions of dollars and tourists into Spain and the strong Hispanic heritage of the United States. Yet cultural factors never superseded political, economic, or military issues within each government or society; indeed they seemed to follow from political and military relations. Thus every aspect of Spanish-American diplomacy remained closely linked following the civil war in Spain. To cite an example, the bases with the presence of American military personnel on Spanish soil encouraged some interest and friction with the United States. Following the investment of millions of dollars in Spain, American tourism subjected Spaniards to new attitudes, social mores, and language and increased already existing tensions.

The apparent or visible influence of one on the other suggested an obvious and important avenue, which dramatically outlined part of their relationship. Included in this vein are such apparent bits of evidence as American movie marquees in Madrid and rock and roll records. The coverage given American affairs in Spanish newspapers, magazines, books, radio, and television also indicated cultural contact. But this worked for the United States as well. Books continued to appear on Spain, especially travel guides and histories. Moreover Americans recognized Spanish as their second language. While evidence suggests that direct influence came from one country to the other (for example, American movies in Spain), other factors grew out of related experiences (for example, Spanish language in the United States coming from Mexico, Cuba, and Puerto Rico). Therefore visible proof of cultural relations remains cluttered and confusing.

Another avenue of approach was the traditional view each society had of the other, measuring its changes after 1939 against the background of their political and economic relations. Such images evolved out of previous experiences in the nineteenth century (which were anything but pleasant) and from more current events, particularly the Spanish civil war and World War II. Complicated by political differences and national philosophies of varying traditions, difficulties grew out of each nation's attitudes as, for example, from racial theories of North American culture versus Hispanic civilization. This peculiar line of thinking has continued drawing adherents, especially in Spain, during the past thirty-five years.

More intimate ties between the two countries following World War II mimicked the pattern visible throughout Western Europe. Subsequent to the Marshall Plan came American dollars, businessmen, more soldiers, and tourists, who influenced national politics, entertainment, and industrial development, even Spain's. Spaniards reacted much like their European neighbors. They enjoyed the material prosperity that the Americans brought and willingly absorbed some—but not all—of the cultural exports. Spanish parents, for example, worried that their children might become too Americanized, or—worse—decadent, by listening to rock and roll music. Most Spaniards falsely thought of the United States as a nation of rich people with no poor citizens or problems—an image that can be blamed on Hollywood and its movies as much as on affluent American tourists and businessmen.

Yet during the 1950s, Spaniards viewed the United States more sympathetically than they had since the 1920s and early 1930s. They studied its economy, artistic and literary traditions, political philosophy, and public administration. Spaniards once again visited the United States in limited numbers, and some wrote about their trips. As in previous decades, they found much to admire in the material and economic life of the nation and less when it came to societal traditions, beliefs, and behavior. Literary developments in the United States became fashionable among Spanish writers as they sought to reestablish intellectual relations with European, Latin, and North American authors. The American penchant for massive economic expansion particularly caught the imagination of many articulate Spaniards searching for remedies to their nation's problems. Thus one could notice in the 1950s growing cultural exchanges paralleling political and economic rapprochement.[1]

While some ultraconservative elements, such as the Falange, mistrusted the United States and found widespread sympathy among members of the Spanish Catholic church, aristocracy, and middle class on this issue, others praised the world power. Some who found positive points to admire in American society wrote of them. One of the most popular and certainly more astute commentators during the 1950s was the philosopher Julián Marías. He spent the academic year of 1951 in the United States. For the rest of the decade he wrote on what he thought of Americans. Marías enthusiastically and perceptively described their society from a variety of angles, noting its dynamism and creativity. Of particular delight to him was the fact that Americans took great interest in Hispanic affairs. Students learned Spanish, universities offered courses in Spain's literature, and publications appeared on the Iberian peninsula.[2] He argued that the Spanish life-style was far more comfortable than the sped-up one in the United States but tempered this complaint with the suggestion that both societies had attractive attributes.

Marías lamented anti-Americanism, which continued to exist among large segments of Spanish society. In fact, he believed it had grown more intense in those who had always been critical of the United States. Attributing this development to the presence of the military bases in Spain, he countered such prejudice by arguing that many Spaniards knew little or nothing about the United States.

---

1. For examples, see Alvaro Alonso Castrillo, *Estados Unidos, país en revolución permanente* (Madrid, 1956); Antonio Heras, *De Nueva York á California* (Madrid, 1956); Vicente Aguilera Cerni, *Arte norteamericano del siglo XX. Arquitectura, artes industriales, escultura, pintura* (Valencia, 1957).

2. Julián Marías, *Universidad y sociedad en los Estados Unidos* (Madrid, 1954); *Los Estados Unidos en escorza* (Buenos Aires, 1956); and "Spanish and American Images," *Foreign Affairs* 39, no. 1 (October 1960): 92–99.

Moreover he argued that Americans posed no political or cultural threat to Spain in the 1950s.[3]

Another important Spanish commentator on the United States came from the ranks of Catholic intellectuals. A powerful molder of public opinion among educated young Spaniards, Rafael Calvo Serer was a leading exponent of the views of Opus Dei (the Catholic lay organization that provided Franco with skilled economic advisers in the late 1950s and early 1960s). He often commented on the United States. Opus Dei, although politically weak in the 1950s, took particular interest in administrative and economic innovations in Europe and the United States, introducing to Spanish audiences some of their views. American institutions that Calvo Serer and others admired soon were reflected in their publications. Writing his first book on the Americans in the late 1950s, Calvo Serer detailed American political life, updating Spanish information on the subject.[4] Once again new data became available to interested Spaniards on technical economic and administrative matters. Like Marías, Calvo Serer admired the creativity evident in some parts of American society and, also as the philosopher, he did not condemn Spanish institutions in comparison. He simply wanted to borrow from those in the United States which he believed might help Spain modernize and improve her economy and public administration.

Despite the writings of such individuals as Marías and Calvo Serer, a deep-seated Spanish distrust for the American way of life existed throughout the 1950s. While American publications became more readily available in Spain, the most popular seemed critical of the United States.[5] Of greater importance, however, was the fact that American books were popular enough to warrant publication in Spanish—the opening door that had been virtually closed since 1936. The first few translations were of old American novels and historical studies on Spain. Thus in a country where anti-Americanism was a

---

3. Marías, "Spanish and American Images," 96.
4. Rafael Calvo Serer, *La fuerza creadora de la libertad* (Madrid, 1958).
5. Arthur P. Whitaker, *Spain and the Defense of the West* (New York, 1961), 88–89.

normal state of affairs, some Spaniards read about the United States, even learning to admire its society.

This interest proved mutual. The establishment of the bases triggered a new American concern for Spain. Interest in Spanish affairs proved greater in the United States than Spain's for American developments. The larger size of the United States, in comparison to Spain, accounted for more publications and people interested in Spanish topics. An enormous Hispanic subculture in North America linked both nations by language and social mores.

Course offerings in high schools, colleges, and universities provided telling evidence of interest in Hispanic subjects. Classes in the language, civilization, and literature dramatically increased in number following World War II as educational facilities expanded. By the end of the 1950s, over one thousand colleges and universities listed courses on Spanish subjects in their catalogs. Nevertheless only a few thousand Americans actually understood much about Iberia, and they hardly exposed the public to their knowledge. The public as a whole, however, expressed little interest in learning more about Spain during the 1950s and the 1960s. Newspapers and magazines, for instance, rarely commented on Spain; Spanish publications, on the other hand, covered various American affairs almost on a daily basis.

One other point should be stressed regarding Hispanic culture in the United States. There existed large Puerto Rican, Mexican, and Cuban subcultures in North America. These families understood Spanish civilization, since it was their own, yet their knowledge of it came from American sources contemporary to them in the New World rather than from Spain. Just because millions of Americans knew the Spanish language and something about its literature did not necessarily mean that they understood contemporary Spain or its history. Many simply had no interest in the Iberian nation, expressing greater concern for events in Puerto Rico, Cuba, Mexico, or Latin America.

Despite the existence of two sources of Hispanic culture flowing into the United States, with the Latin American dominating, some interest in Spain existed nonetheless. Descriptive literature reflected this concern and followed the same pattern of previous publications. Books described tourist attractions, bullfights, food, restaurants, hotels, and entertainment. Romantic images still appealed to Americans; Kay Fulling's *Mantillas and Silver Spurs*, for instance, suggested that such an ideal continued to survive. Other books in a similar vein romanticized Spain while reflecting continued American fascination with the blend of modernity and historical antiquity in Spanish society. Even the bitter emotional and ideological feelings aroused by the Spanish civil war and World War II failed to curb this type of literature.[6]

Any isolation separating both societies during the 1940s and 1950s became part of the past in the 1960s. Contacts between the two multiplied in trade, politics, literature, academic affairs, and military activities. The Spanish government led the way by encouraging closer cultural bonds as a means of furthering political and economic intimacy. This campaign surfaced in many ways. The government's Institute of Hispanic Culture, established to help implement Spain's *hispanidad*, promoted closer relations with the United States. It supported research, sponsored conferences, organized classes for American students in Spain, and flew professors to the United States for conventions. Results of American research were made available to Spanish professors. Statistics suggested the volume of business done by the institute. Between 1963 and 1968, it financed the travel expenses of 7,074 people between the United States and Spain. Since its founding in 1946, the institute's United States Department allowed more than 1,500 American professors and students to use its facilities.[7]

The Spanish government sponsored various publications on American themes. Most recently it underwrote a large volume written by a member of the Foreign Office, Carlos M. Fernandez-Shaw, dealing with Spanish influence in the United States. Publication of this book indicated that the campaign would continue in the 1970s.[8]

---

6. Kay Fulling, *Mantillas and Silver Spurs* (New York, 1952); Mackinley Helm, *Spring in Spain* (New York, 1952); James Reynolds, *Fabulous Spain* (New York, 1953); Frank E. Howell, *Let's Visit Spain* (New York, 1954); William E. Strand, *Exploring Spain* (New York, 1959).

7. *The Institute of Hispanic.Culture in Madrid* (Madrid, 1969), 36, 39.

8. Carlos M. Fernandez-Shaw, *Presencia española en los Estados Unidos* (Madrid, 1972). A study of American presence in Spain would be useful.

Private citizens also wrote on the United States. Calvo Serer published a booklet on Washington's role in international affairs in the early 1960s. Santiago Nadal, editor of *La Vanguardia*, Barcelona's most important newspaper, also wrote a book on the United States. Although highly inaccurate and in some ways biased against Americans, it received wide publicity. The release of Nadal's volume suggested that many Spaniards still found much to criticize in American society but hinted that interest in the United States remained strong. And the prestige of the author made the book an important one on the Americans. Another publication resulted from a Spaniard's fascination with American politics. Eduardo Tarragona, a member of the cortés, published a study of the 1968 presidential election. In the 1970s more books appeared on American politics and minority groups written by Spaniards.[9]

A survey indicates that virtually every best-seller released in the United States in recent years quickly appeared in Spanish-language editions. These included novels and others on American history, politics, economics, Vietnam, racism, and Spanish themes. American literature, philosophy, and politics have sold particularly well in Spain as evidenced by the fact that every major Spanish publisher felt compelled to offer translated American titles and by the sales ratings published in most leading newspapers.

The U.S. government hardly took as great an interest in cultural relations. On occasion, however, a high-ranking official would comment on the subject, and his remarks would be widely publicized in Spain. Press censorship allowed the regime to limit anti-Americanism from appearing too often in newspapers and magazines. By publicizing stories that talked of friendlier relations or about the Fulbright-Hayes program for the exchange of students and scholars, the government hoped to reinforce its foreign policy. Thus it discouraged publication

---

9. Rafael Calvo Serer, *La política mundial de los Estados Unidos* (Madrid, 1962); Santiago Nadal, *Los Estados Unidos vistos de cerca* (Barcelona, 1964); Eduardo Tarragona, *Las elecciones norteamericanas vistas por un procurador familiar* (Barcelona, 1971); Francesco Leoni, *El movimiento conservador en los Estados Unidos* (Madrid, 1973); R. Padilla and J. Bollo, *USA: Guerras internas. Negros y puertorriqueños* (Madrid, 1973).

of complaints about the American military presence, anti-Protestant pieces, or accounts about how Spanish drug problems grew out of American tourism. While such stories appeared, less controversial material was more readily available and, when publicized, served the regime well, paralleling official rapprochement.

Marías in the late 1960s and again in 1970 published more observations on the American scene. As in the 1950s, his views received considerable attention both in Spain and in the United States. His work could be compared in quality to that of Alexis de Tocqueville. While his was not as comprehensive, Marías's exhibited the same depth of perception. He still viewed the United States favorably although he found much to criticize in his discussions on such issues as Vietnam, drugs, racism, politics, education, cultural mores, and university life.

Of particular value were his remarks on the nation's personality and social patterns. Citing one small example, hippies interested him as they did most other Spaniards since they came to Spain by the thousands during the 1960s. He suggested that they were not the first such group to appear in the Western world, citing the seventeenth-century variant described by Cervantes. One character in *La Ilustre Fregona*, Carriazo, left his wealthy parents, lived in squalor, and traveled to various parts of Spain. Like Carriazo, American hippies ran away from home because "respectability, the sober conscientious discipline, the boredom, and the reasons for the tedium that dominates so many worthy, decent, fine families, repel the young." Marías did not condemn hippies; instead he called them an "antidote against boredom, a stimulus for overcoming inertia."[10]

Publications by Marías and other Spaniards grew in large part out of a greater development in Europe: American travels. Throughout Europe in the 1960s and 1970s, Americans appeared everywhere on vacation, as members of NATO, attached to bases, consulates, and the embassy in Spain, as missionaries, businessmen, students, and

---

10. Quoted in Marías, *Americans in the Fifties and Sixties: Julian Marías on the United States*, trans. Blanche DePuy and Harold C. Raley (University Park, Pa., 1972), 339. The Spanish edition of his latest book is *Analisis de los Estados Unidos* (Madrid, 1968).

professors. They came to Spain no less than to other European countries. By their numbers and actions, they affected European society. Spain proved to be no exception. American rock and roll music dominated certain Spanish radio programs, strongly suggesting that it was an important cultural export from the United States. Middle- and upper-class Spanish teenagers listened to it faithfully on radios, on records, and—for those over eighteen years of age—at their favorite discotheques. Along with British rock and roll, American music could be heard on transistor radios in small Andalusian villages and in the Catalan hinterland as easily as in Madrid or Barcelona. Young Spaniards knew the words of popular American songs even though they might not have understood their meaning.

American movies, another cultural conduit from the United States, became popular. Hollywood's image of America became for some Spaniards their primary source of information on the United States. The social values expressed in such productions, while hardly adopted by Spaniards, appeared to be those of all Americans. As in the rest of the world, cowboy and Indian movies were box office successes along with detective stories, Jerry Lewis's comedies, and Elvis Presley's musical films. Urbanites of all classes saw these movies. But the lack of movie theaters in small villages meant that many Spaniards were rarely exposed to American society as reflected in films. Farmers, some factory workers, and older Spaniards who reached adulthood before 1960 found little to admire—let alone understand—in these cultural imports.

Older and more conservative Spaniards blamed American society for problems in Spain, such as the apparent increase in the use of marijuana, hashish, and other stimulants. What such individuals failed to realize, however, was that not all such dangers grew out of American presence in Spain. Spaniards had used narcotics for centuries and thus could not blame the Americans entirely for the apparent rise in their use during the 1960s and 1970s. Hashish, for example, had come from North Africa long before the United States even existed. Yet misleading images of American society suggested that those who disliked the United States would blame it for problems that were either increasing in Spain or just appeared more open than before.

On the positive side, the rapid influx of Americans into Spain led to an increased study of the English language. School systems near the American bases began, as early as the 1950s, to offer English-language courses so that local citizens could obtain employment at these installations. Spaniards found over the years, as did their West European neighbors, that they increasingly needed to know English for business, diplomacy, and academic purposes. Many working in the tourist industry as waiters, desk clerks, hotel managers, airline ticket clerks, or in the Ministry of Tourism and Information learned English. (Along with the American impetus to learn English, the number of British tourists pouring into Spain furthered the use of the language.)

No accurate statistics on the number of Spaniards claiming to speak English are available; however, those who lived in Barcelona, Madrid, Granada, Cordova, Seville, and Mallorca learned it first. Areas usually overrun by American and British tourists also acquired a large number of bilingual residents. Little villages along the Costa del Sol, in the Balearic islands, and on the Costa Brava each year were invaded by tens of thousands of English-speaking tourists. This is not to say that English became widespread in Spain—far from it—but when compared to the situation before the Spanish civil war, the number of those speaking it had increased.

Both the British and American governments encouraged the study of English. Each established institutes in Madrid and Barcelona offering language courses for Spaniards and built libraries filled with books in English. Throughout the post–World War II period, thousands of Spaniards received language instruction at these centers. The British also helped spread the use of English in yet another way. During the 1960s and early 1970s, thousands of Spaniards worked in Britain at better paying jobs than they could obtain in Spain, often in hotels and restaurants. This way they acquired a language that they could use at home by working in the local tourist industry.

More needs to be said about tourists dominating certain villages where much of this English was spoken. Towns on the Costa Brava on the Catalan coast during the month of August are overrun by certain national groups. One community might fill with Germans, another with Frenchmen, and a third with Englishmen. Americans usually flock to Ibiza in the Balearics or rush southward to Torremolinos. In such communities, road signs, billboards, notices in bars, restaurants, shops, historical sites, and hotels appear in the appropriate language. Permanent residents usually speak the necessary idiom, however haltingly, and take care that their menus and prices are posted in two or more languages. Such a phenomenon had existed for decades, though the real surge came after World War II. Earlier in the twentieth century the British had gathered in towns along the Costa del Sol and the French on the Costa Brava. Americans have only begun to repeat this process within the past fifteen years, although they had followed a similar pattern in certain parts of France during the 1920s.

The idea of American or other foreign tourists virtually dominating a particular community worried some Spaniards, both in the Ministry of Tourism and Information and in the villages, because of the threat to the Spanish way of life this posed, not to mention the effects of tourism on pollution, overcrowding, inflation, and crime. Even local newspapers complained of American "colonization" of areas once considered completely Spanish but that now resembled some West European or American communities.[11]

Americanization of certain aspects of Spanish life appeared in other, less dramatic ways over the years. It became possible to drink Coca Cola even in remote villages. In Madrid and Barcelona large American companies maintained office hours as in the United States, forcing Spaniards doing business with them to observe these different time schedules. Congestion in the streets of large cities at noon, when Spaniards rush home for their lunch and siesta, have led some to advocate a one-hour break at midday instead of the usual two. They believe since most of their time is spent traveling back and forth from work, that it would be better to leave the office earlier in the evening. While stores in Madrid, for instance, closed between 2 P.M. and 4 P.M. Monday through Saturday even in the 1970s, some conversion to American hours is evident, particularly in Barcelona. Clothing styles occasionally mimicked American fashions as well. It became more common to see upper-class Spanish youth wearing blue jeans. In addition some American television serials

---

11. For an idea of this, see James A. Michener's novel—based on Torremolinos—*The Drifters* (New York, 1971).

appeared in Spain during the 1960s and 1970s as they did throughout Europe, Latin America, and Asia.

A similar although far less intense pattern of Spanish influence on the United States has occurred. The number of Americans interested in Spain has remained small. Yet millions have visited the country and thus have been exposed to Spanish society. As a result of increased tourism to Spain, the number of travel books, guides, and descriptions of the Iberian nation have grown. They range in quality from the light prose of William J. Bryant to practical hotel and restaurant guides to the even more detailed manuals.[12] Travelogue articles occasionally appeared on Spain in such leading journals as *Holiday*, *Travel and Camera*, and *Atlantic Monthly*.[13]

One guide particularly stands out: James A. Michener's *Iberia*, undoubtedly one of the best introductions to Spain written by any non-Spaniard in the twentieth century.[14] This gifted American novelist did for Spain what Marías accomplished for the United States. Marías directed his volume less to the tourist and general reader or historian than to philosophically and sociologically inclined readers. Michener covered similar Spanish ground by regions, lacing his text with literary and historical bunting. As with all his earlier volumes, Michener researched his subject well before writing *Iberia*. In it he discussed each area's foods, literature, history, entertainment, cultural peculiarities, and some of his experiences. Like Marías, he admired the land of which he wrote, commenting more often on

---

12. William J. Bryant, *The Magic of Spain* (Springfield, Vt., 1967); Stanley Mills Haggart, *Spain on $5 a Day* (New York, 1968, and subsequent editions); Pan American World Airways, *Complete Reference Guide to Spain and Portugal, Including the Balearic and Canary Islands, Madeira and the Azores* (New York, 1962).

13. For examples, see Alexa Atkinson, "By Rocking Chair Across Spain: An Imaginary Tour," *Holiday* 34, no. 3 (September 1963): 70–74, 76; Elaine Flamholtz, "Majorca: The Haunted Island," *Travel and Camera* 32, no. 3 (March 1969): 46–48; Lawrence Merloyd, "Barcelona," *Atlantic Monthly* (August 1963): 108–113.

14. James A. Michener, *Iberia: Spanish Travels and Reflections* (New York, 1968).

its virtues than on its faults, and he became enamoured with the blend of old and new in Spain. His book sold well in the United States considering that many Americans still found much to criticize about Spain.

American academicians in varied fields wrote more about the Spanish than did their counterparts in any other country. During the 1950s and 1960s, a whole generation of outstanding scholars tackled contemporary Spanish problems and studied Spain's history and literature, producing articles and books. Thousands of graduate students studied Spanish literature and hundreds of professors wrote about it. By the mid-1960s, major works began appearing, particularly on Spanish history, following a long tradition of American historical publications on Spain: Gabriel Jackson's *The Spanish Republic and Civil War*; Stanley G. Payne's numerous books on the Falange, army, and politics; Richard Herr's study on eighteenth-century Spain, published at the end of the 1950s, which quickly became a minor classic. Other productive historians, sociologists, and economists also worked on Spain during the same period.[15]

Academic interest in Spanish history, for instance, grew increasingly over the years. The American Historical Association's bibliography of recent articles, published several times each year, contains a section on Spain and Portugal, which lists publications by Americans. In April 1969 Iberian specialists formed the Society for Spanish and Portuguese Historical Studies; as of late 1977, it had over two hundred members. It meets annually for a convention lasting several days to hear papers on history, sociology, economics, and politics. A much smaller group, based at the University of Nevada, formed the Basque Studies Program in the 1960s. Its news-

---

15. Gabriel Jackson, *Spanish Republic and Civil War* (Princeton, 1965); Stanley G. Payne, *Falange* (Stanford, 1961), *Politics and the Military in Modern Spain* (Stanford, 1967), *Franco's Spain* (New York, 1967), and *Spanish Revolution* (New York, 1970); Richard Herr, *The Eighteenth Century Revolution in Spain* (Princeton, 1958). For other titles see my "A Select Bibliography of Materials Published Outside of Spain on the Franco Period of Spanish History, 1939–1971," *Cuadernos de Historia Económica de Cataluña* 6 (1971): 1–113; 8 (1972): 223–248.

letter has a circulation of about five thousand copies. (The high number is attributable to the thousands of Basques who live in the Far West.) Both the Basque group and the SSPHS encourage academic research and in the case of Nevada's organization, collect materials on Iberian subjects and work with the state university press to publish books on the subject. The membership size in each suggests that more American professors are working on Spanish history than even in many individual Latin American and European nations.

Spanish-language instructors in the United States overwhelmingly outnumber historians and political scientists working on the Iberian peninsula and also have their own professional organizations, conventions, and journals, which include concern for Latin American affairs.

National demographic statistics offer some insights into Spanish-American cultural relations as well. In the 1970s the number of Americans claiming to be Catholic exceeded 45 million. The entire population of Spain totaled 10 million less than all the Catholics in the United States. Supposedly 99 percent of all Spaniards are Roman Catholic even though their bishops complain that only a minority of those actively practice the faith. These statistics suggest that the United States is a far more Catholic country than Spain were it not for the dominating Protestant influence on American culture. Nevertheless, the United States is more of a Catholic country, in terms of numbers and activity, than many Spaniards would readily admit.

As of 1972, 9.2 million Americans claimed to be of Hispanic descent; as of this writing, one can assume that number has increased. Of these 6 million use Spanish as the primary language at home. Cuban immigration into the United States during the 1960s (much of it by way of Madrid) accounted for only 629,000 or 6.9 percent of the total Spanish-American population; thus one can reject the notion that the largest number of Hispanic Americans are Cuban and have come only recently to the United States. The majority of these bicultural Americans, 57.2 percent or 5.254 million, are of Mexican extraction and have lived in the United States for generations. Those of Puerto Rican background amount to 16.5 percent of the Hispanic population and also have been tied to the United States for generations. Central and Latin American descendants account for another 6.5 percent and other undesignated members of Hispanic origin 12.8 percent with various lengths of ties to the United States.[16] Even with the latter two groups amounting to more than 19 percent of the Hispanic population, the majority had lived in the United States for a long time.

The number of people with American citizenship intimately familiar with Hispanic culture and its language equals 25 percent of Spain's population. These figures suggest not Spain's direct influence on the United States but rather their shared Hispanic heritage. Spain itself hardly affected the course of events in the United States during the twentieth century. American influences on Spain instead proved greater. What happened in the United States was that Spain's Hispanic culture attached itself to North American life by way of Latin America. A culture larger than either Spain's or the United States'—that is to say Hispanic—has affected both nations, even in the 1970s. The two share a common cultural bond formed over time; Spain did not export it to the United States or control its contemporary features. While irritating to Spaniards who like to think that they influenced Spanish-Americans or claim that the United States was not part of their world, the fact remains that many North Americans are very much members of the *raza hispanica*.

The process of comparing demographic characteristics suggests that misconceptions of each remain strongly embedded in the other, even today. Spaniards continue to think of Americans as Anglo-Saxons, and when they meet one completely fluent in Spanish, they consider him or her a rare exception. Undoubtedly the fact that many Hispanic Americans are too poor to visit Spain explains why the more Protestant and financially better off element in the United States travels to the Iberian peninsula, giving many Spaniards the impression that North Americans are hardly Hispanic. Yet in truth,

---

16. U.S., Bureau of the Census, *Current Population Reports*, P-20, No. 250, "Persons of Spanish Origin in the United States: March 1972 and 1971" (Washington, D.C., 1973), 1–2. Tentative figures as of March 1973 indicated a rise in the number of Hispanic Americans to 10.59 million: *Parade Magazine*, March 24, 1974, p. 11.

there are more citizens of the United States of Hispanic descent using Spanish as their primary language than people living in at least nine Latin American countries. However, Spaniards contradict themselves by complaining that Americans generally do not understand Spain while simultaneously acknowledging close cultural bonds. Americans have also been guilty of misconceptions and contradicted themselves when dealing with Spain. If a general blanket difference exists, it is that American dollars, commercial production, and technology have influenced Spain directly and can be measured, while its civilization remains difficult to define. Moreover, Spain's direct cultural influence on the United States is also unmeasurable in precise fashion. Yet cultural contacts suggest that relations among nations are anything but simple to identify.

15
SOME CONCLUSIONS

It is clear from the record of previous relations between Spain and the United States that their diplomats and policy makers are prisoners of past traditions, prejudices, geographical realities, present national goals, and cultural heritages, which can be counted upon to influence their actions in future years. Some of those include mistrust, political rivalry, economic accommodations, cultural misconceptions, and differing value systems. Besides these, however, are several others that are important when assessing future relations.

The first in significance relates to Spain's geopolitical attitudes. In the past it always considered itself European; consequently Spaniards never allowed their foreign policy toward the United States to damage their contacts with Europe. While seemingly an obvious fact, many Americans failed to realize this during the nineteenth century. After Spain's loss of Cuba, both countries became more aware of Spain's European orientation. The Spanish civil war, World War II, attempts to gain membership in the Common Market, and alignment with the Mediterranean world indicated how important Spaniards viewed their relations with the rest of Europe. Even Madrid's ties to Latin America rated second in significance. As the twentieth century grew older, Spanish foreign policy, which had been distracted away from Europe in the nineteenth century by the New World, recoiled to more traditional lines of concern. When coupled with the tensions Spain and the United States had shared in the Americas during the past century, one could understand why they were often at odds. Spaniards viewed themselves first as Europeans in their geopolitical view of the world—as they do today—and Americans did not. Since this difference of perspective had an impact on political and economic relations in the past, it probably will again in the future.

Throughout this book, cultural influences on both nations emerged as a factor in relations because Spaniards considered themselves a society different from the North Americans'. The United States made a similar comparison to Spain. Diplomats today are more aware of this hidden factor, and no foreign office ignores the complications it poses. When, for instance, American diplomats receive language training at the Foreign Service Institute in Washington, they are required to study the culture and history of the people who speak that particular idiom. Spaniards, more conscious of cultural matters than Americans, are continually pointing to the differences in value systems and manner of operations between them and the North Americans.

In both countries, ignorance of each other and a lack of respect for another's national characteristics often led to criticisms. This will continue to cause friction by confusing analyses of events and motives in each country. There will be complaints (particularly in newspapers), embarrassing situations never intended to insult, and personality differences. Examples abound of these at work in the past. Minister Carl Schurz irritated the Spanish in the 1860s; the U.S. State Department found Fernando de los Rios (ambassador, 1936-39) a nuisance. As recently as the 1960s, Marías felt compelled to comment on American characteristics irritating to Spaniards.

Americans have also been trapped by their past. For instance, despite their stature as a major world power, they still express a geographical preference for the New World in much the same manner and for similar reasons as Spain does for Europe. All nations think in geopolitical terms so there is no reason to suggest that Americans will deviate from the pattern. On both conscious and subconscious levels, they have always thought that the Atlantic Ocean separated them from Europe's problems. Despite advances in transportation and communications and increased participation in international affairs, a quadi-isolationist mentality still exists. Allegiance to this old idea will undoubtedly lead many American citizens to consider relations with Spain anything but urgent.

Events in the twentieth century have altered relations between the two countries. With the end of the war of 1898, Cuba—their major bone of contention—no longer plagued them. Both now considered the other of lesser importance. From the Spanish civil war to the present, relations became complementary. Each nation's diplomats argue that ties remain important in the 1970s. International political situations are changing the basic relationship of Spain to Europe, to the United States, and Washington's impact on Western Europe. Today both are concerned with the Common Market, tourism, and bilateral trade and consider the bases useful (particularly their military forces) even though these installations have lost the sense of importance evident in the 1950s. Therefore in years to come, if no major upheavals disturb Spain or Europe, Washington and Madrid may acknowledge that the bases are no longer valuable and count their relations as being significant in other ways.

Economic aspects of their contacts still do not attract the greatest attention of both since officials consider political issues of more relevance. Spain still feels the need to prove itself and gain international respectability. This reasoning remains during the reign of King Juan Carlos as Spaniards gain the approval of such parliamentary governments as France and Britain. Moreover, the Spanish still worry about their military security. Although Spain is prepared to turn to Europe for respectability and military security, while simultaneously drawing upon its own national resources for defense, Europe's lack of interest forces Madrid to rely on the United States at a time when its economic and military destiny is linked closer to Europe's. The bases thus serve as the conduits of Washington's support and remain a symbol of Spain's international aspirations.

One of the key elements in the political formula is NATO despite all the stones of irrelevancy hurled at it by European and American editors, professors, and politicians. The United States officially supports NATO, and most policy planners in Washington still believe in its usefulness, especially the military who never fail to talk of the Soviet threat to Europe without it. Thus officials in Madrid argue that Spain will support NATO while using it as an excuse for continued Spanish-American military ties. Within the Department of State and at the Pentagon, some want Spain made a member of NATO. If not possible, they at least wish the bases maintained by both governments.

The Spanish today are less enthusiastic about joining NATO than they were fifteen or twenty years ago. Since its organization, NATO has acquired a northern European orientation of little significance to Spain. Spaniards have always identified more with the southern half of Europe toward the Mediterranean anyway. Thus NATO's northward alignment might actually reduce Spain's political options in the Mediterranean. The oil crisis in the fall and winter of 1973, with its shades of European and Middle Eastern economic friction, suggested the potential danger if Spain turned its back on the area where its concerns had been strongest for hundreds of years. It is further believed within Spanish circles that if Spain joins NATO, it might be forced to spend considerable sums to upgrade its armed forces to the standards currently prevailing within the alliance. There is also the question of the operating expenses of the bases along with the auxiliary economic benefits accruing from them now. The United States would probably want Madrid (if it joined NATO) to shoulder most, if not all, the expenses of the bases as its contribution to the defense of Western Europe. This would cost Spain millions of dollars in lost support from Washington, distort even further its balance-of-trade deficit with the Americans, and possibly hurt the economic sectors that are dependent on the foreign military presence.

Yet Spaniards do not discourage talk of such membership when they discuss the status of the bases with Americans. Publicly and privately, Spain mentions membership in NATO along with veiled hints of why it would be better to remain outside that organization. Madrid wants a bilateral military defense pact with the United States since no European power will grant this either by way of NATO or on an individual basis. American diplomats refuse this because they believe the Senate would not approve such a treaty. The State Department argues that a de facto alliance exists anyway because of the close military ties brought about by the bases. Some American military officers agree, yet others want a more formal arrangement. Thus each time the base agreement comes up for renegotiation, Americans and Spaniards argue among themselves on the nature of the new settlement. This occurred each time during the 1960s, down to the renewing of the treaty early in 1976, has continued to the time of this writing, and can be expected to arise again until the bases are no longer a major issue—probably sometime, say diplomats, in the mid-1980s or later.

Crises in the Middle East also affect relations and undoubtedly will do so for the next few years. Because Spain considers the Mediterranean world of importance in the long run, it is imperative that it maintain intimate ties with its Arab neighbors. Today the Spanish muster strong geopolitical and economic (oil) reasons for this position. During 1973 and 1974, Spain supported Washington's position that Europe should adhere to a unified energy policy when dealing with the Middle East. Yet at the same time, Madrid did not offend the Arabs. This policy became evident in public and private exchanges between Madrid and Washington. During 1974 Spanish officials expressed resentment at not being consulted by Henry Kissinger on his recommendation that Europe follow a united fuel policy. Madrid believed that it should have been made a party to such a consideration since its mediatory influence in the Middle East might have proven potentially useful to most European governments. Yet partially because the United States failed to call upon Spain to take sides against the Arabs, Madrid never feared losing its supplies of oil.

In October 1973 Madrid publicly announced that the United States could not use the bases in Spain to refuel airplanes involved in the Middle East. This may have been the cause of Washington's reluctance to include Spain in oil diplomacy. At that time, however, Washington privately told Madrid that the bases would be used only for routine purposes and not in new operations in the Middle East. The Spanish knew this statement meant that reconnaissance planes flying over the Middle East would continue to refuel in Spain. They suspected that data gathered from these flights would end up in the hands of the Israeli government. Yet neither Madrid nor Washington raised that point. The Arabs, undoubtedly aware of all this, realized that both Washington and Madrid wanted to settle the crisis in the Middle East and probably therefore publicly raised no objections to Spanish policy toward the bases. As confirmation of the Arab position, Madrid continued negotiating bilateral oil and trade agreements with Middle Eastern governments in 1974 and after.

Part of Spain's behavior toward the Middle East and the United States stemmed from Europe's objection to Madrid's participation in its military and political life. As long as such countries as Britain, France, the Benelux group, Sweden, and others refused to include

Spain in their affairs more fully, Madrid had no choice but to make friends with the United States and the Arabs. Washington fully understood this and recognized that Spain's ostracism from the mainstream of European activity had been the normal state of affairs for over a century. Thus the Americans saw no point in criticizing Spain for its Arab position.

Earlier in this chapter I suggested that economic issues were important in Spain's diplomacy, particularly in regard to its relations with the United States and Europe. The cases of Western Europe and the Middle East neatly illustrate the point. For the same reason that Europeans kept Spain out of NATO in the mid-1970s, the Spanish did not seek membership in the Common Market. Using much the same logic, Spain sees fewer advantages now for joining EEC than it did fifteen years ago. Its currency is no weaker than those of most other European nations, and its industrial production, as measured by GNP and GNI, is comparatively solid. Despite economic problems that took the luster away from the phenomenal boom of the 1960s (such as rising unemployment and pernicious inflation), Spain developed a complex system of bilateral commercial agreements with Europeans, North and South Americans, Arabs, Asians, and even communist countries tailored to its own needs. Similar negotiations have continued down to the present day, offering Spain greater commercial flexibility in the international marketplace than might have been possible within the context of EEC. Spain's relative friendliness with the oil-rich Arabs ensured that its economy would continue to receive adequate supplies of energy. In turn, Spain's ties to the Middle East have consequently made it more attractive to Europe.

The oil crisis may thus further Spain's economic integration into Europe by way of more bilateral arrangements. Factors other than the recent fuel fury suggest this. For instance, the percentage of American trade within the Spanish economy is declining in the 1970s while the volume of Spain's business with EEC members is increasing within the Iberian market. Diplomats from both nations expect this trend to continue at least through the early 1980s, barring any unforeseen economic crisis in the Western world. Each sees Spanish-American trade in dollar values increasing along with the volume of exchanged goods, such as Spanish fruits, wines, ships, and shoes, for

American machinery and grains. And there is always the massive tourist industry to consider. But the percentage of volume in either domestic market will actually decline since each, particularly Spain, is finding other trading partners.

The economic impact for both should be beneficial and evident by the 1980s. The shifting exchange of sales would in effect redress the balance of trade between them at some point. The net result might be continued commercial intimacy while further bonding Spain's economy to that of Western Europe. Americans and Spaniards could be trading an almost even volume of goods—which each wants—by the 1980s while helping all noncommunist European states integrate more readily without artificial aid from various governments. The situation in which Spain finds itself by not being a member of EEC, with the flexibility of bilateral negotiations that comes with that status, may well mean that Madrid can achieve the sort of economic ties to Europe that the EEC members blocked in earlier years. Washington will try to make sure that any trading advantages it has in Spain are not lost either because of Madrid's bilateral arrangements with others or through EEC membership; the Spaniards will attempt to correct their unfavorable balance of trade with the Americans.

There is also the Congress to think about when assessing political and economic relations between the two countries. Over the next ten years, Congress may find the expense of maintaining the bases unjustifiable. During the 1960s this attitude became apparent. The State Department expects congressional antipathy toward these installations to grow. The objections raised are less the result of criticism of the Spanish government and more the by-product of current opinion regarding the American role in Europe's defense. If troops are withdrawn from NATO, particularly out of Germany, it will become increasingly difficult to justify having any military personnel in Europe. For the time being it seems clear that American presence in Europe will decline over the next ten to fifteen years. That trend inevitably will lead to most or all of the installations being evacuated. It also appears equally obvious that the 1980s will be a critical period in regard to the Spanish bases. By then the United States may have decided to pull its troops out of Europe and leave only the navy in the Mediterranean—based at Naples—and some air force units in Germany and possibly Spain. The base agreement (usually negotiated in increments of five years) will undoubtedly come up for renegotiations in 1979–80 and again in the mid-1980s at a time when the installations may be of declining value to the United States.

Congress, along with other elements of American society, can be expected to argue that intercontinental missiles or détente diplomacy make the expense of carrying the bases and their 9,000 or more personnel unjustifiable. Dependence on Arab oil will probably be less of a factor in terms of American security needs; thus Madrid's ties to the Middle East would decline in relevance for Washington. Moreover the nature of the post-Franco government and economy would have developed more fully into the current forms existing in Western Europe. This in turn could lead to further integration of Spain into European affairs and away from a dependency on the United States. If, on the other hand, political and economic instability plague the Spanish, Americans can be counted upon to shy away from Spain, falling back on the neoisolationist formula employed during the 1930s. Prosperity and a more parliamentary form of government might push the Spanish into its more traditional role of siding with France, as was the case in the nineteenth and early twentieth centuries. Turmoil at home would cause the Spanish to do what they have always done during such difficult times as world wars and their own civil wars: declare neutrality in international affairs and try to block any foreign intervention into its own.

Since it appears that in either instance Spain will move toward greater identification with the goals and destinies of the rest of Europe, the bases suggest yet another situation, particularly for the 1980s. If Madrid decides to join EEC, then it is difficult to imagine the Spanish not in NATO, since membership in both has been the pattern with many other participants of EEC and the alliance. For Spain not to do what the others found advantageous might make little sense. If Madrid joins NATO, then the bases would be part of the defense system linking Madrid formally to the rest of Western Europe. The differences between NATO's members and the United States might therefore be juxtapositioned on the Spanish along with the obvious effects on relations with Washington. The bases would then become less important in their diplomacy. By the 1980s, one could reasonably expect that political relations between Madrid and Washington would have to broaden to take into fuller account the international state of affairs existing throughout Europe rather than as solely involving Spain.

A nation's foreign policy is largely predicated upon national goals and influenced more by domestic than by international events. Thus internal effects on Spanish-American relations that might take place over the next ten or more years must be taken into account. In the United States, inflation, Watergate's aftershocks, and the economic and social problems generally faced by a nation following a war are clearly evident. Europeans view American inflation and the fluctuating value of the dollar with alarm and exhibit a measurable concern for the political and economic stability of the country. Some of the current problems faced by the United States not only are also evident in Europe but will undoubtedly be present for years to come. Included are inflation, a concern for materialism and rising consumer expectations, a reordering of political philosophies, the energy crisis, and new adjustments in basic moral values. When compared to the same problems found in Greece, Italy, Britain, Spain, Portugal, Sweden, and Germany, the Americans are weathering their storms with greater ease and stability.

Neither Washington nor Madrid feels at this time that there will be any major upheaval in the United States. They do not anticipate any radical departure from previous American political or diplomatic positions as they apply to Europe. The rhetoric of President Nixon's "peace for a generation or more" coupled to Henry Kissinger's attempt to create a balance of power reminiscent of nineteenth-century European models suggested that the lines of Washington's international policies are now set for the next few years, irrespective of which political party dominates the government. The statements and actions of the Carter administration, for example, are no different in regard to Spain. Thus on the American side of the diplomatic ledger, it seems fairly clear that policy makers in Europe will face no major surprises from Washington.

The Spanish domestic situation is another question with complicated cross-currents. In the declining years of General Franco's rule, serious problems surfaced with their traditional Spanish militant overtones. The Basque nationalist terrorists (ETA) in the past several years have assassinated one Spanish president, many paramilitary police, and one police chief. They have robbed banks and kidnapped wealthy businessmen for ransom. They promise even more violence in the future. Spain's laboring class, both in industry and in agriculture, faces rising inflation and increased consumer aspirations with one of the lowest wage levels in Western Europe. Militant labor organizations, legalization of the Communist party in 1977, increasing number of illegal strikes, and clashes with the police strongly indicate the dissatisfaction of this sector of Spanish society. The Catholic church is also involved in turmoil at the moment. Rome is worried and wants to preserve and expand its influence in Spain by taking up the causes of the poor, the intellectuals (particularly university students and professors), and the bourgeois as a means of preventing the recurrence of anticlericalism as the country moves in the direction of less conservative government. Yet in the process, it clashes with some conservatives and thus can be counted among the ranks of the concerned, if not discontented, groups.

On the more positive side, Spain's economic growth over the past ten years has usually meant low unemployment. The development of a large middle class both in Madrid and in Barcelona hints of stability since criticism of Spanish society threatens their material prosperity and personal ambitions. Memories of the civil war, although fading rapidly, are still strong enough to make most Spaniards hesitant to start another revolution. But the question remains how serious Spain's problems are. Are the Spanish headed for a succession of ministries such as has been Italy's misfortune to endure for a generation and which seems to be Portugal's immediate fate? And what impact will the resurgence of regional nationalism and labor unrest since the death of Franco have on Spain's domestic affairs?

None of Spain's worries is critical enough to plunge the country into a nightmare of violence or political instability reminiscent of the 1930s. To cause that, most dissident groups would have to unite, augment their ranks considerably, or become more militant—doubtful possibilities at the moment. Moreover as long as the government enjoys the support of the military, prevents an economic recession or depression, and allows a nominal amount of domestic political debate, serious threats to its existence might be avoided. Yet the possibility of some violence and economic difficulties growing out of inflation, labor troubles, rumors of terrorism in Spain (which could seriously harm the tourist industry), and particular internal political situations still remain. Diplomats and other officials worry about these possibilities. Americans may wonder if the effectiveness of the bases and of Spain's related ability to support NATO might not be compromised.

At the moment American officials are hardly concerned with the possible future course Spain's domestic life may take to the degree that they should be. They assume Spain will always be around and part of Europe. Such a cavalier attitude has always crippled American reaction to Spanish affairs in and out of government and will probably continue to do so in the future. Americans assume optimistically that the official machinery will continue functioning for years without significant change. Reliance on events over the past four decades supports this contention. However, if one takes a longer view toward the future, then this reasoning becomes questionable. Spain has sported one of the most unstable collections of governments since the eighteenth century; these were characterized by increased turmoil following long periods of rule by one individual. The future, which cannot be free from the past entirely, will probably reflect some patterns of this historical record.

Spanish diplomats are more sensitive to this issue and consequently display less optimism on Spain than the Americans do. These Spaniards generally feel that Spain's international situation will improve both politically and economically within Europe throughout the 1980s, although not to the point where Madrid would have to implement a foreign policy hostile to the United States as Paris maintained through much of the 1960s. The Spanish agree with their North American counterparts that Spain will have a more moderate political life as ultraconservative features of the government are pried from their generation-old moorings by the new monarchy of Juan Carlos. Both believe that by the end of the 1970s, Spanish public administration will be more similar to parliamentary Europe's than they are at the present and each sees this development as portending better relations between Spain and the United States.

Diplomats, historians, and other Iberian specialists hardly mention tendencies in Europe that could lead to difficult years ahead. Although the Europeans seem to have a strong economy and confidence in their political systems and claim to be socially stable, there are danger signs that diplomats can no longer ignore. One is that Europeans are facing economic tensions unparalleled in force since the 1940s. Their economy is marked by rapid inflation, running from a low of 5 percent to a high of 40 percent, with an average of just under 18 percent annually as of this writing. Such a situation is a brutal strain on any nation's economy and the standard of living of its people. A result of this inflation, coupled with a rise in consumer demands not matched by increases in productivity, is increased labor strikes with crippling effects on a country's economic capability. One has only to think of what the postal employees did to Italy or the coal strikers to Britain in 1973 and 1974 to understand the dangers involved. Surging consumer expectations to the level of an international obsession is in itself disturbing. Worst of all, since it has political parallels with European developments between 1914 and 1933, the obvious inability to some regimes to cope effectively with their nation's problems also emerges as a major concern.

Parliamentary governments have notably shown their helplessness in dealing with their nation's economic and even cultural crises. In Britain, Parliament and the cabinet have failed to curb inflation, shortages, labor strikes, and racial unrest. New governments are continually set up in Italy, and in France the public complains that parliamentarians are too caught up in partisan politics to govern the nation effectively. Even in the United States, opinion polls have indicated a serious lack of confidence in Congress, not to mention in the government as a whole. Over fifty years ago, a perceptive Spanish businessman-politician, Francisco Cambó, complained of the "sterility of parliamentary government." Its ineffectiveness made the advent of dictatorships a welcome development for many Europeans. His comments on the 1920s reach out to us as equally relevant in the 1970s. He struck close to current trends when he noted that "a materialistic society has no other preoccupation but the maintenance of material order and the tranquil enjoyment of its wealth. And it generally considers that the maintenance of this order is more secure under the absolute government of a man with the most complete control of institutions."[1] Today parliamentary states too often

---

1. Francisco Cambó, *Las dictaduras* (Madrid, 1929), 96.

reflect the pattern Cambó saw in the same countries in an earlier period.

What evidence exists to indicate the relevancy of the type of remarks made by Cambó? The Greeks turned to authoritarian government during the 1960s, and Spain kept its to the end of Franco's life. The Italians, faced with a multitude of serious problems, talk more of dictatorship and explore Mussolini's as a nostalgic voyage into a sunnier time. In West Germany, ultraconservative and even neo-Nazi parties are growing as they are in Italy. The Dutch discuss the need for stronger administration. Most of Eastern Europe remains under such regimes. And in Portugal, a series of quasi-military governments rapidly come and go with the passage of time. Europe today lacks dynamic leadership. Consequently many Europeans—and even Americans—are calling for more "dynamic" governments, using such other euphemisms as "law and order" and "responsive" or "effective" administration even at the cost of some civil liberties—shades of fascist rhetoric and certainly authoritarian dialogue. Europeans might adopt more authoritarian regimes, especially during the 1980s, in some Mediterranean countries although they will probably not be of the East European variety. A trend to the right is not inevitable, simply a possible option. On the other hand, the political instability in France following the death of President Georges Pompidou in the spring of 1974 suggests that once again a popular front government might arise in Paris. In short, the Atlantic community displays many of the characteristics that once before caused substantial changes in its political life. Officials in Madrid and Washington should be aware of these potential developments and begin to think of what effects they might have on relations during the next decade.

The implications of future events for Spanish-American diplomacy are not easy to define with certainty. The foreign policy of one toward the other may undergo significant changes during the 1980s, particularly if the political climate in Europe veers sharply to the left or right and is accompanied by serious economic problems. After 1980, both will have to reassess their policies in some fundamental fashion. By then the nature of Spain's government for succeeding years should be more evident, another American presidential term (with a possible change of political party in power) will begin in

January 1981, and the fruits of North America's diplomatic efforts in Asia and with the Soviet Union can be assessed in terms of European and Arab problems.

It appears with the start of a third century of diplomacy that both nations have less to quarrel about than ever before. Past relations have not always been amicable, but that is no bar to better days. While national self-interests will not be foresaken by either to please the other, the world, by being smaller, must force accommodations on all. Consequently Spain and the United Sates cannot afford to be two nations at odds; instead they must be friends linked by the wisdom that has grown from the bonds of time.

APPENDIX A
SPANISH ENVOYS TO THE UNITED STATES[1]

Diego de Gardoqui, chargé d'affaires. Presented credentials to Congress May 21, 1785. Withdrew on leave October 3, 1789.

José Ignacio de Viar, secretary of legation. Acted as chargé d'affaires ad interim from October 3, 1789, to about December 1, 1791, and from April 25 to about August 1, 1796.

José Ignacio de Viar and José de Jaudenes, joint chargés d'affaires ad interim. Commission dated February 12, 1791. Their joint services commenced about December 1, 1791. Jaudenes began acting independently of Viar sometime between March 5 and August 22, 1794. He gave notice of intent to return to Spain April 25, 1796. Viar terminated his services on May 3, 1794.

Carlos M. de Irujo, envoy extraordinary and minister plenipotentiary. Arrived in the United States at the end of July 1796. Presented credentials August 25, 1796. Last note to secretary of state, February 4, 1806.

Valentin de Foronda, chargé d'affaires. Presented credentials July 7, 1807. Took leave by letter October 14, 1809.

Luis de Onís, envoy extraordinary and minister plenipotentiary. Gave notice of arrival in the United States October 7, 1809. Left the United States on leave May 10, 1819.

---

1. Dates in some cases are approximate since it was not always clear when an envoy terminated his service for either government. Sometimes these dates represent when they received orders to return home or their actual departure. The names of the Spanish envoys from 1785 through 1872 came from the *Register of the Department of State, 1872* (Washington, D.C., 1872), 122–123; those through April 1931 came from an unpublished card file maintained by the U.S. National Archives and Records Service based on diplomatic dispatches; for the post-1931 names, the various issues of *Foreign Relations of the United States* were consulted along with annual publications of the *Diplomatic List*, issued by the Department of State.

APPENDIX A 275

Mateo de la Serna, chargé d'affaires ad interim. From May 10, 1819, to April 12, 1820.
Francisco Dioniso Vives, envoy extraordinary and minister plenipotentiary. Presented credentials April 12, 1820. Last official communication was September 23, 1821.
Francisco Hilario Rivas y Salmon, secretary of legation. Acted as chargé d'affaires ad interim from September 30 to October 31, 1821, and from March 15, 1823, to July 25, 1827.
Joaquin de Anduaga, envoy extraordinary and minister plenipotentiary. Presented credentials October 31, 1821. Gave notice of intended departure March 15, 1823.
Francisco Tacon, minister resident. Presented credentials July 25, 1827. Presented credentials as envoy extraordinary and minister plenipotentiary November 11, 1833. Died in Philadelphia, June 22, 1835.
Miguel Tacon, secretary of legation. Acted as chargé d'affaires ad interim from June 30 to December 7, 1835, and from October 4, 1837, to April 28, 1838.
Angel Calderon de la Barca, envoy extraordinary and minister plenipotentiary. Presented credentials December 7, 1835. Took leave September 26, 1839.
Pedro Alcantara Argaiz, envoy extraordinary and minister plenipotentiary. Presented credentials September 26, 1839. Took leave January 2, 1844.
Fidencio Bourman, chargé d'affaires ad interim. From January 2 to August 5, 1844.
Angel Calderon de la Barca, minister resident. Presented credentials August 5, 1844. Took leave August 2, 1853.
José María Magallon, secretary of legation. Acted as chargé d'affaires ad interim from August 2, 1853, to May 30, 1854, and from November 11, 1856, to February 21, 1857.
Leopoldo Augusto de Cueto, envoy extraordinary and minister plenipotentiary. Presented credentials May 30, 1854. Last communication July 30, 1855.
Alfonso Escalante, envoy extraordinary and minister plenipotentiary. Presented credentials October 1, 1855. Took leave November 11, 1856.
Gabriel García y Tassara, envoy extraordinary and minister plenipotentiary. Presented credentials February 21, 1857. Took leave March 11, 1867.
Facundo Goñi, envoy extraordinary and minister plenipotentiary. Presented credentials March 15, 1867. Successor presented March 19, 1869.

Maurício López Roberts, envoy extraordinary and minister plenipotentiary. Presented credentials March 19, 1869. Placed legation in charge of first secretary on March 23, 1872. Took leave April 1, 1872.

José Polo de Bernabé, envoy extraordinary and minister plenipotentiary. Presented credentials April 5, 1872. Took leave July 1, 1874.

Luis de Potestad, secretary of legation and chargé d'affaires ad interim. Acted as such from July 1, 1874, to September 15, 1874.

António Mantilla, envoy extraordinary and minister plenipotentiary. Presented credentials on September 15, 1874. Terminated duty on August 14, 1878.

José Brunetti y Gayoso, secretary of legation and chargé d'affaires ad interim. Acted as chargé from August 14, 1878, to February 3, 1879.

Felipe Mendez de Vigo y Osorio, envoy extraordinary and minister plenipotentiary. Presented credentials on February 3, 1879. Terminated duty on March 2, 1881.

José Brunetti y Gayoso, secretary of legation and chargé d'affaires ad interim. Served as chargé from March 2, 1881, to April 30, 1881.

Francisco Barca del Corral, envoy extraordinary and minister plenipotentiary. Presented credentials on April 30, 1881. Terminated duty on July 29, 1883.

Juan Valera y Alcalá, envoy extraordinary and minister plenipotentiary. Presented credentials on January 29, 1884. Terminated service on April 6, 1886.

Enriqué Dupuy de Lôme, secretary of legation and chargé d'affaires ad interim. Served as chargé from July 29, 1883, to January 29, 1884.

Emilio de Muruaga, envoy extraordinary and minister plenipotentiary. Presented credentials on April 6, 1886. Terminated service on November 7, 1890.

Miguel Suarez Guanes, envoy extraordinary and minister plenipotentiary. Presented credentials on November 14, 1890. Terminated service on November 28, 1891.

José Felipe Sagrario, secretary of legation and chargé d'affaires ad interim. Served as chargé from November 28, 1891, to September 30, 1892.

Enriqué Dupuy de Lôme, envoy extraordinary and minister plenipotentiary. Presented credentials on September 30, 1892. Terminated service on March 2, 1893.

Emilio de Muruaga, envoy extraordinary and minister plenipotentiary. Presented credentials on March 2, 1893. Terminated service on April 16, 1895.

José Felipe Sagrario, secretary of legation and chargé d'affaires ad interim. Served as chargé from April 16, 1895, to May 6, 1895.

Enriqué Dupuy de Lôme, envoy extraordinary and minister plenipotentiary. Presented credentials on May 6, 1895. Terminated service on February 11, 1898.

Juan du Boso, chargé d'affaires ad interim. Served from February 11, 1898, to March 12, 1898.

Luis Polo de Bernabé, envoy extraordinary and minister plenipotentiary. Presented credentials on March 12, 1898. Terminated service on April 20, 1898.

Duke de Arcos (José Brunetti y Gayoso), envoy extraordinary and minister plenipotentiary. Presented credentials on June 3, 1899. Terminated service on November 22, 1901.

Juan Riaño, secretary of legation and chargé d'affaires ad interim. Served as chargé from November 22, 1901, to July 22, 1902.

Emilio de Ojeda y Perpiñan, envoy extraordinary and minister plenipotentiary. Presented credentials on July 22, 1902. Terminated service on April 11, 1905.

Manuel Walls y Merino, second secretary of legation and chargé d'affaires ad interim. Served as chargé from April 11, 1905, to April 30, 1905.

Luis Pastor, first secretary of legation and chargé d'affaires ad interim. Served as chargé from April 30, 1905, to March 13, 1907.

Ramón Piña y Millet, envoy extraordinary and minister plenipotentiary. Presented credentials on March 13, 1907. Terminated duty on June 24, 1909.

Luis Pastor, first secretary of legation and chargé d'affaires ad interim. Served as chargé from June 24, 1909, to July 31, 1909.

Marqués de Villalobar (Rodrigo Saavedra y Vinent), envoy extraordinary and minister plenipotentiary. Presented credentials on July 31, 1909. Terminated service on February 25, 1910.

Francisco de Zea Bermudez, secretary of legation and chargé d'affaires ad interim. Served as chargé from February 25, 1910, to May 24, 1910.

Juan Riaño y Gayangos, envoy extraordinary and minister plenipotentiary. Presented credentials on May 24, 1910. Terminated service on December 1, 1913. Served as ambassador extraordinary and plenipotentiary from December 1, 1913, to August 23, 1926.

Manuel Walls y Merino, minister resident. Served from March 18, 1917. Date of service termination not known.

Mariano Amoedo y Galarmendi, second secretary of embassy and chargé d'affaires ad interim. Served from August to September 1926.

Eduardo Garcia Comin, counselor of embassy and chargé d'affaires ad interim. Served as chargé from September 21, 1926, to October 11, 1926.

Alejandro Padilla y Bell, ambassador extraordinary and plenipotentiary. Presented credentials on October 11, 1926. Terminated service on April 15, 1931.

Salvador de Madariaga, ambassador extraordinary and plenipotentiary. Presented credentials on June 30, 1931. Terminated service in either December 1931 or January 1932.

Juan Francisco de Cárdenas y Rodriguez de Rivas, ambassador extraordinary and plenipotentiary. Presented credentials on January 19, 1932. Terminated service in May 1934.

Luis Felipe Calderon y Martin, ambassador extraordinary and plenipotentiary. Presented credentials on June 14, 1934. Terminated service on September 6, 1936.

Fernando de los Rios, ambassador extraordinary and plenipotentiary. Presented credentials on October 20, 1936. Terminated service in late March or early April, 1939.

Juan Francisco de Cárdenas y Rodriguez de Rivas, ambassador extraordinary and plenipotentiary. Presented credentials on June 6, 1939. Terminated service in June, 1947.

Germán Baraibar, minister plenipotentiary, counselor of embassy, chargé d'affaires ad interim. Served as chargé from June 1947 to September 20, 1949.

Eduardo Propper de Callejón, minister plenipotentiary, chargé d'affaires ad interim. Served as chargé from September 20, 1949. Terminated service in January 1951.

José Félix de Lequerica y Erquiza, ambassador. Presented credentials on January 17, 1951. Terminated service about November 1954.

Count de Motrico (José María Areilza), ambassador. Presented credentials on November 6, 1954. Terminated service in August 1960.

Mariano de Yturralde y Orbegoso, ambassador. Presented credentials on August 19, 1960. Terminated service in June 1962.

Antonio Garrigues y Diaz-Canabate, ambassador. Presented credentials on June 20, 1962. Terminated service in May 1964.

Marques de Merry del Val (Alfonso Merry del Val y Alzola), ambassador. Presented credentials on May 19, 1964. Terminated service by February 1970.

Jaime Arguelles, ambassador. Presented credentials on February 20, 1970. Terminated service by March 1972.

Angel Sagaz, ambassador. Presented credentials on March 27, 1972. Terminated service in May 1974.

Jaime Alba, ambassador. Presented credentials in June 1974. Terminated service in December 1976.

Juan José Rovira, ambassador. Presented credentials in January 1977.

APPENDIX B
AMERICAN ENVOYS TO SPAIN[2]

John Jay, minister plenipotentiary. Began duties at end of 1779. Terminated service about May 20, 1782.

William Carmichael, chargé d'affaires. Served from April 20, 1790, to September 5, 1794. Had served in same position intermittently in the 1780s.

William Short, minister resident. Presented credentials on September 7, 1794. Terminated service on November 1, 1795.

David Humphreys, minister plenipotentiary. Presented credentials September 10, 1797. Terminated service about December 28, 1801.

Charles Pinckney, minister resident. Presented credentials in January–March 1802. Terminated service on October 25, 1805.

George W. Erving, minister plenipotentiary. Presented credentials on August 24, 1816. Terminated service on May 15, 1819.

John Forsyth, minister plenipotentiary. Presented credentials on May 18, 1819. Terminated service on March 2, 1823.

Hugh Nelson, minister plenipotentiary. Presented credentials on December 4, 1823. Terminated service on July 10, 1825.

Alexander Hill Everett, envoy extraordinary and minister plenipotentiary. Presented credentials on September 4, 1825. Terminated service on August 1, 1829.

Cornelius P. Van Ness, envoy extraordinary and minister plenipotentiary. Presented credentials on December 9, 1829. Terminated service on December 21, 1836.

William T. Barry, envoy extraordinary and minister plenipotentiary. Took oath of office but died en route to post in 1835.

---

2. Extracted from Richardson Dougall and Mary Patricia Chapman, *United States Chiefs of Mission, 1778–1973* (Washington, D.C., 1973), 139–143.

APPENDIX B

John H. Eaton, envoy extraordinary and minister plenipotentiary. Presented credentials about February 1, 1837. Terminated service on May 1, 1840.

Aaron Vail, chargé d'affaires. Served from November 5, 1840, to August 1, 1842.

Washington Irving, envoy extraordinary and minister plenipotentiary. Presented credentials on August 1, 1842. Terminated service on July 29, 1846.

Romulus M. Saunders, envoy extraordinary and minister plenipotentiary. Presented credentials on July 31, 1846. Terminated service on September 24, 1849.

Daniel M. Barringer, envoy extraordinary and minister plenipotentiary. Presented credentials on October 24, 1849. Terminated service on September 4, 1853.

Pierre Soulé, envoy extraordinary and minister plenipotentiary. Presented credentials on October 24, 1853. Terminated service on February 1, 1855.

Augustus C. Dodge, envoy extraordinary and minister plenipotentiary. Presented credentials on June 17, 1856. Terminated service on March 12, 1859.

William Preston, envoy extraordinary and minister plenipotentiary. Presented credentials on March 12, 1859. Terminated service on May 24, 1861.

Carl Schurz, envoy extraordinary and minister plenipotentiary. Presented credentials on July 13, 1861. Terminated service on December 18, 1861.

Gustavus Koerner, envoy extraordinary and minister plenipotentiary. Presented credentials on November 4, 1862. Terminated service on July 20, 1864.

John P. Hale, envoy extraordinary and minister plenipotentiary. Presented credentials on September 30, 1865. Terminated service on July 29, 1869.

Daniel E. Sickles, envoy extraordinary and minister plenipotentiary. Presented credentials on July 29, 1869. Terminated service on January 31, 1874.

Caleb Cushing, envoy extraordinary and minister plenipotentiary. Presented credentials on May 30, 1874. Terminated service on April 9, 1877.

James Russell Lowell, envoy extraordinary and minister plenipotentiary. Presented credentials on August 18, 1877. Terminated service on March 2, 1880.

Lucius Fairchild, envoy extraordinary and minister plenipotentiary. Presented credentials on March 31, 1880. Terminated service on December 20, 1881.

Hannibal Hamlin, envoy extraordinary and minister plenipotentiary. Presented credentials on December 20, 1881. Terminated service on October 17, 1882.

John W. Foster, envoy extraordinary and minister plenipotentiary. Presented credentials on June 16, 1883. Terminated service on August 28, 1885.

Jabez L. M. Curry, envoy extraordinary and minister plenipotentiary. Presented credentials on December 22, 1885. Terminated service on July 5, 1888.

Perry Belmont, envoy extraordinary and minister plenipotentiary. Presented credentials on February 13, 1889. Terminated service on May 1, 1889.

Thomas W. Palmer, envoy extraordinary and minister plenipotentiary. Presented credentials on June 17, 1889. Terminated service on April 19, 1890.

E. Burd Grubb, envoy extraordinary and minister plenipotentiary. Presented credentials on December 23, 1890. Terminated service on May 26, 1892.

A. Loudon Snowden, envoy extraordinary and minister plenipotentiary. Presented credentials on October 6, 1892. Terminated service on June 3, 1893.

Hannis Taylor, envoy extraordinary and minister plenipotentiary. Presented credentials on July 1, 1893. Terminated service on September 13, 1897.

Stewart L. Woodford, envoy extraordinary and minister plenipotentiary. Presented credentials on September 13, 1897. Terminated service on April 21, 1898.

Bellamy Storer, envoy extraordinary and minister plenipotentiary. Presented credentials on June 16, 1899. Terminated service on December 10, 1902.

Arthur S. Hardy, envoy extraordinary and minister plenipotentiary. Presented credentials on March 2, 1903. Terminated service on May 1, 1905.

William Miller Collier, envoy extraordinary and minister plenipotentiary. Presented credentials on May 15, 1905. Terminated service on June 9, 1909.

Henry Clay Ide, envoy extraordinary and minister plenipotentiary. Presented credentials on June 9, 1909. Terminated service on July 8, 1913.

Joseph E. Willard, envoy extraordinary and minister plenipotentiary with title changed to ambassador extraordinary and plenipotentiary. Presented original credentials on October 31, 1913. Terminated service on July 7, 1921.

Cyrus E. Woods, ambassador extraordinary and plenipotentiary. Presented credentials on October 14, 1921. Terminated service on April 18, 1923.

Alexander P. Moore, ambassador extraordinary and plenipotentiary. Presented credentials on May 16, 1923. Terminated service on December 20, 1925.

Ogden H. Hammond, ambassador extraordinary and plenipotentiary. Presented credentials on March 26, 1926. Terminated service on October 13, 1929.

Irwin B. Laughlin, ambassador extraordinary and plenipotentiary. Presented credentials on December 24, 1929. Terminated service on April 12, 1933.

Claude G. Bowers, ambassador extraordinary and plenipotentiary. Presented credentials on June 1, 1933. Terminated service on February 2, 1939.

H. Freemon Matthew, chargé d'affaires ad interim. Presented credentials on April 13, 1939. Terminated service on or about June 15, 1939.

Alexander W. Weddell, ambassador extraordinary and plenipotentiary. Presented credentials on June 15, 1939. Terminated service on February 7, 1942.

Carlton J. H. Hayes, ambassador extraordinary and plenipotentiary. Presented credentials on June 9, 1942. Terminated service on January 18, 1945.

Norman Armour, ambassador extraordinary and plenipotentiary. Presented credentials on March 24, 1945. Terminated service on December 1, 1945.

Phillip W. Bonsal, chargé d'affaires ad interim. Served between March 1946 and June 1947.

Paul T. Culberston, chargé d'affaires ad interim. Served between June 1947 and December 1950.

Stanton Griffis, ambassador extraordinary and plenipotentiary. Presented credentials on March 1, 1951. Terminated service on January 28, 1952.

Lincoln MacVeagh, ambassador extraordinary and plenipotentiary. Presented credentials on March 27, 1952. Terminated service on March 4, 1953.

James Clement Dunn, ambassador extraordinary and plenipotentiary. Presented credentials on April 9, 1953. Terminated service on February 9, 1955.

John Lodge, ambassador extraordinary and plenipotentiary. Presented credentials on March 24, 1955. Terminated service on April 13, 1961.

Anthony J. Drexel Biddle, ambassador extraordinary and plenipotentiary. Presented credentials on May 25, 1961. Terminated service on October 12, 1961.

Robert F. Woodward, ambassador extraordinary and plenipotentiary. Presented credentials on May 10, 1962. Terminated service on February 1, 1965.

Angier Biddle Duke, ambassador extraordinary and plenipotentiary. Presented credentials on April 1, 1965. Terminated service on March 30, 1968.

Frank E. McKinney, ambassador extraordinary and plenipotentiary. Appointed on May 11, 1968, and took oath of office but did not serve.

Robert F. Wagner, ambassador extraordinary and plenipotentiary. Presented credentials on July 4, 1968. Terminated service on March 7, 1969.

Robert C. Hill, ambassador extraordinary and plenipotentiary. Presented credentials on June 12, 1969. Terminated service on January 12, 1972.

Joseph J. Montllor, deputy chief of mission. Served from January to October 1972.

Horacio Rivero, ambassador extraordinary and plenipotentiary. Presented credentials on October 11, 1972. Terminated service March 1975.

Wells Stabler, ambassador extraordinary and plenipotentiary. Presented credentials in March 1975.

BIBLIOGRAPHIC ESSAY

The purpose of this essay is to review some of the basic sources for Spanish-American relations. It is not a definitive survey of the bibliography on the subject since it is meant only to introduce the subject in general terms. Moreover, only some of the important titles listed in the notes are mentioned below; materials of lesser significance have been left out. For more details on any particular issue or era, consult the bibliographies accompanying many of the monographs cited below.

Manuscript collections are massive on the subject. For the American half of the story, the fundamental documents are the diplomatic dispatches from Spain written by envoys and consuls. The most useful are the ministerial dispatches, housed at the National Archives in Washington, D.C., which cover the years from 1792 through 1951 (as of this writing), with a new year of papers opening to researchers approximately every twelve months. The dispatches through 1906 have been microfilmed on 134 rolls and may be purchased. For a list of these, consult National Archives pamphlet for Microcopy No. 31, *Despatches from United States Ministers to Spain, 1792–1906* (Washington, D. C., 1959). Materials after 1906 are currently being filmed and are not yet available. Consular dispatches for at least seventeen posts in Spain and its colonies to 1906, totaling over 100 rolls, are also on film. Price lists for these may be obtained upon request from the National Archives. Also available on microfilm are "Diplomatic Instructions of the Department of State, 1801–1906 (M-77): Spain," for which one dozen rolls exist. Other valuable collections include "Notes from the Spanish Legation in the United States to the Department of State, 1790–1906 (M-59)" containing 31 rolls and "Notes to Foreign Legations in the United States from the Department of State, 1834–1906 (M-99): Spain, 1834–1906," rolls 85–90.

All of these papers are basic to understanding American policy toward Spain. There are also other groups of minor consular, State, and Navy Department records not on microfilm. For a list of these, consult the catalog prepared by Daniel T. Goggin and H. Stephen Helton for the National Archives, Preliminary Inventories No. 157, *General Records of the Department of State* (Washington, D. C., 1963); Mark G. Eckhoff and Alexander P. Mavro, *List of Foreign Service Post Records in the National Archives*, rev. ed. (Washington, D. C., 1967), and Natalia Summers, *List of Documents Relating to Special Agents of the Department of State, 1789–1906* (Washington, D. C., 1951). For relevant private papers of diplomats and politicians, see the bibliographies of the specialized monographs below.

On the Spanish side, the basic papers are the diplomatic dispatches written by ministers and consuls assigned to the United States and copies of correspondence from the Ministerio de Asuntos Exteriores (Foreign Office), known also as the Ministerio de Estado in the nineteenth century. These papers are housed in two locations. Those from the 1770s through 1833 are kept at the Archivo Histórico Nacional. A partial catalog of these, listing what has been put on microfilm, is the Archivo Histórico Nacional's (Sección de Estado), *Relaciones diplomáticas entre España y los Estados Unidos (Años 1737–1819)* (Madrid, 1972). The rest of the diplomatic papers are preserved at the Foreign Office in Madrid in an archival bureau. Both sets are open to scholars through 1930. A card file exists that may be consulted at the Foreign Office. For a short description of the post-1833 papers dealing with the United States, see my "Spanish Foreign Office Archives," *SHAFR Newsletter* 4, no. 3 (September 1973): 2–4. Two other collections are the papers of the Spanish consulate in Charleston, South Carolina, 1794–1898, and of the vice-consulate in Savannah, Georgia, 1835–1935, both of which are at Duke University in North Carolina. Private papers of individual Spanish diplomats and politicians relevant to Spanish-American diplomacy are almost nonexistent.

The study of Spanish-American relations through documents can be augmented by consulting the colonial files of the Spanish government for Cuba and Puerto Rico housed at the Archivo Histórico Nacional. There, bibliographic guides suggest some of the basic groups of documents. These colonial files are voluminous and especially useful for the twentieth century as a whole and more specifically for the years 1868–78 and 1895–98 on Cuba. The diplomatic dispatches of the British envoy to Madrid from the eighteenth century through World War II are often useful and may be consulted at the Public Records Office in London. The PRO has published various volumes of *Lists and Indexes*, which break down the files by years and countries. These papers are vast; therefore the guides are necessary. French diplomatic papers are also massive, particularly for the nineteenth century. These are housed at the French Foreign Office (Quai d'Orsay). The archivists there have published several useful guides, Archives du Ministère des Affaires Étrangères, *État numérique des fonds de la Correspondance Politique de L'Origine a 1871* (Paris, 1926); *Inventaire sommaire des archives du Département des Affaires Étrangères, Correspondance Politique*, II, *Espagne* (Paris, 1919), and *Inventaires des Mémoires et Documents: Fonds France et Fonds divers des Pays D'Europe jusqu'en 1896* (Paris, 1964). The French dispatches from Madrid are far more informative as a whole than those from Washington.

Some documentary collections have been published. On the American side, a selection of diplomatic correspondence between Spain and the United States from 1831 to 1861 on the Caribbean is available in William R. Manning, ed., *Diplomatic Correspondence of the United States: Inter-American Affairs, 1831–1861*, vol. 11: *Spain* (Washington, D. C., 1939). From 1861 through the 1940s there are the Department of State's *Foreign Relations of the United States* collections of dispatches and other diplomatic papers arranged by country and continuously being augmented by new volumes now covering the 1950s. They are invaluable for the study of American diplomatic history, particularly the volumes from World War I forward. Unfortunately there is no Spanish equivalent. For the Revolutionary War period, however, there are Miguel Gómez del Campillo, *Relaciones diplomáticas entre España y los Estados Unidos, según documentos del Archivo Histórico Nacional*, 2 vols. (Madrid, 1954–55), and the detailed publication by the Ministry of Foreign Affairs, *Documentos relativos a la Independencia de Norteamerica existentes en archivos españoles*, 5 vols. to date (Madrid, 1976–).

General published surveys of Spanish-American diplomacy appeared early in the twentieth century. A retired American naval officer and member of the naval board investigating the explosion of the U.S.S. *Maine*, French Ensor Chadwick, wrote *The Relations of the United States and Spain*, 3 vols. (New York, 1909–11), a detailed discussion about Cuban problems. The second and third volumes concerned only the war of 1898. Another general survey is Willis Fletcher's *A History of Cuba*, 3 vols. (New York, 1920). More recently the American envoy to Madrid from 1942 to 1945 and a historian in his own right, Carlton J. H. Hayes, wrote a short book designed to foster closer relations by minimizing the differences between the two nations, *The United States and Spain: An Interpretation* (New York, 1951). Philip S. Foner wrote four volumes on Cuban-American relations with a Marxist interpretation, *A History of Cuba and Its Relations with the United States*, 2 vols. (New York, 1963), which takes the story through the mid-nineteenth century, and *The Spanish-Cuban-American War and the Birth of American Imperialism, 1895–1902*, 2 vols. (New York, 1972). One other American publication worth mentioning is Eula McDonald, "Highlights in the History of the United States Post at Barcelona, Spain, 1797–1959," *Cuadernos de Historia Económica de Cataluña* (1969–1970): 21–63. For a detailed list of hundreds of titles from the 1770s to the present, consult my *A Bibliographic Guide to Spanish Diplomatic History, 1460–1977* (Westport, Conn., 1977).

Spaniards wrote fewer general accounts of diplomatic relations between the two countries. The one dominating figure here was Jerónimo Becker, director of the archive at the Foreign Office during the 1920s. His books were based on the Spanish diplomatic papers, the most useful of which included *Historica política y diplomática desde la independencia de los Estados Unidos hasta nuestros días, 1776–1895* (Madrid, 1897), *La independencia de América: su reconocimiento por España* (Madrid, 1922), and *Historia de las relaciones exteriores de España durante el siglo XIX*, 3 vols. (Madrid, 1924–27). Of some use is a cultural history by Stanley T. Williams, *The Spanish Background of American Literature*, 2 vols. (New Haven, 1955). Three other publications offer interpretations of relations. A noted Spanish historian, Rafael Altamira, discussed their significance in a pamphlet, *Cuestiones internacionales: España, América y los Estados Unidos* (Madrid, 1916). On treaties and more current relations, consult a booklet by Ildefonso Cuesta Garrigos, *Los convenios entre España y los Estados Unidos* (Madrid, 1955). A good survey of the colonial problems plaguing Spain in the last century with references to the United States is Roberto Mesa, *El colonialismo en la crisis del XIX español* (Madrid, 1967).

The period from 1776 to the 1840s attracted much historical attention. For the American Revolution, see Samuel Flagg Bemis, *The Diplomacy of the American Revolution* (New York, 1935, various editions subsequent), and his earlier study, *The Hussey-Cumberland Mission and American Independence* (Princeton, 1931); Edward S. Corwin, *French Policy and the American Alliance of 1778* (Hamden, Conn., 1916); Buchanan P. Thompson, *La ayuda española en la guerra de la independencía norteamericana* (Madrid, 1967), and its English translation, *Spain: Forgotten Ally of the American Revolution* (North Quincy, Mass., 1976); Mario Rodríguez, *La revolución americana de 1776 y el mundo hispanico: ensayos y documentos* (Madrid, 1976); and Juan F. Yela Utrilla, *España ante la independencía de Estados Unidos*, 2 vols. (Lerida, 1925)—all based on archival work.

More recently, new Spanish studies have appeared on various aspects of the American Revolution. Pedro Voltes Bou published a series of items, "Repercusiones de la guerra de la Independencía de Estados Unidos en el comercio español de Indias," *Revista de Indias*, no. 76 (April–June 1959): 213–221; "La tentative de mediación de España en la Guerra de Independencía de los Estados Unidos," ibid., nos. 109–110 (1967): 313–334; and *Catalunya i la llibertat del comerc amb America* (Barcelona, 1964). Two other serious contributions include a letter on Spanish recognition of the Americans, Jacques Donvez, "La première démarche, faite en 1776 pour la reconnaissance des Etats-Unis par l'Espagne fut l'oeuvre de Beaumarchais," *Revue Historique* 218, no. 2 (1957): 279–283, and Matero Rafael Sanchez, "La misión de John Jay en España, 1779–1782," *Anuario de Estudios Americanos* 24 (1967): 1389–1431. Recently some historians have tried to revive the notion that Spain's aid to the colonists was decisive: Francisco Morales Padrón, *Participación de España en la independencia política de los Estados Unidos* (Madrid, 1952); Manuel Ballesteros, "Participación de España en la Independencia de Estados Unidos," *Revista Cubana* 31, nos. 3–4 (1957): 29–48; Luis Merino, "La ayuda española a la independencia de Estados Unidos," *Religión y Cultura* 15 (July–September 1969): 409–428; and on the key Spanish military figure in Louisiana, see José Rodulfo Boeta, *Bernardo De Galvez* (Madrid, 1976). Also useful is J. Leitch Wright, *Florida in the American Revolution* (Gainesville, Fla., 1976).

The immediate post-Revolutionary War years have also been the subject of much research. One of the earliest works was by Samuel G. Coe, "The Mission of William Carmichael to Spain" (Ph.D. dissertation, Johns Hopkins University, 1926). More recently Sandra Sealove produced "The Founding Fathers as Seen by the Marqués de Casa-Irujo," *The Americas* 20, no. 1 (1963): 27–32, and a summary of her doctoral dissertation done at the University of Madrid, "La relaciones diplomáticas entre España y los Estados Unidos de Norteamérica a través de la embajada de Carlos María Martínez de Irujo, marqués de Casa-Irujo, 1796–1807," *Revista de la Universidad de Madrid* 12 (1963): 803–805. Relations past the turn of the century may be gleaned from José Navarro Latorre and Fernando Solano Costa, *¿Conspiración española? 1787–1789. Contribución al estudio de las primeras relaciones históricas entre España y los Estados Unidos de América* (Zaragoza, 1949), and from Norman Fulton, *Relaciones diplomáticas entre España y los Estados Unidos a finales del siglo XVIII: relaciones económico-comerciales* (Madrid, 1970). Also useful are Mary P. Adams, "Jefferson's Reaction to the Treaty of San Ildefonso," *Journal of Southern History* 21 (1955): 173–188, and Raymond Arthur Young, *La influencia de Godoy en el desarrollo de los Estados Unidos de América, a costa de Nueva España* (Mexico, 1968).

More standard works on territorial rivalry are by Americans. Samuel Flagg Bemis contributed to the subject with *Pinckney's Treaty: A Study of America's Advantage from Europe's Distress, 1783–1800* (Baltimore, 1926); Arthur P. Whitaker, *The Spanish-American Frontier: 1783–1795, The Westward Movement and the Spanish Retreat in the Mississippi Valley* (Boston, 1927); P. C. Brooks, *Diplomacy and the Borderlands: The Adams-Onis Treaty of 1819* (Berkeley, 1939); Thomas M. Marshall, *A History of the Western Boundary of the Louisiana Purchase, 1819–1841* (Berkeley, 1914), and most recently, Warren L. Cook's monumental *Flood Tide of Empire: Spain and the Pacific Northwest* (New Haven, 1973).

The specific problems posed by Florida have been covered in a series of monographs by H. B. Fuller, *The Purchase of Florida* (Cleveland, 1906); Isaac J. Cox, *The West Florida Controversy, 1798–1813* (Baltimore, 1918), and Robert L. Gold, *Borderland Empire in Transition: The Triple-Nation Transfer of Florida* (Carbondale, 1969). On aspects of the question see J. Leitch Wright, Jr., *William Augustus Bowles: Director General of the Creek Nation* (Athens, 1967), *Anglo-Spanish Rivalry in North America* (Athens, 1970), *Britain and the American Frontier, 1783–1815* (Athens, 1974). Regarding Georgia's frontier warfare consult R. W. Patrick, *Florida Fiasco: Rampant Rebels on the Georgia-Florida Border, 1810–1815* (Athens, 1954). Each of these monographs is well researched and deals with the problems on a broad basis, encompassing relations among Spain, the United States, France, and Britain.

The Latin American revolutions have generated dozens of excellent monographs, thousands of polemical publications, and large collections of documents. Many of these deal with relations between the United States and Spain. For a detailed bibliography arranged by topic and country, see David F. Trask, et al., *A Bibliography of United States-Latin American Relations since 1810* (Lincoln, 1968). To understand the story, one need only consult a few works. Among these, the most comprehensive are Charles C. Griffin, *The United States and the Disruption of the Spanish Empire, 1810–1822* (New York, 1937); Arthur P. Whitaker, *The United States and the Independence of Latin America, 1800–1830* (Baltimore, 1941); Bradford Perkins, *Castlereagh and Adams: England and the United States, 1812–1823* (Berkeley, 1964); and J. Fred Rippy, *Rivalry of the United States and Great Britain over Latin America, 1808–1830* (Baltimore, 1929). The best surveys of the Monroe Doctrine were written by Dexter Perkins, *Hands Off: A History of the Monroe Doctrine* (Boston, 1941), and *A History of the Monroe Doctrine* (Boston, 1963). Ernest R. May has written an excellent monograph on the same subject, *The Making of the Monroe Doctrine* (Cambridge, Mass., 1975). On the early Pan-Americanism of the United States, see Ralph Sanders, "Congressional Reaction in the United States to the Panamá Congress of 1826," *The Americas* 11, no. 2 (1954): 141–154. One of the best overall surveys of the revolutions is by John Lynch, *The Spanish-American Revolutions, 1808–1826* (New York, 1973).

During the following decades when Spanish-American rivalry settled on the Caribbean, events multiplied, eventually attracting the attention of American, Cuban, and Spanish historians. A distinguished Cuban scholar, Herminio Portell Vilá, wrote a study covering the entire nineteenth century, *Historia de Cuba en sus relaciones con los Estados Unidos*, 4 vols. (Havana, 1938–41). On related topics, see Charles C. Tansill's *The United States and Santo Domingo, 1798–1873. A Chapter in Caribbean Diplomacy* (Baltimore, 1938), and Mark J. Van Aken, *Pan-Hispanism: Its Origin and Development to 1866* (Berkeley, 1959). J. M. Callahan studied the multinational problems posed by the Caribbean in "Cuba and Anglo-American Relations," American Historical Association, *Annual Report, 1897* (Washington, 1898), 195–215, and in *Cuba and International Relations* (Baltimore, 1899). For a Spanish account see Isidro Fabela, *Los Estados Unidos contra la libertad* (Barcelona, 1921).

On narrower themes there are various publications. Cuban documents were printed in "Correspondencía reservada de los Cónsules de Expaña en los Estados Unidos con el Gobernador y Capitán General de ... Cuba, 1819–1834," *Boletin del Archivo Nacional* (Havana) 27 (1928): 129–273. A detailed study based on Spanish, French, and American documents is José Luciano Franco, *La batalla por el dominio del Caribe. Política continental americana de España en Cuba, 1812–1830* (Havana, 1964). On the Mexican War, see David M. Pletcher, *The Diplomacy of Annexation, Texas, Oregon and the Mexican War* (Columbia, 1973). Also of use are Glen T. Harper, ed., "The Spanish Diary of Arthur Middleton," *The Southern Quarterly* 7, no. 3 (April 1969): 207–249, and no. 4 (July 1969): 393–423, and Juan Llabrés' pamphlet, *La estación naval norteamericana en Mahon (1815–1826)* (Palma de Mallorca, 1969).

The Cuban slave issue was recently studied by Arthur F. Corwin, *Spain and the Abolition of Slavery in Cuba, 1817–1886* (Austin, 1967), and Franklin W. Knight, *Slave Society in Cuba during the Nineteenth Century* (Madison, 1970). The expanding role of the Monroe Doctrine came under examination by several historians. The best monographs were written by Dexter Perkins: *The Monroe Doctrine, 1826–1867* (Baltimore, 1933) and *The Monroe Doctrine, 1867–1907* (Baltimore, 1937). More recently Clifford L. Egan wrote "The Monroe Doctrine and Santo Domingo in Spanish-American Diplomacy, 1861–1865,"

Lincoln Herald 71 (Summer 1969): 55–68. The most useful Spanish account is by L. Izaga, *La doctrina de Monroe: su origen y principales faces de su evolución* (Madrid, 1929).

On López there are Anderson C. Quisenberry, *Lopez's Expeditions to Cuba, 1850 and 1851* (Louisville, 1906); the best account in English by Robert Caldwell, *The Lopez Expeditions to Cuba, 1848–1851* (Princeton, 1915); and the most detailed, Herminio Portell Vilá, *Narciso López y su epoca*, 3 vols. (Havana, 1930). See Portell Vilá for that and earlier years in the above article in the *Boletin del Archivo Nacional*. Other studies of value include L. A. Yanow, "Washington Irving as United States Minister to Spain: The Revolution of 1843" (Ph.D. dissertation, New York University, 1969); Amos A. Ettinger, *The Mission to Spain of Pierre Soulé, 1853–1855* (New Haven, 1932); Emeterio S. Santovenia, *El Ptesidente Polk y Cuba* (Havana, 1936); Basil Rauch, *American Interest in Cuba, 1848–1855* (New York, 1948); A. C. Wilgus, "Official Expressions of Manifest Destiny Sentiments Concerning Hispanic-America, 1848–1871," *The Louisiana Historical Quarterly* 15 (July 1932): 486–506; and C. S. Urban, "The Ideology of Southern Imperialism: New Orleans and the Caribbean, 1845–1861," *The Louisiana Historical Quarterly* 39 (January 1956): 48–73.

In recent years a number of articles and books have explored the active decade of the 1860s. R. Olivar Bertrand commented on the age in "Notas sobre la visión norteamericana de España de 1860 a 1870," *Revista de Occidente*, no. 22 (January 1965): 50–71, "Conflictos de España en el Caribe juzgados por los Estados Unidos, 1860–1870," *Cuadernos Americanos* 150 (January–February 1967): 157–173, and *España y los españoles: cien años atras* (Madrid, 1970). On Spain's intervention into Mexico, the most useful study is by Carl H. Bock, *Prelude to Tragedy: Negotiation and Breakdown of the Tripartite Convention of London, October 31, 1861* (Philadelphia, 1966). The standard account of the Chilean war is William Columbus Davis, *The Last of the Conquistadores: The Spanish Intervention in Peru and Chile, 1863–1866* (Athens, 1950). For a version of the later war more favorable to Spain, see my "Diplomatic Rivalry between Spain and the United States over Chile and Peru, 1864–1871," *Inter-American Eeconomic Affairs* 27 (Spring 1974): 47–58.

An early survey of relations during the American Civil War was by Donaldson H. Jordan and Edwin J. Pratt, "Spanish Opinion of the North American Civil War," *Hispanic American Historical Review* 10 (February 1930): 14–25. Other publications include Emeterio S. Santovenia, *Lincoln el precursor de la buena vecindad* (Havana, 1951); Clifford L. Egan, "Cuba, Spain and the American Civil War," *The Rocky Mountain Social Science Journal* 5 (October 1968): 58–63, and his "An American Diplomat in Spain: Selected Civil War Letters of Horatio J. Perry," *Lincoln Herald* 73 (Summer 1971): 62–75. I have also commented on the period in "A Case of International Rivalry in Latin America: Spain's Occupation of Santo Domingo, 1853–1865," *Revista de Historia de América*, no. 82 (July–December 1976): 53–82; "Relaciones diplomaticas entre los Estados Unidos y España, 1861–1865," *Cuadernos de Historia Economica de Cataluña* 4 (1969–70): 107–123; "Pierre Rost and Confederate Diplomacy," *Louisiana Historical Quarterly* 54 (Summer–Fall 1971): 18–28; Charles J. Helm, "Cuba and the Confederacy," *The Journal of the Southern Confederacy* 2, no. 2 (1972): 12–32, "Spanish Views on Abraham Lincoln, 1861–1865," *Lincoln Herald* 76 (Summer 1974): 80–86, and "Rivalry in the New World: United States-Spanish Relations, 1855–1868" (Ph.D. dissertation, Florida State University, 1973).

For the period from 1868 to 1895 useful studies exist. On American influence in Spanish politics, see Joaquin Oltra, *La influencia norteamericana en la constitución española de 1869* (Madrid, 1972). On diplomacy see Roderick Hiram Conrad, "Spanish-United States Relations, 1868–1874" (Ph.D. dissertation, University of Georgia, 1969); Edgumb Pinchon, *Dan Sickles, Hero of Gettysburg and "Yankee King of Spain"* (Garden City, 1945), and W. A. Swanberg, *Sickles the Incredible* (New York, 1956). Two useful studies on the Ten Years' War are Emilio Roig de Leuchsenring, *Cuba y los Estados Unidos, 1805–1898* (Havana, 1949), and Ramiro Guerry Sanchez, *Guerra de los Diez Años, 1868–78*, 2 vols. (Havana, 1950–52). For American policy seen from Washington, see Allan Nevins, *Hamilton Fish: The Inner History of the Grant Administration* (New York, 1936).

Two monographs on Spain's foreign policy set Spanish-American relations into the context of European diplomacy: Leonar Melendez, *Cánovas y la política exterior española* (Madrid, 1944), and Julio Salom, *España en la Europa de Bismarck* (Madrid, 1967). In English there is

F. J. D. Lambert, "The Cuban Question in Spanish Restoration Politics, 1878–1898" (Ph.D. dissertation, University of Oxford, 1968–69). On Caleb Cushing's dealing with the Spanish in 1876–77, see Ignacio Herrero de Collantes, "Notas diplomáticas sobre Cuba colonial en sus ultimos años," *Boletín de la Real Academia de la Historia* 138, no. 2 (1956): 135–149. On Lowell's tour of duty in Spain, see Martin Duberman, *James Russell Lowell* (Boston, 1966). The career of the Spanish envoy of the mid-1880s is covered in Cyrus C. Decoster, "Valera en Washington," *Arbor* 27 (1954): 215–223.

Many historians have studied diplomatic aspects of Cuba's revolution of 1895 and Madrid's war with Washington in 1898. On the literature of this period one might begin with Nancy Leonore O'Connor, "The Spanish-American War: A Reevaluation of Its Causes," *Science and Society* 22 (Spring 1958): 129–143. Most of the published works deal with domestic American affairs and their influence on Washington's foreign policy. One of the earlier studies was Julius W. Pratt, *Expansionists of 1898* (Baltimore, 1938). For a short survey of the same theme, see Charles Velvier, "American Continentalism: An Idea of Expansion, 1845–1910," *American Historical Review* 65 (January 1960): 323–335. Also useful are Nelson M. Blake, "Background of Cleveland's Venezuelan Policy," ibid. 47 (January 1942): 259–277; Walter LeFeber's important book, *The New Empire: An Interpretation of American Expansion, 1860–1898* (Ithaca, 1963); Louis J. Halle, *Dream and Reality* (New York, 1958); Robert E. Osgood, *Ideals and Self-Interest in America's Foreign Relations* (Chicago, 1953); and Christopher Lasch, "The Anti-Imperialists, the Philippines, and the Inequality of Man," *Journal of Southern History* 14 (August 1958): 319–331.

Diplomatic accounts abound. Horace E. Flack's *Spanish-American Diplomatic Relations Preceding the War of 1898* (Baltimore, 1906) was a major work for years, as was Walter Millis, *The Martial Spirit* (New York, 1931). A good survey is H. Wayne Morgan, *America's Road to Empire* (New York, 1965). A Spanish diplomat, Orestes Ferrara, wrote *The Last Spanish War: Revolution in Diplomacy* (New York, 1937), setting the event within the context of European affairs. Becker, *Historia de las relaciones exteriores*, vol. 3, also relies on Spanish documents. The role of the U.S. consul in Havana during the 1890s is covered by Gerald G. Eggert, "Our Man in Havana: Fitzhugh Lee," *Hispanic American Historical Review* 47 (November 1967): 463–485. Elbert J. Benton dealt with the subject as a problem of international law in *International Law and Diplomacy of the Spanish-American War* (Baltimore, 1908). Jesús Pabón y Súarez de Urbina summarized its diplomatic implications in *El 98: Acontecimiento internacional* (Madrid, 1952). A more detailed Spanish account is by Pablo de Azcárate, *La guerra del 98* (Madrid, 1968). The best volume on the war's diplomacy is Ernest R. May's *Imperial Diplomacy: The Emergence of America as a Great Power* (New York, 1961). For a general account of the *Maine*, see John E. Weems, *The Fate of the Maine* (New York, 1958). The most useful book on how the ship blew up, which convincingly argues that it exploded as a result of spontaneous combustion of coal on board, is H. G. Rickover, *How the Battleship Maine Was Destroyed* (Washington, D. C., 1976).

Shirley F. Jackson's "The United States and Spain, 1898–1918" (Ph.D. dissertation, Florida State University, 1967) utilizes American papers but no Spanish manuscripts. M. A. S. Hume's *The United States and Spain* (New York, 1909) briefly summarizes relations from 1898 to 1909. The U.S. minister from 1905 to 1909, William Miller Collier, wrote *At the Court of His Catholic Majesty* (Chicago, 1912). On World War I, see Thomas A. Bailey, *The Policy of the United States toward the Neutrals, 1917–1918* (Baltimore, 1942). On the 1920s the only study is by Diana F. Todd, "The United States and Spain during the Regime of Primo de Rivera" (Master's thesis, Florida State University, 1967).

The most useful study of cultural rivalry in the New World is Frederick B. Pike, *Hispanismo, 1898–1936: Spanish Conservatives and Liberals and Their Relations with Spanish America* (Notre Dame, 1971). For an explanation of the anti-Hispanic attitudes of the United States toward Latin America and Spain for the past two centuries, consult Philip Wayne Powell, *Tree of Hate: Propaganda and Prejudices Affecting United States Relations with the Hispanic World* (New York, 1971).

A considerable number of books dealing with the international aspects of the Spanish civil war have appeared, none supported by Spanish diplomatic papers. Three general studies worth examining are Gabriel Jackson, ed., *The Spanish Civil War: Domestic Crisis or International Conspiracy?* (Boston, 1967); Dante A. Puzzo, *Spain and the Great Powers, 1936–1939* (New York, 1971); and Claude G. Bowers, *My Mission to Spain: Watching the Rehearsal for World War II* (New York, 1954), the memoirs of an American ambassador to Spain. The first monograph on Spanish-American relations was by F. Jay Taylor, *The United States and the Spanish Civil War, 1936–1939* (New York, 1956). Allen Guttmann, *The Wound in the Heart: America and the Spanish Civil War* (New York, 1962), deals mainly with domestic American reaction to the conflict. The most recent study is a diplomatic one by Richard P. Traina, *American Diplomacy and the Spanish Civil War* (Bloomington, 1968). Allen Guttman, ed., *American Neutrality and the Spanish Civil War* (Boston, 1963), is an anthology of American opinions on the war.

More specialized works also exist. The best studies on American volunteers in the civil war are Arthur H. Landis, *The Abraham Lincoln Brigade* (New York, 1967); Cecil D. Elby, *Between the Bullet and the Lie: American Volunteers in the Spanish Civil War* (New York, 1969); and Robert A. Rosenstone, *Crusade of the Left: The Lincoln Battalion in the Spanish Civil War* (New York, 1969). On domestic reaction to the conflict, see Hugh Taylor Lovin, "The American Communist Party and the Spanish Civil War, 1936–1939" (Ph.D. dissertation, University of Washington, 1963), and John D. Valaik, "American Catholics and the Spanish Civil War, 1931–1939" (Ph.D. dissertation, University of Rochester, 1964).

Relations during World War II are just now coming under thorough research because American, British, and German documents currently allow scholars to write a fuller account. Yet the story was commented on almost from the end of World War II. Augustín del Río Cisneros wrote two books defending Spanish diplomacy: *Replica al cerco internacional, 1945–1946* (Madrid, 1946) and *Viraje político español durante la II Guerra Mundial* (Madrid, 1947). One Spanish foreign minister, Ramon Serrano Suñer, wrote his memoirs, *Entre Hendaye y Gibraltar* (Madrid, 1947). A more balanced account written by another diplomat is José María Doussinague's *España tenía rázon, 1939–1945* (Madrid, 1947).

Americans active in the period also wrote. Ambassador Carlton J. H. Hayes published *Wartime Mission in Spain* (New York, 1946).

Others included State Department official Herbert Feis, *The Spanish Story: Franco and the Nations at War* (New York, 1947); David L. Gordon and Rayden Dangerfield, both involved in economic warfare, *The Hidden Weapon* (New York, 1947); and embassy employees Charles Foltz, Jr., *The Masquerade in Spain* (Boston, 1948), and Emmet John Hughes, *Report from Spain* (New York, 1947).

Much of the polemical literature is listed in my "A Bibliography of Materials Published Outside of Spain on the Franco Period of Spanish History, 1939–1971," *Cuadernos de Historia Económica de Cataluña* 6 (1971): 79–90, and 8 (1972): 240–241. On Ambassador Weddell's two years in Spain, see Charles R. Halstead, "Diligent Diplomat: Alexander W. Weddell as American Ambassador to Spain, 1939–1942," *The Virginia Magazine of History and Biography* 82 (January 1974): 1–39. For the role of Carlton Hayes, see John P. Wilson's "Carlton J. H. Hayes in Spain, 1942–1945" (Ph.D. dissertation, Syracuse University, 1969), and my *United States-Spanish Relations: Wolfram and World War II* (Barcelona, 1973).

Historians have commented on Spanish-American relations since World War II. A general survey to about 1960 is Arthur P. Whitaker, *Spain and the Defense of the West: Ally and Liability* (New York, 1961). A more recent volume with sections on Spanish-American diplomacy is by J. Lee Shneidman, ed., *Spain and Franco, 1949–1959* (New York, 1973). On the bases there is Theodore J. Lowi's *Bases in Spain* (Indianapolis, 1963) and on congressional participation, Albert J. Dorley, Jr., "The Role of Congress in the Establishment of Bases in Spain" (Ph.D. dissertation, St. John's University, 1969). The American ambassador of the early 1950s, Stanton Griffis, wrote his memoirs, *Lying in State* (New York, 1952). For a discussion of the United Nations in Spanish-American relations, see R. E. Sanders, *Spain and the United Nations, 1945–1950* (New York, 1966). Beyond 1960, information must be gleaned mainly from newspapers. The most recent monographic accounts in English on relations are by Edmund A. Gullion, "U.S. Security Policy in the Western Mediterranean: Spain and North Africa," in Alvain J. Cottrell and James D. Theberge, eds., *The Western Mediterranean: Its Political, Economic, and Strategic Importance* (New York, 1974), 205–215, and Samuel Chavkin et al., *Spain: Implications for United States Foreign Policy* (Stamford, Conn., 1976). The most detailed surveys of diplomatic, economic, and cultural relations between the two nations since World War II are by Manuel Vázques Montalbán, *La penetración americana en España* (Madrid, 1974), and Eduardo Chamorro and Ignacio Fontes, *Las Bases Norteamericanas en España* (Barcelona, 1976).

On cultural relations during the past generation, one has to consult a variety of materials since there is no study of the subject. For a list of Spanish publications on the United States and for translations of works from English, consult the annual and sometimes semiannual *Libros en venta en Hispanoamerica y España* (Buenos Aires). *Books in Print* serves the same purpose for Spanish publications released in the United States. My bibliography on the Franco regime also contains some useful titles. Spanish and American newspapers provide much information. Dennison Nash wrote a sociological study on the American community in Barcelona, *A Community in Limbo: An Anthropological Study of an American Community Abroad* (Bloomington, 1970). On American academic research on Spain, see the *Newsletter of the Society for Spanish and Portuguese Historical Studies*, which appears four times each year. At least once a year the *American Historical Review* lists recent publications and constantly reviews books. Beyond these few suggestions, there is no substitute for living in both countries.

INDEX

Abolition in Cuba and Puerto Rico, 86-87
Abraham Lincoln Brigade, 199-200
Acheson, Dean, 221, 226
Adams, John, 55
Adams, John Quincy: and Florida, 30; and Latin America, 39
Adams-Onís Treaty, 30
Agnew, Spiro, 241-242
Alfonso XIII, press image of in the United States, 150-151, 161, 162, 168-169, 173
American movies in Spain, 252
American Revolution, significance of, 18
Amiens, Treaty of, 23
Anduaga, Joaquín de, and Latin American revolution, 44
Arab-Israeli conflicts, 240-241
Aranda, Pedro de, 12
Aranjuez, Treaty of, 7-8, 13
Atomic bombs in Spain, 239-240

Bancroft, George, 135
Barcelona, 19th-century ties to the United States, 144-145
Basque Studies Program, 256-257

Black Warrior, 72; compared to *Virginius* affair, 96
Blaine, James G., 103-105
Blue Division, 212
Bolívar, Simón, 49
Borderlands, Spanish-U.S. discussions of (1700s), 10, 11, 14-17
Borrego, Andrés, 69
Bourbon, Juan Carlos, 241, 242, 262, 270
Bowers, Claude, 177
Bravo Murrillo, Antonio, 67-68
Britain: and American Revolution, 6-15; in Caribbean, 52-53, 57, 67-68; Cold War, 220-221, 233; Common Market and, 264-265; and Cuba, 57, 61; on filibustering, 74; and Gibraltar, 240-242; in Latin America, 38-41, 45, 105-106, 180; and Louisiana Purchase, 19-26; and Mexico, 82-83; Monroe Doctrine, policy toward, 45-48; music of, 252; in New World (1500s-1700s), 3-5; and Oregon, 26; and Pacific Northwest, 33; role of in acquisition of Florida, 26-33; and Santo Domingo, 61,

76; Spanish-American War and, 114-115, 124-125; Spanish Civil War and, 187-189, 191-192, 195, 197, 202-203; during Ten Years' War, 93, 96; tourism of, 236-237, 253-254; trade of, 165; and War of 1812, 28-29; during World War I, 153-154, 160-161; during World War II, 207, 210-211, 213-215
Brunetti y Gayoso, José, 146
Buchanan, James, 65-68, 72-73, 75, 76
Butler, Benjamin F., 85

Calderon Collantes, Saturnino, 82
Calderon de la Barca, 138
Calderon y Martin, Luis Felipe, 192
Calvo Serer, Rafael, views on U.S.A., 247-248, 250
Calvo Sotelo, José, economic policies of, 172
Cambó, Francisco, 271-272
Canning, George: and Cuba, 58; and Latin America, 45, 59
Cánovas del Castillo, Antonio, 97-98, 106, 108, 111-112, 127
Caribbean, during American Revolution, 54-55. *See also* Cuba; Santo Domingo
Carlists, 91, 99
Carlos III, 13
Carranza, Venustiano, 159
Carrero Blanco, Luis, 237, 241
Carter, Jimmy, 241, 242
Castejon, Marqués de, 18
Catalan trade, 101-102
Cazneau, William, 77. *See also* Santo Domingo
Cervera, Admiral Pascual, 120
Céspedes, Manuel de, 90

Chamberlain, Neville, 194
Chapman, Charles, 183
Chilean-Peruvian War (1864-1871), 87-88
Cleveland, Grover, 105; policy of on Cuba, 113
Cold War, diplomacy of, 217-222
Collier, William, 152-153
Columbus, Christopher, anniversary celebration (1892), 106
Common Market, and Spain, 237-239, 262, 265
Concert of Europe, and Latin America, 38-39
Congress of Aix-la-Chapelle, 41-42
Conolly, Admiral Richard L., talks with Franco, 227
Cortina Mauri, Pedro, 242
Costa, Joaquín, 127
Cuba, 74-77, 86-87, 92-109; and American Civil War, 84-86; claims of the United States against (1899-1910), 148-149; Congress and, 75-76; Europe and, 57; United States rivalry in, 52-70
Cultural relations between Spain and the United States, 130-139, 182-185, 245-249
Cultural rivalry: in Latin America, 49-50; in New World, 69
Cushing, Caleb, 132, 137

Dewey, George, 120
Díaz, Porfirio, 158-159
Dodge, Augustus C., 74
Don Quixote, United States views on, 132
Dorado, El, 73, 75
Dos Passos, John R., 184
Dupuy de Lôme, Enrique, 115

Economic relations (1950s-1960s), 232-235, 236
Eisenhower, Dwight D., 230; visits Spain (1959), 235
English, study of the language in Spain, 252-253
Espartero, Baldomero, 71
ETA (Basque terrorist group), 268-269
Europe: influence on United States-Spanish relations (1890s), 271-273; policy of toward Spain (1939-1945), 207

Family Compact, third (1761), 3-4
Fernandez-Shaw, Carlos M., 249
Fernando VII: and Florida, 30, 32; Latin American policy of, 39, 42
Ferrer de Couto, José, 80, 142
Filibustering, in Cuba, 66-67, 68-69, 72-74, 97-98, 100
First Republic, Spanish, 91
Fish, Hamilton, 92, 97
Floridablanca, Conde de, 6-7, 9-11, 13. *See also* American Revolution, significance of
Foner, Philip S., 117-118
Forsyth, John, 61
Foster, John W., 102; and Cuba, 100-101; and Spanish society, 137-138
France: American Revolution and, 6-15; Caribbean ties of, 53, 57, 67-68; in the Common Market, 264-265; cultural influence of, 140-142; and filibustering, 74; acquisition of Florida, 26-33; rivalry over Florida, 19, 26-33; invasion into Spain (1823), 42; Louisiana Purchase, 19-26, 27; in Mexico, 82-83; Napoleonic invasion of Spain,
effect of on colonies, 35-36; and Santo Domingo, 61, 76; Seven Years' War, role in, 4-5; during Spanish-American War, 114-115, 124-125; during Spanish civil war, 187-189, 191-192, 197, 202-203; and Ten Years' War, 93, 96; tourism in, 236-237, 254; trade with, 165; World War I, 160-161; World War II, 206, 208
Franco, Francisco: during Civil War, 187, 188, 189, 190, 194; concludes civil war, 197, 201-202; Eisenhower visit with, 235, 241; foreign policy of during Civil War, 202-203; Latin American policy of (1939-1945), 216-219, 224-225; United States relations of, 228-229, 230; World War II foreign policy of, 206-207, 213
Fulbright-Hayes Program, 250-251
Fulling, Kay, 249

Gálvez, Bernardo de, 11
García Tassara, Gabriel, 74-75, 79
Gardoqui, Diego de, 15
"Generation of '98," 126-127
Gibraltar, and Britain, 240-241
Godoy, Manuel, 20, 25
Gómez Jordana, Count Francisco, policy of, 212
Goñi, Fecundo, 86
Grant, Ulysses S., 92, 94, 96
Griffis, Stanton, 229
Guernica, United States reaction to, 195

Harrison, Benjamin, 105
Hay, John, 133
Hayes, Carlton J.H., 211-212, 213

Hayes-Tilden campaign, Spanish views on, 98-99
Hearst, William Randolph, 112-113
Hemingway, Ernest, 184
Herr, Richard, 256
Hispanic population, in the United States, 257-258
Hispanismo, 103, 154-160, 216, 249-250
Holy Alliance, and Latin American revolution, 44
House, Colonel E.M., and Spain, 164
Hull, Cordell, 192, 193, 195, 216

Ibero-American Union, 103
Irving, Washington, 132-133, 137

Jackson, Andrew, invasion of Florida, 29
Jackson, Gabriel, 256
Jay, John, 9-11, 12
Jefferson, Thomas, 28
Juarez, Bénito, 82

King, Georgiana G., 183
Kissinger, Henry, 242, 264
Korean War, Spain and, 227

LaFeber, Walter, 117
La Granja, Treaty of, 20-21
Latin America: effect of French invasion of Spain on, 35-37; rivalry in (1899-1920s), 154-160; rivalry in (1914-1920s), 164-166; United States involvement in (1830s), 63; United States involvement in (1930s), 178-182; United States-Spanish relations during Spanish civil war, 197-199, 203-204; World War II and the United States, 216-217

Laughlin, Irwin B., 175-176
League of Nations, 169, 178, 181
Lee, Henry Charles, 135-136
Leitch Wright, Jr., J., 17
Lequerica, José Felix de, 225, 229
Lewis, Jerry, 252
Lewis and Clark, 25-26
Liberal Union (1858-1863), 91
Lincoln, Abraham, 79
Livingston, Robert, 24-25
Longfellow, Henry Wadsworth, 132, 136
López, Narcisco, 66-69, 72-73
López Bravo, Gregorio, 241, 242
López de Santa Anna, Antonio, 81
López Roberts, Mauricio, 94
Louisiana Purchase, 19-26; influence on rivalry in Florida, 27-29
Lowell, James Russell, 136; on Spanish society, 137, 138

Madero, Francisco I., 159
Madison, James, 28
Maine, U.S.S., 115-116; cause of destruction, 149-150; effect on United States-Spanish relations after 1899, 149-150
Marías, Julian, 246-247, 251
Marshall Plan, 225
Martí, José, 106, 110
Martín Artajo, Alberto, 218, 233
Martínez Campos, General Arsenio, 99
Mason, James Y., 72
Masonic incident, 102
Mateo Sagasta, Práxedes, 106-107
Maura, Antonio, 106-107
McKinley tariff, 102-113; and Cuban policy, 113-117
Merriman, Roger Bigelow, 183
Metternich, Clemens, 47
Mexico, French intervention in and

INDEX 303

Anglo-United States reaction, 81-84; relations over (1911-1918), 158-160
Michener, James A., 254, 255-256; compared to Marías, 255
Middle East, 264-265
Mississippi River, rivalry over (1780s-1790s), 14-16
Mondale, Walter, 242
Monroe Doctrine, 45-49, 61, 63, 88, 155, 183; European reaction to, 47; Spanish reaction to, 47-48; United States reaction to, 46-47
Moret, Segismundo, 111
Motley, John L., 135

Nadal, Santiago, 250
NATO, 262-263, 265-267, 270
Neutrality Act (1937), 195-196
Nixon, Richard, 240, 241
Non-Intervention Committee, 192

O'Donnell, Leopoldo, 81; Mexico and, 82-83; Santo Domingo and, 76-79
Oltra, Joaquin, 142-143
Onís, Luis de, 30-31; on Latin American policy, 39
Ostend manifesto, 72

Pact of Madrid: benefits of to Spain and the United States, 231-232; construction of bases under, 231; negotiations for, 223, 229-230; relations under the treaty (1950s), 232-234, 242-243
Payne, Stanley G., 256
Philippines, 102; boundary problems, 147-148; during Spanish-American War, 120-122
Pierce, Franklin, 71; and Ostend manifesto, 72

Pinckney, Thomas, 16
Polk, James K., 64-66
Pompidou, Georges, 272
Prescott, William H., 133-135
Presley, Elvis, 252
Prim, Juan, 83
Primo de Rivera, General, 168-169; economic policies of, 171, 173; fall of, 174; Latin American policy of, 178-180
Puerto Rico: and New World politics, 61-62; United States-Spanish rivalry over, 60-61
Pulitzer, Joseph, 112-113

Queen Isabel II, 66

Race (*raza*), in relations between Spain and the United States, 18. *See also* Cultural rivalry
Rayneval, Gérard de, 12
Raza, 18
Riaño y Gayangos, Juan, 165
Rios, Fernando de los, 192, 261
Rip Van Winkle, 140
Rivalry, between Spain and the United States (1795-1800), 17-18
Rock and roll music, in Spain, 252
Rogers, William, 241
Romanones, Count of, 173
Roosevelt, Franklin D., 181-182, 194, 196, 197, 214, 217
Ruiz Gómez, Servando, 101
Russia, 38, 41, 46, 47-48, 93, 96, 114, 214, 221, 232, 239

Samaná Bay, 63, 76. *See also* Santo Domingo
Sanjurjo, José, 173
Santana, Pedro, 77, 79
Santo Domingo, 61-62, 76-81
Schurz, Carl, 261

Second Spanish Republic: establishment of, 173; relations with the United States (1931-1936), 176-182; United States recognition of, 176
Segovia, Antonio María, 76-77
Serrano Suñer, Rámon, 208-210; relations with Germany, 212
Seven Years' War (1756-1763), 3-5
Seward, William H., 79, 84, 85, 88
Sickles, Daniel E., 92, 94
Slavery, and the Caribbean, 55, 64-65
Society for Spanish and Portuguese Historical Studies, 256-257
Soulé, Pierre, 71-72
Stein, Gertrude, 184-185
Suarez, Adolfo, 241, 242
Suez crisis, 232-233
Spain: American Revolution and, 5-14; cultural interest in the United States, 138-145; domestic history of (1918-1923), 168; domestic influence of on relations (1980s), 268-271; Florida and, 26-33; foreign policy of (1936-1939), 202-203; policy of toward the United States (1940s), 225-226, 227; general trends of, 260-268; reaction of to United States-Latin American policy during French occupation of Spain, 37-38; relations of with Germany during World War II, 208-210, 212-213
Spanish-American War, 110-129; background of, 110-113, 117-120; Europe's view on the crisis, 115; military events of, 120-121; peace treaty of, 121-122; reasons for United States intervention in, 117-120; significance of on Europe, 122-123; significance of on Spain, 124-127; significance of on the United States, 123-124; United States relations and, 127-129; United States views on, 112-114
Spanish civil war: origins of, 186-187; United States and European reactions to, 187-197; United States public opinion on, 200-202
Spanish Embargo Act (1937), 193

Tarragona, Eduardo, 250
Ten Years' War (1868-1878), 89-99, 100, 103, 106
Ticknor, George, 136
Tourism, in Spain, 236-238, 253-254
Trade relations, 151-153, 156-158, 162-165, 169-175, 220
Transcontinental Treaty (1819), 31-32
Truman, Harry S, 217, 224

United Nations, 219, 221, 226; Spain joins, 232
United States: Civil War of and Spain, 83-86; Cuban policy of, 54-56, 64-69, 107-109; domestic history of (1918-1923), 168; domestic influence of on relations (1980s), 268; Florida acquisition by, 26-33; and Latin America during French occupation of Spain, 35-37; literature of in Spain, 141; and Mexican War, 62-63; NATO and, 226-228, 229-235, 240-241; policy of in Latin America (1810-1818), 40-41, 43-45; politics and influence on Spanish views, 141-145; publications of translated in Spain, 250; reaction of to end of Civil War, 197; relations of (1947-1952), 224-230; relations of

(1960s-1970s), 241-242; relations of after Franco, 242-243
United States volunteers in Spanish Civil War, 199-200

Valera y Alcalá, Juna, 138
Vayo, Alvarez del, 196
Venezuela (1893), 105-106
Vietnam War, and Spain, 240
Villa, Francisco "Pancho," 159
Virginius incident, 89, 94-96

Walker, William, 74
Washington Brigade, 199-200
Weddell, Alexander W., 209-210
Weyler, Valeriano, 111, 113

Wilkinson, General James, 28-29
Wilson, Woodrow, 159-162, 164
Woodford, Stewart, 113-114; diary of, 137
World War I: peace initiatives, 163-164; United States-Spanish relations during, 153-154, 160-164
World War II: Allied economic warfare in Spain during, 213-216; relations during, 206-207; World War I compared to, 205-206

Zamora, Alcalá, 173
Zanjón, Treaty of, 99-100
Zapata, Emiliano, 159

About the Author

James W. Cortada has published articles in several journals, including the *Journal of Contemporary History*, the *Review of Politics, Il Politico*, and *Renaissance and Reformation*. He is the author of *A Bibliographic Guide to Spanish Diplomatic History, 1460-1977* (Greenwood Press, 1977) and is preparing a volume on Spanish diplomatic relations in the twentieth century.